"Affliction"

God would not send you the darkness, dear,
  If He felt you could bear the light,
But you would not cling to His guiding hand
  If the way were always bright.
And you would not care to walk by faith
  Could you always walk by sight.

'Tis true, He has many an anguish
  For your sorrowful heart to bear
Many a cruel thorn-crown
  For your tired head to wear—
He knows how few would reach Heaven
    at all
  If pain did not guide them there.

So He sends you the blinding darkness
  And the furnace of seven-fold heat,
'Tis the only way, believe me
  To keep you close to His feet.
For 'tis always so easy to wander,
  When our lives are glad and sweet.

Then nestle your hand in your Father's
  And sing if you can as you go,
For song may cheer some one behind you
  Whose courage is sinking low;
And well if your lips do quiver—
  God will love you better so.

Joe Kotcka

105A

DESIGN COPR. 1950 DEVOTIONAL PUBLISHING CO. LITHO IN U. S. A.

GERMANY
AND THE
EAST-WEST CRISIS

GERMANY
AND THE
EAST-WEST CRISIS

The Decisive Challenge to American Policy

By WILLIAM S. SCHLAMM

DAVID McKAY COMPANY, INC.

New York

Contents

Introduction

~~~~~~

I AM an Austrian by birth, an American by choice. I love the
Mediterranean sun, the elegant wit of Paris, the heartbeat and
beauty of Rome. And I say all this to show my credentials: all my
instincts and prejudices are provoked by anything Teutonic. In fact,
when Karl von Ossietzky, the late Nobel Peace Prize winner, disappeared in a Nazi jail in 1933, I took over the editorship of the
Weltbühne, Germany's best-known and most vehement weekly
attack on all that was mean, provincial, dusty, and cruel in pre-
Hitler Germany. (The *Weltbühne* was also, at least as long as I
edited it, an attack on the intellectual premises of Stalinism.) And
yet this book is going to propose that Germany be given, in American policies as well as in American notions, the place it already
occupies in forceful reality—as the decisive European power in the
West's struggle with communism.

I shall propose, in other words, not to separate emotion and
judgment, but to comply—as rational people should—with both,
and in a correct order of values. In the sphere of policies and politics my own formative emotion is a revulsion against the moral
insanity of communism. And my judgments, arrived at on the basis
of serious study, will be presented in this book. It is my desire to

convince the reader who shares my emotion that the judgment goes properly with it.

To assume that only a medication that tastes good can cure—this is the kind of silliness that makes politics the silliest of all human plays. And such a bias would be inconceivable in any other sphere of human curiosity and search. Yet in politics an alliance with the most attractive people is always being considered the sanest and safest of all possible alliances; and no one is guiltier of such irrational behavior than Americans.

As it happens, the Russians (the nucleus of the explosive communist mass) are very attractive people. It also happens that the Germans—lovable as some of them are—remain awkward and definitely born with original sin. And Germany's lunatic fringe is every bit as lunatic and large as, for example, America's. Yet to base policy decisions on the kind of aesthetics that goes under the name of "national psychology" is frivolous. It is also absurd.

Policy decisions must be based on rationally viewed facts. To study these facts, I went to Germany in November 1957 and I stayed there, or in its vicinity, until November 1958. During this year I must have talked to more than a thousand Germans—and I have talked to them in a colloquial German that made them speak, I should like to think, without those self-conscious distortions the conspicuous foreigner encounters. Thus, the sample I have taken is about as large as those from which Dr. Gallup derives his social oracles; but my kind of "polling" has the advantage over his that I have lived a lifetime with the poll's subject: I have lived, with conscious urgency, for forty-one years with the problems of communism; and with the Germans I have lived half of my adult life, plus one year. This does not necessarily make me right, but it makes me knowing.

This book undertakes to report what and who the new Germans are. It then proceeds to discuss the confused premises on which the West, and America in particular, has built its policies. And it finally proposes an attitude and a policy that, to me, seem to promise an end to the uninterrupted succession of miserable and dishonorable western defeats. Since I moved to the United States, in 1938, I have often returned to Europe, and each time I was animated by its sweet and tender glories; but not before this year's stay in Germany have I felt with such pressing certainty that the Old World remains the area of decision and destiny for the entire West. And though this was a year of a prosperous European comfort that I have never witnessed before, I felt a choking urgency move in on all of us. The year in Germany persuaded me that there is only a short time left to ponder and to choose between attitudes. My book ponders and chooses. It was written with an aching love for the Old World that once was mine, and a loving apprehension for the New World that now is my home. It is dedicated to both these worlds. Between them, they own all the splendor of man's fate. May they retain it.

WILLIAM S. SCHLAMM

GERMANY
AND THE
EAST-WEST CRISIS

CHAPTER ONE

Anatomy of a Miracle

THE German "economic miracle" is neither a miracle nor particularly economic. There is nothing miraculous about a perfectly rational response of profitable supply to urgent demand. Exhausted by an absurd war to the point of naked starvation, 50 million Germans went to work and produced, from scratch, a modern economy. The reason for their spectacular success was precisely that they started from scratch.

Neither an outdated machinery nor petrified trade traditions stood in their way. There was nothing at all; and so, once they went to work, there was soon the newest and most adequate European economy. The world has seen this before—in America, for instance. America's unparalleled growth in the nineteenth and twentieth centuries is fully understandable only if one takes into account America's unique freedom from the dead hand of a complex economic past. There was in America neither the corset of feudal traditions nor the mortgage of venerably old investments which habitually insist on being amortized over and over again before anyone can dare make new ones. Modern America, compared to the Old World, started from scratch; and so it overtook Europe in a few decades. There is nothing miraculous in America's speed of achievement—and in Germany's economic feat.

And yet an almost incomprehensible factor enters the German picture: that the suppliers were *politically* allowed to make money by satisfying demands. How it happened that the celebrated Dr. Erhard mustered enough courage to do the reasonable—to lift, with one stroke, all regimentations of Germany's decimated economy— has often been told, and usually correctly. Ten years after the event, in 1958, Dr. Erhard laughingly admitted that the Allied military authorities allowed him to do what he did only because *nothing* seemed to matter any more: The country had reached the bottom of a hopeless pit—so it might just as well try the reasonable. It did. And in a few years it had grown rich.

The only miraculous element in it remains that there existed, at a time when the whole world was run by planners, a group of articulate and persuasive people in Germany who believed in the ancient rules of the market. The astonishing part in the German success story is the personal character of a few Germans (most important among them was and remains the naturalized Swiss Professor Wilhelm Röpke, from whom Dr. Erhard learned all he knows), who had the wit to oppose National Socialism not only because it was national but also because it was socialism.

From 1933 on, Germans such as Röpke confronted the massive reality of Nazi economic regimentation with imaginative notions of economic freedom. And when, by a fluke of history, that small group of neo-Liberals got a chance to act decisively, they did what is no longer known in western society—they acted according to their convictions. This faith of a few accidentally powerful men in the principles they professed, this unmitigated faith in first principles, was the German miracle. For it all happened under the eyes and stringent military controls of a British Labor Government and of Truman's Fair Deal administration, both deeply committed to the regimentations of the welfare state. And it happened in the midst of a continent that seemed completely sold on statist controls, west as well as east of the Iron Curtain. Against these infinitely superior forces a few Germans trusted their convictions, which were diametrically opposed to those of all world powers. I remember, in my generation, no more daring act of nonconformism.

Everything that followed was as magic as the multiplication table. Once Germans were allowed to satisfy unlimited demands with profit-making supplies, the normal and predictable things occurred. (At least they would seem normal and predictable to anyone who studied economics before the Keynesian era.) In seeing profitable German enterprises mushroom, in response to desperate demand, an American may have felt constantly reminded of some heroic chapters in his own economic history.

For example, he would feel familiarly at home with a young friend of mine, a former Sudeten-German, who in 1948—when he was thirty-two—crossed the border of the German Soviet Zone and started to manufacture nylon stockings in West Germany. At the end of 1957, nine years later, he marked an annual business volume of DM 18 million. His plant would be the pride of any United States chamber of commerce. Beautifully remodeled in 1957, it is an authentic example of shrewd rationalization techniques, of mechanical perfection, of tidiness and profitability. There was no magic and not even a trick involved in this particular Horatio Alger story. A young Sudeten-German refugee, from an old family of weavers, put his preciously small savings and his unlimited diligence to work in 1948; and because a few theoreticians of the free market had created sound ground rules for the convalescing German economy, the enterprise grew in nine years to the annual equivalent of $4.2 million—or, rather, $8.4 million in terms of American purchasing power. My friend, I should add, still possesses no house of his own; he still lives, with a growing family, in a rented home because he puts practically all his earnings into the plant.

This man was eighteen years old when Hitler came to power, thirty when Hitler evaporated. My friend was born and raised in the notoriously nazified Sudeten territory and, as an officer of the Nazi Army, held a locally important position with the German occupation forces in France. Yet I have not met a more genuinely European mind in all of Europe. What he has learned in Hitler's war is a touching and slightly exaggerated respect for the French and an almost accent-free French. His attitude vis-à-vis the Jews is almost normal; I say "almost" because he is one of the many Germans I have met who tend to idealize the Jews. I would trust him in all private matters implicitly, and I would very much want him on my side in any public crisis. Besides, if I were an American business-man, I could not find a more attractive business partner than this German.

And it is no digression to speak of him in the context of the German "economic miracle." There has been far too much talk of German *Tüchtigkeit,* German working prowess, and German sweat. Not that these clichés are altogether untrue. But they remain a poor explanation of what was happening in Germany between 1948 and 1958 and what is happening there today. The conclusive German recovery, to the point of indisputable German economic hegemony on the Continent, is a result of *a character mutation* rather than of continuity of national character.

The Germans are back in front—with the United States and the Soviet Union, one of the world's three great industrial powers—be-cause, for the first time in their history, they did *not* return to the ancient patterns of the tribe. They are today the most potent nation of western Europe because they are the one western nation on the Continent that does *not* want to be connected with its own past. And the common denominator of all that is new in this Germany seems to me a momentous change in the German scale of personal values. On the top of this scale stands—for all that it is worth—"personal improvement," and neither Fatherland nor *Weltanschauung.* Busi-ness, and nothing else, is the new German's business.

If he wants to refresh his memories of fading American indi-vidualism, an American had better go to Germany. The Germans, to be sure, have not yet acquired the French degree of social atomization which, in just two generations, has brought about the demise of France as a great power; that is, the Germans have still retained a social cohesion that permits the body politic at least to exist, if not to expand. But today's Germans are social creatures by reflex rather than by deliberate choice—a reflex still responding to a repressed past rather than today's ready cooperation. Their *deliberate* preference—the new factor in the German mind and the

German reality—is a clearly egotistic and yet somehow dedicated self-concern. And one cannot understand a single political, economic, or cultural event of most recent German history without comprehending this revolutionary change in the German value system.

There was, for instance, the *ohne mich* ("without me") period in German politics; a time when it looked unlikely that Germany would rearm again and thus vitalize the pale NATO concept. *Ohne mich* was the authentic attitude of the German generation between the ages of eighteen and forty which, quite literally, wished to cancel its membership in the nation and to withdraw from history into a comfortable realm of wealthy privacy. Never before and nowhere else had old Henry Ford achieved that kind of echo for his bold contention that "history is bunk." This German *ohne mich* generation had not only debunked history—it had resigned from it.

True, Germany is today nonetheless rearming, and young Germans have begun to serve in the new armed forces without noticeable difficulties. But this is possible only because Dr. Adenauer had in the meantime achieved his monumental stature as the German statesman who must be followed implicitly (though by no means be implicitly trusted), even when going off on such a "juvenile" tangent as rearmament. The very indifference with which the *ohne mich* generation finally submitted to a policy it had so outspokenly opposed before was proof of the depth of its affliction. National conduct was presumed to be so unimportant, personal self-advancement so evidently all-important, that nobody was going to lose much sleep, let alone his career chances, by heated opposition to the Old Man's whims. As it happens, those whims became the decisive factor in Europe's potential firmness in the face of Soviet expansion. But to the lethargy of the German *ohne mich* generation it did not really matter one way or the other.

What mattered, and mattered alone, was personal prosperity. And toward that goal the Germans started with a ferocious zeal, an impersonal dedication that, in the German past, had been serving "idealistic" schemes only. In this respect Germany has not

changed much. There has remained in the Germans an irreducible
need for impersonal dedication, even when it is mobilized for
nothing but personal improvement. The contemporary German still
builds with religious fervor, though he is now building his personal
career. This must have been the spirit in which the original
Calvinists created modern capitalism. It is a strange sight to see
Catholics of the Rhineland, the Palatinate, Bavaria behave like
early Calvinists. But they do—and nowhere so conspicuously as in
the economic area. They seek private success the same way America's early settlers did: the way one seeks earthly proof of transcen-
dental salvation.

The country is growing rich in the speediest "initial" capital
accumulation Europe has seen since England's first industrial jumps
in the early nineteenth century. With the amount of capital that
was at Germany's disposal in 1948 no other modern economy
would have dared to expand. There was no governmental pump
priming, no foreign aid to speak of. (The United States Marshall
Aid that went to Germany was a fraction of the billions that poured
into the French and British economies—with notoriously modest
results.) The only capital available to German entrepreneurs at
the beginning of the prosperous decade was the reinvested profit
of the first few transactions. And there was, therefore, sometimes
a neck-breakingly high profit rate. (I have seen some convincing
evidence of 100 and 150 per cent profit taking in the commodity-
starved German market of 1948 and 1949.)

Erhard's Germany went through phases when the more or less
unavoidable conditions of "initial" capital accumulation were no
less unattractive than those that prevailed in Britain and the
United States a hundred years ago. But the difference was the
brevity of the ordeal: the "initial" German capital snowballed,
and multiplied many times over, in three or four years. Since
1955 the German banking system has functioned with an audacity
unknown anywhere else in Europe and seldom matched by America's increasingly overcautious banks. In 1958, after only nine
years of domestic profit taking, Germany was the only nation out-

side the United States that qualified, on a grand scale, as capital investor abroad.

Banalities such as "German sweating" do not help much in explaining the event. In fact, nowhere in Europe, not even in France, have I seen as massive an insistence on "relaxation," ordinary fun, and general comfort, as in Germany. Average working hours are down, in German mining, to a most comfortable thirty-eight hours a week, to thirty-seven in textile industries, to thirty-eight in electrotechnical enterprises. A recent German study estimates that, adding vacations to Sundays and holidays, the German worker stays home on 108 out of the year's 365 days; and on the remaining 257 days he works an average of 7.5 hours a day—fewer than 2,000 working hours per year.

From 18 to 20 million Germans, of a total population of 52 million, can be considered "working population." Of these people, almost 10 million Germans went on vacation trips in 1957; and 2 of these 10 million Germans spent their vacation in foreign countries. It has been estimated that about DM 3 billion—1.5 per cent of the total national gross product—have been paid for these trips. To match such largesse, about 35 million Americans should have gone in 1957 on vacation trips, about 7 million of them traveling outside the United States, spending between them more than $6 billion. Actually, fewer than 30 million Americans took vacation trips, only 1,250,000 went abroad, and the total vacation expenditures in the United States have been estimated at $2 billion for 1957.

Germans in 1957 were three times more frequent tourists abroad than the people of the next most-traveling nation of Europe. I cannot honestly say that I have found German mass tourism, or any other kind of German mass relaxation, a very attractive type of human conduct. But the point is that the Germans of today have no resemblance to the conventional image of the German who enjoys sweating and would not know what to do with an idle hour. The German weekend has become an elaborate and plush affair. The relaxing German may be loud, but he certainly enjoys relaxing.

And yet the size of annual German savings, turned into investments, is tremendous. In 1957 Germany's new investment of the
year amounted to DM 49 billion, out of a gross national product of
DM 207 billion—more than 23 per cent. To match this investment rate, the United States should have invested in 1957 about
$100 billion; it actually invested $30 billion. The spectacular German investments are taken out of every year's capital profits which,
to repeat, are still considerably higher than those tolerated in
Anglo-Saxon welfare states. In 1957 Germany's corporate capital
income was more than 35 per cent of the gross national product,
i.e., DM 70 billion. Of these 70 billion marks, after taxes and personal expenditures, the stately sum of DM 49 billion was reinvested.

But this immense rate of profit taking and reinvesting by no
means results in low average incomes for the working men. The
average annual income of the German worker was about DM
4,800 ($1,150) in 1957. However, if Americans want to visualize
the living standards supported by an annual income of DM 4,800
they must substitute a realistic index of purchasing power for that
of the official currency exchange rate. And it is a rather conservative estimate that a dollar buys in America, not what DM 4.20 buy
in Germany, but at the most the commodity equivalent of DM 2.10.
So that in purchasing power and living standards the average
German worker earned in 1957 the equivalent of $2,300. This
is still less than the average worker's income in the United States,
but it is indisputably the highest income of any working man in
the Old World (excepting Switzerland); and it is more than the
German worker of past generations ever dreamed of making.

Indeed, the German air is heavy, if not sticky, with physical
well-being. In the better residential sections of the cities the professional beggar still keeps ringing the bell at his appointed hours;
but this is a display more of folklore than of misery. True misery
is confined to the typical victims of world-wide inflation—the
pathetic dregs of the middle class, the dupes of "social" and private
insurance who must try to live on insanely low annuities. If these
were not old people, candidates for nothing but death, the distress

of these "social rentiers" could blow up even the sturdy German structure. But their whisper is hardly audible. They die in the shadow of a noisy prosperity. The rest of the German people have never known better times. And they are even aware of it. A recent public poll produced the amazing result that almost one half of all Germans, asked how they were satisfied with their private state of affairs, actually answered that they *were* satisfied—a rather incredible percentage, if one takes into account man's normal habit of insatiable greed.

Prosperity has been the one immense, the one new experience of the Germans since 1945; and it has utterly fascinated them. The sense of getting on, of getting richer every day, has replaced all conventional German emotions. Collectivism is blooming as fully in Germany as anywhere else in the world; but in Germany the common denominator of collective cravings is paradoxically a drive toward individual self-improvement. The joke, as always in such social paradoxes, is of course ultimately on the individual; and the collective German urge to succeed individually will end, no doubt, in the same fashion all such jokes do—in some kind of equalitarian nirvana. But this is still far off. For the time being, for an unusually long stretch of prosperity, everybody seems to run after his own sweet fortune.

The essence and the aroma of this German prosperity can be appreciated only in terms of the Germans' ever-present memory. There is not a single German above the age of eighteen who does not remember, in stark personal recollection, the terrors of a social breakdown without precedent in human history. The women whom the Russians had raped in 1945 were still young matrons in 1958; the men who had chewed filthy leather in Soviet PW camps were still the young generation in 1958; and the bombed-out civilians, the cavemen of 1945, were still the active core of the population. There was not a single prospering German who did not recall—silently but every day—the lowest recesses of human existence. To these people, overwhelmed by their progress in such an incredibly short time, no other experience could possibly matter. This material redemption, it was almost like Faust's pact with the devil. Only there was no devil. There was nothing but these Germans' own efforts. There was every reason for pride. But the astonishing fact, at least for this critical observer, was the absence of such pride—at least the apparent absence of it.

True, from time to time some tasteless German Caliban let go with the traditional German war cry of self-admiration. But each time he has been cut down by a mighty public display of regret over such poor manners. The Germans who in the old days could not get over the fact that the German Rhine was German, and the German maidens German as well as maidens, the same Germans, in 1958, were the epitome of impeccable reserve and correct understatement. Inside, indubitably, they were proud. But it was pride in the single person's achievements—not the nation's. The nation, in fact, was an irrelevant category—a real one, to be sure, but irrelevant.

Briefed by stacks of printed matter and my own lifetime knowledge of "the German character," I had, for instance, expected I would find "the reunification problem" in control of all German emotions. Was not this, after all, the people that twice, in a single generation, had readily gone to war to correct some sloppily drawn borderlines? And now the whole nation was cut in two. But one of the fundamental surprises of my year's coexistence with the new Germans was to discover how bored and embarrassed they were with "the problem."

Not once, literally not once, did I encounter a German who got emotional about it. Some of the Germans I met felt obliged to advance, rather lifelessly, a formal position of national protest, considerably short of the "irredenta" type of emotionalism that remains par in the rest of a Europe that is perpetually busy with some kind of "nationality problems." But the numerous Germans with whom I made, or renewed, a trusting acquaintance readily agreed that East Germany, to be honest about it, was not worth any serious trouble. If West Germany could somehow get the 17 million sovietized Germans back, them and their ransacked territory, *without* trouble—well, one would gladly take them back. But should they stay separated forever from the 52 million prosperous citizens of West Germany—well, just too bad. I have found in Germany much more emotional participation in Empress Saroya's marital fate, or Princess Margaret's heart affairs, than in what the outside world expects to encounter as the great German tragedy.

And yet this remains a thoroughly irritated or, at any rate, irritable area of the German mind. These new Germans can easily rationalize and even justify their comfortable lethargy of the moment; but to the West Germans the East Germans are, so to speak, the current Jews—an ever-present thorn in the somnolent national conscience. These East Germans—silenced, helpless, herded in a ghetto, debased—are a ubiquitous reminder of a sinister reality which, of course, one can try to ignore by looking the other way. But the reality creeps up on everybody, haunts his dreams, and somehow spoils every moment of fun. Yes, one can try once more to protest that one simply does not know what is being done to the captives; just as most Germans still deny that they ever knew what was being done to the Jews. But this time, at least, they *do* know that they know.

Thousands of sovietized Germans still escape every month into West Germany. They keep talking. The newspapers keep talking. The facts keep talking. West Germany is crowded with evidence of the dehumanization that remains the fate of 17 million East Germans: no fewer than 10 of the 52 million West Germans are refugees from the East. Yet at the prosperous moment the very presence of these former refugees in West Germany insulates, through a strange quirk of the human mind, the prosperous country against the surrounding harshness. Americans will understand this phenomenon better than anybody else. In the United States it is the relative newcomer to the country who, far more than the old-timer of New England and the South, swells the ranks of "isolationism"; for it is the recent immigrant's forbidding recollection of the harsh world he left behind that makes him want to close his eyes and his ears to its predicaments. The 10 million refugees from the German East, who have built for themselves new existences in the West, have become in all truth West Germany's "isolationists": they do not want to be reminded of the evil world they left behind.

The conventional admiration for the "German economic miracle" grows usually high-pitched when it comes to praising the absorption of more than 10 million German refugees from eastern Europe in a few years. The feat is unquestionably without precedent; it would amount to the successful immigration of 45 million people into the United States in the course of three years. When the "expellees" began to pour into West Germany, the native inhabitants numbered 40 million destitute people; and no migration expert on earth would have thought it possible that a broken-down economy, satisfying even at its best just about the native population, could provide not only temporary haven but livelihood and even happy normalcy to 10 million people who arrived in a stupor of fear, penniless and emaciated. And yet this is precisely what happened in the Germany of the late forties.

The events followed, as usual, a trend exactly contrary to the accepted axiom of the "experts." For in truth the immigration of vast masses into an expanding economy creates not "a run on scarce jobs," or whatever else the United States labor unions and other foes of immigration claim, but provides a decisive incentive to *prosperity*—a fast increase of national wealth, and a considerable rise of individual standards of living. This, of course, is how the United States grew to its present levels of wealth: because of the mass immigrations of the late nineteenth and the early twentieth centuries.

The forgotten American experience—repressed by the protectionist opponents of a free market and the foes of an economy regulated, not by an omnipotent government, but by incentives— that forgotten but formative American experience has been relived and surpassed by Adenauer's Germany. The next country to learn from that experience—Canada or Australia or Brazil— and to invite mass immigration on an unprecedented scale, will outdo West Germany (and, I am afraid, the United States). It will prove once more—and to the chagrin of "migration experts"—

that national wealth is *always* created by masses of people who are determined to build, from scratch, their personal wealth.

In the German case, the acceptance of 10 million refugees was not so much an act of economic horse sense as a national commitment, politically as inescapable as morally. In fact, appeals to national and human solidarity notwithstanding, West Germany's "man on the street" was his usual amoral self and objected, sometimes in controlled anger, but often with poisonous accents, against the influx of miserable East German refugees; and even today, amidst a fat prosperity for everybody, you can make a prospering old-timer in Munich or Cologne or Hamburg give you a pretty revolting piece of his mind on the subject of "those prospering newcomers." But the slowly reconstituted federal German authorities were adamantly decent and strong-willed. Swimming against the current of West German egotism, they received the refugees and admitted them, without any important reservations, to the social and economic life of the nation.

Ever since—partly thanks to the politically powerful refugee parties and organizations—the German authorities have resisted all temptations to regiment the immigrants in order to please the natives; for, whatever votes a German politician may win with petty conduct, he would lose just as many, if not more, by arousing the ire of the refugees who have the right to vote (and make clever use of it). As it turned out, this official German immunity to xenophobia—as if virtue were really meant to bring even in this world its own rewards—was one of the decisive incentives for the fabulous German prosperity.

Today one encounters former refugees in all places of fast economic growth. They, more than anybody else in West Germany, have worked since 1948 with a stubborn dedication and an almost ferocious urge to rebuild their destroyed lives by rebuilding the economy of West Germany. They brought with them skills, trade secrets, commercial contacts with the outside world—from old Czechoslovakia, for instance, that (to its eternal shame, and to the shame of the Allied military governments which supported such inhumanity), even before the Communists ascended to power in

Prague, chased several million Sudeten-Germans across the German border into the night of destitution. And in ten years the Sudeten-Germans have contributed, man by man, more to the German "economic miracle" than any group of West German natives.

In the town of Kaufbeuren, for instance, near the Austro-German-Swiss border, there is an extraordinary settlement called "Neu-Gablonz." Now the town of Gablonz used to be the center of the Czechoslovak "novelties" industry, mostly glass products, that manufactured the perhaps most widely known items of Czechoslovakia's export. Sudeten-Germans manned that Gablonz industry, and when they were forcibly driven out of Gablonz—where they had lived through long and happier Habsburgian centuries—they took with them all there is to human wealth; namely, skill and a traditional aptitude for special work. Some of them stopped on their flight in Kaufbeuren where they were housed in ugly army barracks in the woods north of town. Ten years later that shabby emergency housing had developed into the town of Neu-Gablonz; and in June 1958 the ten thousandth citizen of Neu-Gablonz was registered—the newly born Markus Feix.

There are in Neu-Gablonz now three new churches, two elementary schools, a stadium, a gymnasium, and a growing number of brand-new apartment buildings. There are no fewer than thirty-one civic clubs and societies, dedicated to everything from philately to chamber music; and there are, above all, five hundred small enterprises that produce the world-famous type of Gablonz trinkets. More than one hundred firms specialize in exporting "novelties." They have sold in 1957 DM 50 millions' worth of them to foreign countries ($12 million—in purchasing power $24 million), a by no means negligible fraction of the export total on which West Germany bases its wealth. A few thousand refugees have built in a few years a brand-new German industry that brings West Germany about DM 15,000 ($3,800 or, in purchasing power, $7,600) per year per adult worker in foreign currency. And Neu-Gablonz keeps expanding, though it currently suffers from a scarcity, not of jobs, but of skilled labor. A federal school for glassworkers has been opened in 1957 to teach about a hundred and fifty youngsters the age-old secrets of old Gablonz's ancient glass industry.

This textbook story of the sources and makings of wealth will not, I am afraid, pierce the thick layer of ignorance and egotistic naïveté that our economic folklore misunderstands for "expertise on immigration." Even so, in Germany the story of Neu-Gablonz stands for scores of similar success stories which, in a tremendous accumulation, constitute the "German economic miracle." Sensible human need to produce wealth in freedom from regimentation, bureaucratic chicanery, and statist intervention rebuilt Germany. Destitute people, driven by hunger and an indefatigable will to live, started doing what they best knew how to do. And in ten years a sacked Germany had grown into the great powerhouse of Europe.

With the obvious exception of the United States, Germany is today the world's largest producer of capital goods; and, consequently, the building of machinery is Germany's largest industry. The construction of machines reaches a business volume of 10 per cent of the national gross product (about $5 billion or, in purchasing power, $10 billion). More than one third of that machinery is sold abroad, most of that export going to other countries of western Europe (DM 4.5 billion in 1957). Almost DM 2 billions' worth of machinery was sold in 1957 overseas—a billion's worth to Asia, DM 700 million sales to Latin America, DM 300 million exports to Africa, and machinery valued at only DM 178 million to the Soviet Empire. But there has recently started a dangerous tendency to seek Soviet markets for German machinery. This tendency originates with, of all people, Alfried Krupp—and thereby hangs a story.

The case illuminates the obstinate inanity of the West and the astute rascality of the Soviets in handling Germany. Herr Krupp, the notoriously thin-skinned and even neurotic heir to an unhappy reputation and the perhaps largest European fortune, cannot forget that the United States Military Court at Nuremberg threw him into jail for years; but—and this makes the case so significant—he has easily forgotten that this undeniable miscarriage of justice was perpetrated on Soviet instigation. On all legal and moral grounds the treatment Alfried Krupp received at the Nuremberg trials came near the lowest low western jurisprudence reached under the corrupting influence of wartime policies: Alfried Krupp was sentenced to years of dishonorable jail for deeds in which, *to the knowledge of the United States Court,* he had demonstrably no part.

The Court made no bones about the motives of this *conceded* miscarriage of justice: The obviously guilty party, Alfried Krupp's deathly sick father, could not be tried; and because the United States Court at Nuremberg considered it propagandistically inadvisable to finish its job without sentencing a Krupp; and because the indubitably innocent Alfried was the only male member of the Krupp family available to the Court—for such dismally cynical reasons Alfried Krupp was jailed. That much is known.

Less known is the essential part the Soviets—i.e., their innumerable sympathizers on the staff of the United States prosecutor in Nuremberg and, *alas,* on the staff of the United States Army of Occupation—played in the outbreak of unmitigated juridical cynicism. To the United States adherents of economic determinism, fascism in general was "the dictatorial system of monopoly capitalism" and nazism in particular the obedient creature of the Ruhr's capitalist bosses (who, in the "anti-Fascist" terminology of the forties, had somehow the mystical function of the Elders of Essen). It seemed insufferable to them that a court of the "anti-Fascist" victors should convene, to sit in trial over those Germans who were guilty of warmongering, without a single Krupp in the dock. And to the non-Marxians among the United States officials it seemed impermissible that such trifles as respect for truth, and judicious processes of the law, should disturb "Allied Unity." Exit Alfried Krupp—innocent, but guilty.

And then, eight years later, he returned. As it happened, he returned to control a family fortune which, while he was in jail, had again become the most massive enterprise of the Ruhr area. In 1957 the business volume of the Krupp enterprises—about 150 plants—was DM 3.4 billion ($820 million). They employed 54,-

000 workers and exported in 1957 capital goods for about DM 500 million. While his father was in command, and indubitably was committing criminal acts in exploiting forced foreign labor, Alfried Krupp had not the slightest influence on Krupp policies; but when he had finished his jail sentence for acts he did not commit, Alfried Krupp *did* assume full responsibility for his family's fortunes. And from that day on Alfried Krupp apparently had only one ambition (beyond being what he already was—one of the world's six or seven richest men): to prove that the tarnished name of Krupp stood for anything but cannons. He now was passionately interested in "international cooperation" and many other catch phrases in the fashionable dictionary of leftism. I hasten to add that Alfried Krupp is anything but a leftist himself; he would be appalled by the mere suggestion that his policies have ever followed any ideological impulses. And, indeed, they have not—if by such impulses we understand conscious rationales.

Still, whenever Alfried Krupp had an opportunity to make a choice, he usually chose the alternative that seemed to go against the western grain. Nor is this difficult to understand. The subconscious works in a German capitalist as surely as it works in a New York *avant-garde* writer; and in Alfried Krupp's case, his subconscious has supplied the hook on which he can hang all his rationalizations—his hatred of what must seem to him a despicable Anglo-Saxon bigotry that dismisses justice at an "allied" gangster's wink. And so ferocious is this hatred, or so it seems to me, that Herr Krupp is perfectly willing to smile at the very same gangster—particularly as such smiles prove profitable.

Ten years after the United States Court, on Soviet instigation, had violated the law, in order to get a Krupp, Alfried Krupp was engrossed in studies of what his enterprise could do to develop "the underdeveloped areas of the world"—which, as it happened, were almost identical with the areas the Soviets *wanted* developed. The obvious intent behind everything the Krupp enterprises had undertaken since 1945 was a desire to vindicate the family name in one respect—Krupp must be proved to be no "merchant of death." But once your motivations are reduced to remorseful pacifism, the Soviets will catch you every time. They now seem to have caught up with Alfried Krupp.

The incorrigible "anti-Fascists" of the West, of course, are still in no mood to acknowledge this crucial German reality: that whatever remains of Germany's nationalistic sickness is today being employed by the Soviets; and that for every secretly unrepenting former Nazi who may have wormed his way into an important position in West Germany a dozen openly unrepenting Nazis are working for the communist overthrow of the West; for genuine Nazis hate the West infinitely more than they hate communism. Those incorrigible "anti-Fascists" (they call themselves in the United States "liberals" today) keep indicting the United States Government for having issued, in 1957, a visitor's visa to Alfried Krupp. Six months after their outcry had dissuaded Alfried Krupp from attending an innocuous public conference in San Francisco, the number-two man in the Soviet government, Anastas Mikoyan, came to Bonn—officially to sign a perfectly irrelevant trade agreement with the Adenauer government, actually to engage in secret negotiations with Alfried Krupp concerning a formidable business deal.

Four weeks later Krupp's entire high command was in Moscow. Alfried Krupp's *Generalbevollmächtigter* (plenipotentiary general), Herr Berthold Beitz, accompanied by two codecisive members of the Krupp directorate, Dr. Hans Kallen and Dr. Joachim Wrede, bargained for seven days with the top men of Mikoyan's ministry. On his return to Bonn, in June 1958, Beitz reported triumphantly that Anastas Mikoyan himself had called the Krupp delegation "the first swallows foreboding good business with the West," and that Krupp, for the time being, had succeeded in lining up orders for DM 55 million. But this was just a token. Actually, Krupp was chosen to produce the *major part* of the capital-goods equipment the Soviets need for the completion of the ambitious 100-billion-ruble "Seven-Year Plan" Khrushchev had designed for the chemical and synthetics industries of the Soviet Union.

In announcing his plan, Khrushchev had named Krupp by name,

praising "the good trade relations the Soviet Union had previously entertained with that firm." Informed guessers in German industrial quarters estimate that Krupp, if his new relations with the Soviets proceed in the same spirit in which they have so sensationally begun, may very soon reach an annual export volume to the Soviet Union of DM 100 million (not counting the extensive Krupp trade with satellite areas). And a hundred million marks' worth of Krupp machinery, every year, means a formidable increase of Soviet productivity which, by the way, may not be confined to pots and pans. It means a fifth of Krupp's normal annual export. Alfried Krupp, in other words, who has made up his mind never again to produce armaments for Germany and the West, has now joined forces with the Soviets in an enterprise that bets 100 billion rubles on a modernized, superior, and battle-ready Soviet industry.

At which point I should like to recapitulate the essential data of the Krupp case. First, the western powers, under Soviet pressure, rape justice against Alfried Krupp. Then they set him free but continue to harass his enterprise with, to put it mildly, unrealistic demands for "breaking up the Krupp empire." Then he is blackballed from entering United States territory twelve years after the war had ended. In the meantime, the Soviets had surrounded Alfried Krupp and his high command with a whole network of researchers, promoters, commission agents, who, as it happens, know an astonishingly great deal about trade prospects in the Soviet area. Then Khrushchev announces a 100-billion-ruble "Seven-Year Plan" which, on careful reading, is based on capital goods which Krupp will produce for the Soviet Union. In less than thirteen years the fall guy of Nuremberg has been groomed to perform as a major asset of the Soviet industry. And the West continues to worry that Alfried Krupp may have been let off too easily. This, in a nutshell, is the whole story of western fallacies in handling Germany.

The name of Krupp stands, in truth, for the strategic main goal of all Soviet policies in Europe—the control of the Ruhr. No matter how Soviet tactics may change, and in what directions, there remains immovably Lenin's concept: that the victory of world revolution is assured only if and when Germany's industrial prowess has joined the Soviet dynamism. And it does not really matter, at least not in an interim phase, whether Germany's industrial areas are *politically* under communist control; to achieve the essential Soviet stratagems it may suffice to have the Ruhr industry *work* for the Soviet Union. To no one's greater surprise than his own, Alfried Krupp may finally discover that he has delivered Germany and the West to world communism.

What West Germany means to the Soviet Union will be immediately comprehensible as one compares the two countries' economic indices. Here are relevant comparative output figures of 1957:

	West Germany	Soviet Union
Coal	230 million tons	462
Steel	24.5 million tons	51.1
Electricity	91.6 billion KWH	209.5
Concrete	19.3 million tons	29

But we must keep in mind not only the population ratio of the two countries—1 to 4—but also the strategically all-important fact that the Soviet Union must diffuse its industrial output over a vast continental expanse, while West Germany has a singularly compact industry. Unlike the Soviet Union, which dispenses its production around an immense periphery, West Germany can at any given moment concentrate its industrial potency on a particular strategic need. In times of war the diffusion of Soviet industries is a strategic advantage. But in any "peaceful" armament or production race, the concentration of West German industries is a priceless asset.

The production ratio in basic industries—1 to 2—corrects the population ratio of 1 to 4 very much in Germany's favor. And the German superiority becomes altogether spectacular if one compares the production figures of complex machinery:

	West Germany	Soviet Union
Cars (1957)	1,212,000	495,000
Motorcycles (1956)	866,000	297,000
Electric tubes (1956)	25,410,000	11,300,000
TV sets (1957)	808,000	600,000
Radio sets (1956)	4,300,000	4,200,000
Cameras (1956)	3,300,000	1,100,000
Watches (1956)	29,700,000	22,600,000

But perhaps the most impressive race of production was run in the humanly momentous area of home building. According to plan, the Soviet Union undertook to build for its population of 200 million people in 1957 about 46 million square meters of housing. In the same year West Germany actually built—not in plan, but in performance—40 million square meters of housing for 52 million people.

True, the state of the consumer's morale does not really affect the Soviet state's power to survive; the effective indices of totalitarian security are not the square meters of available housing but the square meters of available concentration camps. Still, the Soviet lords cannot overlook the fact that West Germany has built in 1957 almost as much housing for 52 million people as the Soviet Union had *promised* to build for 200 million people.

By the way, in home building West Germany has outdone every other country on earth, including the United States. More than 4 million new homes have been built in Germany since 1948. To match the German annual record, the United States should have built in 1957 about 1.7 million homes; it actually finished only about a million. Since 1948 West Germany has produced more new housing than France and England combined. (And just one other German production record: In 1957 West Germany's steel output was 40 per cent of West Europe's total steel production.)

In the face of such results the Soviet strategy assumes the simplicity of necessity: West Germany must be "neutralized" *at all costs;* which means that West Germany must be denied to the West and be gradually adjusted to the economic and strategic needs of the Soviet Empire. Khrushchev may have learned what Dr. Schacht so unsuccessfully tried to teach Hitler: that one can save oneself the trouble of conquering a country *militarily* if one has pressured or seduced it into *producing* for the master. The alliance between the Soviet Empire and the Krupp Empire was a most promising first step in a campaign of penetration that may prove more decisive to the West than the communist conquest of China and of the Near East.

But the West has not yet begun to comprehend the key position of West German industry. For instance, American private investments in West Germany remain on an incredibly low level. In 1956 (later comprehensive figures are not available), total private United States investments abroad amounted to 22 billion dollars. Of these, 7.5 billion were held in Canada, another 7.4 billion in Latin America. In other words, more than two thirds of all private United States investments abroad were tied to the Western Hemisphere: Evidently, United States capital does not like to go beyond its back yard. Of the remaining 7 billion dollars, about one half was invested in all of western Europe, about 3.5 billion dollars in Asia, Africa, Australia, and the other Pacific centers. Now of the 3.5 billion dollars privately invested in western Europe, almost one half ($1.6 billion) worked in Britain, $426 million in France, $204 million in Italy, $182 million in little Holland—and only $424 million in a Germany that is, without a doubt, the most productive, most reliably profit-producing, most capitalist, and most secure nation outside the United States. In short: two cents out of every dollar United States private business has put to work abroad have gone to Germany.

This is astonishing. It becomes downright incomprehensible in the face of the rate and size of private German investment which in the last two years was in the neighborhood of $12 billion annually (or $25 billion in purchasing power). Conservatively estimated, private investments in Germany have amounted to DM 250 billion since 1950—$60 billion or, in purchasing power, $120 billion —in a nation of 52 million people. Thus the private United States investments in Germany since 1950 ($424 million) compare to total private German investments in the same period something like 1 to 140. The United States has participated less eagerly in the profitable development of Germany than in the socialist regimentation of India, Yugoslavia, Indonesia, Haiti, and even the Soviet Union. In spite of Germany's industrial prowess, in spite of the proved earning power of German business, private United States investments in Germany have remained, quite absurdly, relatively the lowest in the whole world.

Why this is so I do not pretend to know. That private United States investors go by the editorial prejudices of America's leftist press is unlikely. And it certainly cannot be bad business experiences in Germany. In 1956 a United States investment in Germany of $424 million brought a net profit of $52 million—an impressive 12 per cent. Now there may be areas in the world where capital, daringly invested, produces higher results. Oil speculations abroad occasionally multiply an initial investment in a few years; smuggling of arms to Cuba and Egypt may produce stunning profit rates; and there are some choice investments in monopolistic French industries that can still account for fabulous results. (I know of a French mining corporation that makes, but naturally does not declare, an annual profit of about 120 per cent of capital.) Now were the general trend of United States investment directed toward such speculative ventures, the low United States investment rate in Germany would be comprehensible. But—with the exception of oil and mining—United States investments move generally toward caution, prudence, long-range security, comparatively low but dependable annual earnings—on the whole, toward the blue-chip type of stock.

If this is so—and I do not think that any competent market analyst will disagree with my assessment—those small United States investments in Germany remain inexplicable. From 1950 to 1956 private United States capital has put four times the amount of its German holdings into Britain. But British profits are considerably lower than German, the infringements of the welfare state far more annoying in half-socialized Britain than in Dr. Erhard's Germany, the rate of expansion, productivity, and the stimuli of profit prospects incomparably higher in Germany. Most certainly Germany, and not Britain, is the one coming capitalist power outside the United States. It is the only nation on earth that almost instinctively takes to United States techniques of production, marketing, and service, to all the characteristically American ways of doing business. It is, I repeat, the only preponderantly capitalist nation amid the global tide of expropriation. And yet private United States capital barely trickles into Germany; while it flows generously into the regimented parts of the world.

Of course a few United States corporations have importantly invested in Germany. General Motors owns the German Opel Werke, Ford runs its own German branch, and Chrysler is about to take roots in Germany. Understandably enough, the United States automobile industry has learned to have a healthy respect for the automotive acumen of a Germany whose *Volkswagen* is changing the habits and perhaps even the structure of the domestic United States automobile market. Several electrical and chemical United States concerns have developed close contacts with their German counterparts, not so much in form of capital investments as through licensing contracts on a fee basis. On the whole, 237 of the 424 million dollars invested in Germany are working in industry, 114 in oil, 43 in trade, and 30 in various services.

One of the possible reasons for the sluggish United States investments in Germany may be the expansion policy of the German government itself. Far from soliciting foreign investments, it almost discouraged them—not by fiscal methods, to be sure (it is easier to transfer profits from Germany to the United States than from anywhere else in Europe, except Switzerland), but simply by refraining from the kind of investment promotion that is at work all over the United States. Italy and Holland, for instance, have immensely stepped up their organized efforts in the United States to draw into their countries every available United States dollar. Britain continues its well-bred propaganda of reserved social superiority and all that Old Country magic. France tempts with monopolies and seduces with occasional earning performances of staggering proportions. India works the con trick of threatening that it will go communist unless United States private capital subsidizes its socialist economy. Everybody has a special pitch in luring United States capital—everybody but Germany. Unless, of course, one wants to interpret such German reluctance as a particularly shrewd "come-on" strategy. If so, it has been very unsuccessful.

I, for one, believe that the Germans—who are anything but subtle in the wiles of the propagandistic understatement—have meant exactly what they were trying to say: that private United States investments in German industry are, from the German entrepreneur's point of view, not desirable. In the first place, the German rate of investment was most satisfactory; and Dr. Erhard is by no means sure he wants an even faster expansion of German industry. Second, Germany is by now in the viable position to do its own investing abroad, even in the United States, and rather substantially: German private investments in Asia and Africa increase faster than those of any other nation in the world. Third, and most important, Germans know the American tendency to buy *sole* ownership rather than *associate* with foreigners or just extend credits to them. And, assuming that private United States capital would naturally tend toward the most viable industrial properties, the Germans cannot see why such choice pieces should be conceded to foreign capital.

Consequently, neither Washington nor Wall Street nor the United States banks are pestered by German promoters. To invest in Germany, Americans would have to go there themselves and engage in pretty serious competitive bidding. This is, altogether, a situation taken from a very old textbook on economics—an economy almost free from regimentation; chances that have to be diligently pursued; and the early bird being back to his proverbial promising routine.

I say this not because I admire period pieces. In fact, I am not at all sure that I found the *pastiche* of a hectic German economy particularly attractive. But we are not here in the region of aesthetics. We are in the uncouth area of economic triumphs and defeats. The German industry is clearly on its way to beat every competitor outside the United States; and there are several industrial fields in which Germany is likely to beat the United States, too, if only because of the wage differentials. If one is allowed to assume that some United States capital still remains in search of solid prospects; and if one likes to think that purely economic motives govern the flow of investment, then there is no rational reason to expect that profit-seeking United States capital will forever avoid Germany. Surely American national interest demands United States investments in Germany. America's political and strategic security requires strong, solidly built, mutually profitable economic relations between the United States and Germany.

To argue first from the negative, an economic collapse of Germany would be not one iota less deadly to the United States than the bankruptcy of United States Steel. And I am not even thinking of the horrid consequences such a German catastrophe would necessarily have for world trade. I am thinking here of its consequences for the staying power of the Atlantic society, very much including the United States.

A serious tremor, let alone the collapse, of the German economy would bring the German Social Democracy to power; and I anticipate here, advisedly, the *least* dramatic alternative. (Actually, such a crisis might lead very fast to the complete rapprochement between a disrupted Germany and the only remaining great power in Europe—the Soviet Union.) As far as the German Social Democratic party is concerned, they are subjectively as anti-communist as they come in Europe. Yet it is, after all, a Social Democratic party; i.e., it cannot comprehend power, and it is congenitally unable to comprehend the most concentrated power phenomenon of our time, communism.

This party is irreparably vulnerable to the type of political communist attack that will blast the walls of the West far more reliably than could the hydrogen bomb. The German Social Democrats respond by reflex to the socialist vocabulary of Marxism, the communist appeals to the socialist bias of "nationalization," "expropriation," equalitarian regimentations, "social reforms," and every other kind of utopianism. The German Social Democrats—

and I do not know a more decent and humanly more disarming species of Germans—are already responding to the communist play on pacificism and anti-militarism. They have an incurable *faiblesse* to deem one former Nazi a thousand times more dangerous to contemporary Germany than a hundred present Communists; and so they can be made to concentrate all public power, once they have obtained it, on the erasure of yesterday's blots, while the operators of the monolithic tomorrow penetrate the German society.

The German Social Democrats, in short, would make the venerable Mr. Kerenski of Russia's 1917 look like the conquering Napoleon—not because they have sympathies for communism (they despise it), but because they combine the power instincts of the Salvation Army, the reasoning habits of the nineteenth century, and the utopian temptations of the twenty-first. And if the German Social Democrats were to achieve governmental responsibility in the cataclysm of a serious economic crisis, the Soviets would make hash of them, and of West Germany, in no time and with very few swift motions—from an irresistible offer to "reunite" West Germany with a German Soviet zone poised to take control all the way to the Rhine and the Ruhr, to a "trade agreement" that would put all of Germany at the economic mercy of the Soviet Empire. None of the obvious Soviet gambits would require a single Soviet soldier to cross a single border—which means, quite simply, that NATO would atrophy in embarrassing uselessness. And none of these gambits would find the German Social Democracy in a political, psychological, and moral position of principled obstinacy (which is Dr. Adenauer's forte).

It is, therefore, as important for the United States to keep Germany protected from a serious economic crisis as it is important for the United States to keep, at all costs, the Red Army from getting to the German Ruhr. Several Indias, with several Yugoslavias and Polands thrown into the bargain, do not begin to equal the strategic momentum of West Germany in the defense of the United States. And if the United States saw reasons to spend about $75 billion in foreign aid since 1945 to retain its *outposts* against the Soviet Empire—how much foreign aid would be justified when it is spent on retaining the heart land of the West?

But the point is precisely that, in the case of Germany, there is no need for the extravagant kind of foreign aid that has driven significant sections of the American people into a sullen suspicion of *any* kind of foreign aid. Germany has an almost frightening Midas touch: every bit of pump priming turns there into an outburst of profitable production. The only sensible and the only necessary act of foreign aid supplied by the United States Government would seem to be a consistent governmental policy to encourage, facilitate, and protect *private,* profit-seeking United States investment in Germany. What forms such a policy would have to assume is unforeseeable; it must depend on the accidents of the instant. But whether it would be the execution of special United States trade agreements with Germany—guaranteeing, for instance, the unmitigated transfer of United States profits in Germany to the United States—or whether it might, in a critical moment of political tension, expand into a United States subsidized insurance of private United States investments in Germany—it would always remain confined to fundamentally *profitable* United States participation in the expansion of German industry.

So far, as I have said, the Germans themselves have not been anxious to engage the services of United States capital on American terms; that is, in the form of United States purchases of viable German properties. But the recession of 1957–58 has changed some of America's investment habits: United States money has grown cautious, almost timidly so, when it comes to industrial investments at home that are bound to increase even further the productive volume of an American industry singed by recent domestic marketing troubles. By the same token, United States money is now, for the first time in years, getting interested in the old-fashioned type of capital investment abroad that expects neither ownership nor partnership but simply an attractive annual interest return. And there are signs that United States money was being lent to Germany in 1958 in growing amounts.

Germany, on the other hand, is currently more eager to engage credits from abroad than it has been in recent years. Its industry is now seriously in the market for long-term loans, partly because the unprecedented rate of German industrial expansion during the fifties has well-nigh absorbed German investment capacities; partly because United States creditors are now ready to make the loans, not in terms of dollars, but in terms of marks. This is a significantly important point. German industry recalls with some horror that, in the inflation years after World War I, industrial loans that had to be repaid in dollars or other hard currencies were often the undoing of German firms which, had they been unburdened by that type of loan, would have easily withstood the crisis. Ever since the German capital market has been weary of dollar loans. But once American investors were sufficiently persuaded that the DM is as hard a currency as any other (and that in all human foresight American capitalism would not for long survive German capitalism anyhow), United States loans are being offered to Germany in German currency obligations of repayment.

Two German developments were particularly helpful in this accommodation of United States investment practices to German fears. For one, Germany's skillfully directed banking system has maneuvered the fast expanding German economy around the obvious inflationary dangers; so that, of all European nations, Germany has today the sanest monetary system, and a creditor has more reasons here than anywhere else in Europe to expect that the money repaid will not be a mere fraction of the money lent. Secondly, Germany is one of the few countries on earth that have established practically unlimited currency exchangeability; Deutsche Marks can freely buy dollars in Germany; and these dollars can be freely exported. Under these circumstances, United States long-term credits have begun to reach Germany at an increasingly important rate. And if the United States Government deliberately encouraged that trend, the two economies could soon reach a high degree of mutually advantageous interdependence—an interdependence, I shall like to add, that will be politically and strategically no less important than economically.

One more word on the present structure of the German economy: Whatever else may be new in Adenauer's Germany, the names of the rich and mighty are not. The economically decisive property remains in the hands of the families that have personified German economic potency throughout the last decades. And the greatest of them all, of course, is still Krupp.

Alfried Krupp, sole owner of the firm Friedr. Krupp, is worth today between DM 2.5 and 3 billion ($600 to 740 million or, in purchasing power, $1.2 to 1.5 billion). But this figure means next to nothing. What matters is the magnitude of the empire over which Alfried Krupp presides—150 plants, an annual business volume of DM 3.4 billion.

The next most important name in German economy is still Thyssen. The widow of Fritz Thyssen, Amélie, is today the owner of Phoenix-Rheinrohr A.G. (which controls Blohm & Voss in Hamburg and considerable interests in the United States and Canada). She owns together with Fritz Thyssen's daughter, Countess Anita de Zichy-Thyssen, the ATH Concern which produced in 1957 more than 3 million tons of steel (more than any other German steel producer) and the Handelsunion A.G., which inherited the giant sales and merchandising organization of the former Vereinigte Stahlwerke A.G. Then there is the Thyssen-Bornemisza branch of the family which rules the Thyssen Gas- und Wasserwerke, the mining corporation Walsum, the Stahl- und Röhrenwerke Resiholz and the August-Thyssen-Bank. Finally, there is the Joseph Thyssen branch of the clan that owns the Hamborner Bergbau A.G. and, together with the rest of the family, about one hundred square miles of Europe's most valuable coal fields.

The Haniel family still controls the Gutehoffnungshütte A.V., the Hüttenwerke Oberhausen A.G., the Bergbau Neue Hoffnung A.G., the Rhein-Preussen A.G. für Bergbau und Chemie, the Deutsche Werft in Hamburg, and the Franz Haniel & Cie.G.b.H.

The Flicks lost some of their legendary power, mainly through the amputation of East and Central Germany, but they still own the Monopol Bergwerke G.m.b.H., the Metallhüttenwerke Lübeck, the Maximilianshütte, the Buderus Eisenwerke, considerable steel

and coal interests in France and Belgium. They have also branched
out into automobile production and own substantial holdings in
Krauss-Maffei, Daimler-Benz, and the Auto-Unjon.

The heirs to Peter Klöckner retain controlling interests in the
formidable Klöckner-Humboldt-Deutz A.G., the Rütgenwerke, and
the Klöckner Werke A.G.

The heirs to Otto Wolff still run the mighty firm of Otto Wolff
K.G., the Eisen- und Hüttenwerke, the Stolberger Zink A.G., and,
gathered around these organizations, a choice selection of minor
iron works.

The Röchlings still own the Volklinger Stahlwerke, the Stahlwerke Röchling-Buderus A.G., the Rheinmetall A.G., the Gollnow-
Werke A.G. Besides, they are very likely Europe's most active
traders of iron and steel.

Germany's steel and coal, in other words, are still, or again, administered by the few families that had been doing this job provocatively well ever since Germany first became a great industrial
nation. This fact is remarkable for two reasons. For one, the Allied
military governments have done all that can be done, and a little
more, to break up these families' hold over the German economy.
Second, the currency reform of 1948 has dissolved most other
property relations. And yet the staying power of Germany's traditional bosses proved stronger than all storms of history. What saved
them was the very depth of the German collapse. When the German
economy slowly began to breathe again, a nation that had lost all
standards, all references, values, beliefs, reached out for the few
names that signified economic solidity. At a time when no one had
credit, simply because there was no credit system, the Krupps and
the Thyssens and the Wolffs got all the credit they wanted just because they were the Krupps and the Thyssens and the Wolffs. When
people began to invest again, they rushed quite naturally to buy
industrial shares on which unforgettably magic names guaranteed
the blue-chips habit of economic success. And so, a few years after
the "German economic miracle" had set in, the rich and mighty
were back in splendor.

They are back not only in steel and coal. The old names are also back in chemical and food industries, machine manufacturing, banking—the Werhahns, the Quandts, the Henkels, the Oetkers, the Boschs, the Oppenheims, the Von Fincks. There are, of course, a few newcomers among the German tycoons—people such as Max Grundig, who built, from scratch, a European empire of radio and TV appliances; and Helmut Horton, who owns innumerable department stores and spends money more conspicuously than any nouveau riche has ever dared before. But, on the whole, the *Gotha* of German wealth reads as if we still lived in 1929.

The traditional German tendency toward cartelization has won out even under a government that the most suspicious watchdog of the Sherman Act could not possibly accuse of connivance in favor of the cartels: the economy in which Germany has prospered since 1949 is the nearest thing to a free economy Europe has ever seen. And yet the concentration of important property in the hands of the mighty few has continued at an increased pace.

In 1958 the Statistische Bundesamt carefully analyzed the structure of the 2,600 corporations that constitute the body of the German industry. On 941 of them, no reliable data could be obtained. But 1,636 corporations reported with revealing precision—and the picture is unequivocal. Before the war, 29 per cent of the stock of these corporations were held by the management groups. By 1958 their stake had grown to 35 per cent; while the total of shares distributed among stockholders on the outside shrank from 34 to 20 per cent; and 45 per cent (as compared with 36 per cent in 1936) were in the hands of investor groups closely affiliated with the controlling interests which, in such way, could count on no less than 80 per cent of stock to back their policies blindly. And the 1,636 analyzed corporations represent three quarters of Germany's total corporate capital.

Unavoidably, therefore, the facile social critics, who populate the German press even more conspicuously today than they did in the twenties, speak of the "Regime of the Three Hundred"—the 300 German families whose names seem indeed to stand for economic control. And they are getting more visible every day because of the new trend in cartel expansion. The favorite form is no longer the conquest of a significant segment in a specific industry (steel production, for instance, owned in Germany by eight combines: Thyssen, Krupp, Rheinstahl, Gutehoffnungshütte, Mannesmann, Hoesch, Klöckner, and Flick). The thing today is "vertical expansion"—the incorporation of all accessible intermediary stations in the economic process, from raw-material sources to the sales organizations that handle the finished consumer product. And in this one respect, it seems to me, the German Government can be correctly accused of favoring the cartels with a somewhat suspect provision of the tax law.

The *Umsatzsteuer* (turnover tax), a very substantial source of German fiscal income, must be paid each time a semifinished product changes hands; and many consumer goods go through twelve or fifteen mutations of ownership before they reach their final destination—which means twelve or fifteen times *Umsatzsteuer*. But if a product is handled inside one and the same organization, from raw-material source to final salesroom, the government charges only one *Umsatzsteuer* of 4 per cent of the final price—a mere fraction of the tax burden hung onto consumer goods that go through the normally manifold channels of preprocessing. The term "one organization" refers to the purely legal aspect of ownership; so that a "vertical cartel," reaching from raw material to supermarket, can split the very considerable saving in *Umsatzsteuer* two ways: it can cut prices in competition with small producers and at the same time still reap much higher profits which, in most cases, are reinvested in the ever-increasing "vertical" expansion of the cartel. Understandably enough, the small entrepreneurs in Germany are engaged in a serious battle against such effects of tax laws that, in a kind of perpetual motion, constantly augment the power of the cartels.

On the whole, the German tax burden is onerous. In 1957 the Germans paid more in taxes and contributions to Social Security than any other western nation—31.7 per cent of the gross national product. (The British paid 29.4 per cent, the French 28.8 per cent, the Americans 25.9 per cent, and the Swiss 20.3 per cent of their respective national gross products.) The total tax burden of the

Germans was in 1957 slightly more than DM 50 billion, for a population of 52 million people; so that the per-capita tax payments of the Germans amounted to almost exactly DM 1,000 per year, taken out of the DM 4,000 that are the German per-capita quota of the national gross product. But in addition to these taxes the Germans also pay contributions to Social Security in the amount of more than 8 per cent of the national gross product—another DM 16 billion, or DM 300 per capita every year.

These enormous demands of Social Security and general bureaucracy on the productive economy remain a serious threat to the free-market system. It can be neglected as long as the extraordinary prosperity prevails. But the first tremors of a recession will make the German economy cringe under its fiscal burdens. This is quite likely the area where the unusual blandness of German political life will turn into combat, the strange social calm—a weird atmosphere, for battle-scarred Germany, of complete social pacification—into acute social conflict.

CHAPTER TWO

How Much Guilt—How Much Atonement?

THE longer I live with the knowledge of the dirty witchcraft that dehumanized Germany for twelve years, the less can I comprehend the nature of man in general and the German's nature in particular. The years that have passed since Hitler's dissolution have added nothing to my (or anyone else's) understanding of the ghastly binge; and the complete normalcy of the Germans who survived subtracts a great deal from a certainty of yesterday—that something, somewhere deep inside a distorted "German soul," is specifically corrupt. During the past few years I have learned anew to love individual Germans, though I still cannot say that I love the Germans. But then, can one love a nation?

Just as "a whole nation cannot be guilty," just so a whole nation cannot be lovable. If there is a nation on earth that I love it's the Americans; and yet, I do not love the red swollen necks that I see prowling the back streets of certain American towns; I do not love the misanthropic faces I keep meeting in certain regions of the country; I do not love the aggressive arrogance of a "Know-Nothingism" that claims to thrive "in God's own country." True, of all generalizations none can be less depended on than the maxim that no generalization is admissible; can there, for example, be a

reasonable doubt that there *is* "a national character" and that a
nation *chooses* to be prevailingly this or that? And yet the ugly pain
of recent historic experience seems to have established that what
happened to the Germans can happen to any other dispirited nation. Recent events have established the distressing truth of that
political cliché, "the lunatic fringe," and established it for all nations with about equal force.

Civilized Frenchmen have tortured human creatures in Algeria
("to extract information") with a refinement and "a sense of duty"
that, so one had for many years believed, were the national characteristics of Prussians. There are "ideologies" in America which are
as "romantically" cockeyed and as untouched by Christian mores
as anything ever propagated in lower Saxony; yet they make prose-
lytes. Some British heirs to seven centuries of Magna Charta behave
with such contempt for civil liberties and the inviolability of private
existence that Hitlerian blockheads would feel immediately at home
among them. The surrender of human sentiments to the subhuman
regimentation that has become civic habit in Russia makes the
German submission to the Gestapo look normal. Jews embark in
Israel upon careers of muscle-bound assassination, Spaniards have
quartered one another with passionate finesse, Czechs—not long
ago the most *petit-bourgeois* people of the Continent—imitate quite
believably the megalomania of ruthless villains, and native Americans talk Wagnerian nonsense as if they had been bottle-fed on
Houston Stewart Chamberlain.

All of which does not excuse a single Nazi murder. Nor does it
explain a single gesture of Nazi insanity. That a Frenchman or a
Briton or an American or a Jew or a Spaniard or a Czech or a
Russian can also flow over with evil and ugliness makes matters, on
the contrary, only less explicable, for it deprives one of the last
crutch of determinism: the horror, likely to break out at *any* of all
conceivable places, cannot be charged to the notorious *"special*
circumstances of time and place." If man can shrink to beastly
stupidity, regardless of his group's tradition and its accumulated
racial experience, then his capacity for evil is indeed metaphysically
ordained. The conduct of one man can neither excuse nor explain

the conduct of another; but the potential misconduct of *all* removes the problem from politics to theology—where it remains unfathomable.

I mean to say that it is not only demonstrably wrong (and Nazistic) to accuse "the" Germans of ethical monstrosity—it is irrelevant. I hope fervently that neither the world nor the Germans will ever forget the gas chambers or minimize the unspeakable guilt that will hang, anonymously and immovably, over this part of the earth for centuries to come. But I also hope that we all shall learn to accept that guilt as the *common* guilt of man. The German who still refuses to acknowledge that guilt (and that means practically every German) is *right* as German—and miserably *wrong* as man. The national entity does not carry "collective guilt," if only because it was itself terrorized; and, under the moral law, no man is *obliged* to be a saint or a martyr. The German, who for this reason shrugs off his personal responsibility and, referring to the *universal* human indifference to the pain of others, claims his relative innocence as "helpless little man," is incontrovertibly right as a little man—and shamefully wrong as the bearer of a soul for which he will have to account.

The human herd, when not beastly, is cowardly. To expect civic courage from a whole nation is therefore naïve; to *demand* it, is folly. The bulk of the German people behaved under nazism exactly, I am afraid, as the bulk of any other people would behave under extreme pressure—namely, despicably. The Germans who deny this today are ludicrous. But a non-German, in passing judgment on the fetid twelve years of nazism, cannot escape the first concern of judicious investigation—the control question, How would any other people have behaved? Hitler was obviously wrong: the Germans *are* no superior race. Consequently, a verdict on their conduct must be based, not on what can be expected from a superior people (if there is one), but on a comparison with what can be considered standard behavior of a comparable national group in our vulgar century.

When the Lord pondered the punishment of Sodom and Gomorrah, He was willing to forgive the debauch, if only ten just men could be found in the land; and ever since, informed moral judgment has been based, not on the predictably contemptible behavior of the average, but on the conduct of those rare beings whose moral essence permeates their normal life processes. By this I mean to say that it does not seem permissible to tie one's judgment over a people to the accidental appearance of extraordinary saints and martyrs. Saints and martyrs are infinitely personal phenomena that neither redeem nor indict a group. They stand for nobody but their own lonely selves. The correct biblical term for socially representative people was, very significantly, "ten just men." Men, that is, who are cut out of the general cloth; but men, also, whose moral essence permeates their normal life processes. No saints—"just men." And today, thirteen years after the absurd events, only the Nazi-in-reverse—the person, that is, who applies the inanities of racialism to a complex group of millions of non-interchangeable individuals—can deny that there *were* just men in Germany, and thousands of them.

Some statistics first. The Nazi tribunals passed death sentences on about 12,000 "Aryan" Germans for what the regime called treasonable acts against the security of the Third Reich. More than 600,000 "Aryan" Germans who survived concentration camps have been found, after a strict postwar investigation, to be "victims of political persecution" under Hitler. The Gestapo, in other words, has "processed" two out of every hundred adult Germans as enemies of the regime. Now some of these people may have been, of course, quite innocent victims of plain denunciation and by no means deliberate foes of nazism. Even so, close to half a million Germans knowingly preferred persecution to submission. And they did so in the face of a *Schrecklichkeit* unparalleled in history. Even more, they had the additional courage and the maturity to act against a "national" regime that was glowing with flamboyant success.

Now we simply do not know what the statistics would be for other national entities going through comparable experiences. I hope there would be more than 2 million Americans (i.e., 2 per cent of the adult population) to defy a government of perverse evil;

but I have no way of knowing. What I do know is that, for instance, far less than 2 per cent of Czechoslovakia's adult population, terrorized not only by hoodlums but by *foreign* hoodlums, defied the Nazi occupation from 1939 to 1945. I also know that *la résistance* in France never—never, that is, before the jig was up for the Germans in 1944—succeeded in mobilizing more than 2 per cent of the adult French population against the Nazi might.

This first redeeming fact—that two out of one hundred adult Germans actively fought the ruling sickness—is accompanied by an even more extraordinary fact: that for years the High Command of the German Army was in demonstrable conspirational opposition to the Hitler regime. The generals who presided from 1933 to 1938 over the Army's High Command, Colonel General von Hammerstein-Equord, Colonel General Ludwig Beck, and General Halder, were constantly engaged in technically treasonable negotiations with foreign governments—chiefly the British Government which, *alas,* under Neville Chamberlain had neither the sense nor the courage to coordinate its policies with the brave anti-Nazi intentions of Hammerstein-Equord, Halder, and Beck.

The immense fact is established beyond the possibility of doubt: not before 1938 was Hitler in formal control of the German Army. For five years its commanding generals remained willing and ready to overthrow what German officers used to call "their legal government," provided there was adequate encouragement from abroad—and the encouragement they insisted on was no more than a resolute policy of the British and French governments that would have denied Hitler his dirt-cheap successes of rearmament and expansion. There is no parallel situation in modern history: The army high command of a great power conspires with foreign governments against the domestic regime, not just for an exuberant moment, but for years, and is willing to renounce the military grandeur of its own nation, if only, by so attaining the failure of the hated regime, conditions could be readied for its overthrow.

Nor was such unprecedented loyalty to moral principle, overruling a conventional loyalty to the national government, confined to a few commanding generals. Six years after Hitler had purged the High Command, the aborted uprising of July 20, 1944, was based on an organized rebellion of essential German army cadres, led by officers who, through years of blinding Nazi triumphs, had remained faithful to the beliefs of Beck, Halder, and Von Hammerstein-Equord. The conspiracy failed. But the list of names of those whom a maddened Hitler hanged after the failure reads like a *Gotha* of Germany's famous military families.

And it is indecently easy today to make fun of the unhappy inefficiency these military conspirators paid for with their lives. More significant, no doubt, remains the fact that the professional German class of officers, notorious for their rigid notions of "duty," "oath," and "unquestioning obedience," has shown itself capable of a loyalty to non-military principles of moral conduct that I am afraid would not necessarily be matched by less traditionalist officer corps of less "militaristic" nations. The Anglo-Saxon world, in particular, retains a concept of patriotism the measure of which is the trite homily, "Right or wrong, my country." And even as penetrating a mind as Rebecca West's has never understood (in her exquisite book on treason) that there are human commitments and loyalties far superior to those that remain rooted in man's rather primitive love for country, the valley where he was born, the community that surrounded him all his life.

The many scores of German (Prussian) officers who were desperately ready—and not just in a fleeting moment of rage, but for endless years of mortal dangers—to conspire with the "enemy" against the "legal government" of their own country, had made a profoundly moral choice between right and wrong; and they were no longer fooled by the banal seductiveness of "my country." This, it seems to me, was the victory of the men who were hanged in 1944.

Out of Nazi Germany, of all places, came a Moltke, a Yorck von Wartenburg, a Trott zu Solz, a Von Stauffenberg, a Von Stülpnagel, a Schwerin von Schwanenfeld, a Von der Schulenburg, a Von Schlabrendorff, a Von Hammerstein-Equord, a Von Kleist, a Von Hardenberg, a Von Gersdorff, a Von Tresckow. These are "Prussian" names, names of *Junkers;* and they are also names which, if truth indeed prevails, will join the short list of superior men who have not hesitated to choose their God over their race. If there is a future for the West, these conservative Prussian officers and noblemen will have died for it. In the face of these names may he who can still speak of racial German guilt. I cannot.

And yet the self-righteousness of inverted racialists who despise "the" Germans is no worse than the self-righteousness of Germans who angrily insist that "the past be forgotten." There are millions of such Germans. If they were themselves former Nazi torturers, trying to bury their past crimes, their outcry would be humanly understandable; for it is an elementary rule of self-preservation to suppress evidence and to repress all memories of unforgettable guilt. But the vast majority of those Germans who today bitterly object to the most modest attempts at punishing the gorillas of Hitler's concentration camps are the mass of German *Bürger* whose fundamental indifference has kept them out of any kind of commitments, even Nazi. They never were Nazis; and they most certainly are no Nazis today. They want to be comfortable; and this, too, would be a humanly understandable motivation of a questionable attitude, if it were not so clearly incompatible with the nation's peace of mind. Comfort-loving people who attend to their comfort are rational; but comfort-loving people who insist on staying uncomfortable make no sense.

The rising chorus of protests against anything that might remind the Germans of the Nazi stench swells to real power each time a German court gets around to trying a former hangman. There were a few major trials in the spring and summer of 1958—truly sickening cases of an unrepenting mass sadism—during which one could sense public outrage, not against the sadists, but against the authorities who attended to their duties. And, I repeat, one hardly ever noticed a conscious or even subconscious sympathy with the beastly; it was essentially a growing impatience with a judiciary policy that, whether or not this is its intention, keeps shameful memories alive. "Yes, yes," I heard countless Germans say in 1958, "I *know* these horrible things happened—but must we still hear about them, thirteen years after the event, just to blacken the German name again, in a world only too anxious to forgive and forget?"

This posture, clearly, is reprehensible and unintelligent to boot. And yet, it seems unavoidable. It was prepared, with the automatism of tragedy, in the first few years of Germany's military occupation. Indeed, seldom in history has the noble intention of bad statesmen and even worse psychologists backfired so fast and so destructively.

The men in charge of Allied military governments, and particularly the men advising them, had a noble intention to purge vanquished Germany of the evil that had ruled it for twelve years. This was the concept of all the military trials at Nuremberg and elsewhere. Yet true statesmen and adequate psychologists would have known that a nation can be purged, if at all, only by itself. Had the United States Army of Occupation hanged all the Nazi leaders it considered criminally dangerous for their military government, but had it done so under the stern military laws of occupation, the defeated Germans would have understood and, more likely than not, applauded. The tragic mistake of statesmanship and the profound psychological blunder were to disguise an act of perfectly correct military retribution as a majestic procedure of incorruptible justice.

I happen to know some of the United States officers who prepared those trials, and I can vouch for the sincere, the burning idealism behind their efforts. They truly believed they were opening the doors toward a new and beneficial concept of international law that would, once and for all, abolish aggressive war and what later became known as "genocide." What these United States officers never understood, and their clever advisers did not tell them, was first that the Germans could not be taught justice by a court on whose bench were sitting the representatives of the Soviet Union that had closed an alliance for the sake of aggression with Göring & Co. in 1939 and had raped Germany in 1945; second, that one cannot teach a vanquished people the fundamentals of justice by demonstrating to them the arbitrary willfulness of the conquerors.

There is no adequate punishment, this side of hell, for Göring,

Streicher, *et al.* But this is entirely beside the point. For the point is not what was done to the "war criminals" and whether they deserved it; they were guilty of much more than what they were indicted for, and their walk to the gallows was as nothing compared with their eternal journey through hell. The only essential point is whether or not what *we* did was consistent with our self-imposed assignment; and, even more important, whether or not it was consistent with our professed dedication. It was neither.

Our professed dedication was to justice and law; but the Nuremberg Tribunal, a joint venture with Hitler's Soviet allies, was acting under an arbitrary and fancy concept of some "new" law, uncodified by jurisprudence and incompatible with the traditional concept of justice. And our self-imposed assignment was to impress the German people with an exemplary shock treatment, so that they might reform in shame and terror; but the German people, when they looked at the "war crime" trials, were not shaken with terror, could not identify themselves in shame with the culprits, and felt no compulsion to reform. Rather, they understood and even approved of the trials as the kind of political revenge the Germans, too, might have taken, had they won the war; and, having been relieved by the Allies of the duty of sitting in court over the horrid crimes committed in their name, they have considered ever since the punishment of Nazis as no concern of theirs. Had not the Allies done their utmost to get even with *all* the Nazis who could be held responsible for the regime? And why, then, should the Germans, deprived of their own judicial powers for years, now duplicate a job the Allies had done with all their superior might?

The net result has been a dreary German cynicism in all matters even vaguely connected with judicial retribution for Nazi crimes. They understood, though not enthusiastically, their government's political need to accept an obligation of financial retribution to victims of nazism. They even understood, as I said, the Allies' desire to hang the vanquished leaders of nazism. And they might have understood their own duty to sit in judgment over their own past had they been invited to do so at the moment of defeat, in 1945; and had they then been entrusted with the means of authoritative justice. But for almost four years they were denied any self-governing authority of a nation. And as if to make them completely numb, cynically indifferent to a judicious conduct of their own affairs, the Allied military governments crushed any instinctive sense of justice by proclaiming the entire German people "guilty until proven innocent"—by the unforgivable inanity of the "denazification screening."

For several years a bureaucratically blind machinery of army officials went to work on the German people, choking the life and pinching the nerves of the whole nation with the notorious techniques of the *Fragebogen;* and, having driven the whole German nation through the mill of a ludicrous investigation—ludicrous because there was not even theoretically a chance to check the self-assessment of 30 million frightened Germans—the Allied military governments left Germany so exhausted with bureaucratic vexation, so drenched with self-pity, so thoroughly accustomed to the black-and-white lies about everybody's past, that the living German generation will never again be willing to sit in judgment over itself. The time has been missed. The task, the moral need for a self-afflicted German catharsis, has never been understood by the Allied military governments. The Germans went through a purgatory all right, but they emerged from it with bulging muscles and an atrophied moral sense.

It is an *atrophied* moral sense—not a perverted one. The German *Bürger* who feels offended by reminders of his nation's recent sickness wants to forget it—*not* to approve of it. His moral sensitivity, crushed in years of military occupation, has been finally reduced by a prosperity of spectacular proportions that would have softened the conscience of far more sensitive nations. And it would be the crowning mistake of a West that has almost forfeited Germany's future in years of a blundering military occupation if the contemporary moral indifference of the German mass were to be misunderstood as a tendency toward neo-nazism.

There is in Germany no demonstrable danger of a nazistic relapse; and not only because that monstrous "romantic" German aberration has fizzled out in ridiculously shameful impotence, but also because the new Germany was successful beyond anyone's dreams. The Weimar Republic bred nazism because it had an unfortunate habit of failing—economically, politically, diplomatically. The Weimar Republic was pathetic. It had the political style of a masochist—always on a beggar's defensive, always exposing its structural weakness, always on its knees. But there is, not only in politics, an absolutely irresistible attraction between masochist and sadist: A weak government will unfailingly be raped by a gang of blackguards. And so it was a stroke of incredibly good luck, for Germany and the West, that the first decade of post-Nazi German convalescence was determined by the calm manliness of Dr. Konrad Adenauer.

For the decisive decade during which the matrix was cast for a whole German generation, this Dr. Adenauer held Germany in the palm of his steady hand. Here was a statesman unaffected by self-doubts and neurotic hesitations, a man of an elementary firmness in conduct, guided by a profoundly secure set of values (quite simply: obedience to Catholic dogma), and an unshakable faith in a West European destiny of his people. Whether or not Adenauer is a genius is beside the point. What of it if he has not contributed a single new thought to German *Weltanschauung* and to learned German state philosophy? At that climactic time of its history Germany was in need, not of a new *Weltanschauung,* but of a safe and preferably old reliance on character.

In convalescence, nations as well as men need above all a reassuring sense of trust in the predictable response of their environment: the crutch must be lying just there and nowhere else, there must be exactly twenty-seven steps from bed to door, and there should be the wonder of a budding tree looking through the window. The profoundly reassuring sight in convalescence is the familiar—not the new. Adenauer—and this made him such a priceless stroke of good luck for Germany—was the personification of everything that, without being Nazi, was totally familiar to all Germans: the solidity of a substantial *Bürger;* the rocklike allegiance to a recognizable set of beliefs; the self-assurance, the unwavering certainty, and, yes, even the *bourgeois* pride of a man who has achieved authority in his personal career; the self-sufficient happiness of a person set in his personal ways, his rather pedestrian tastes, his unbrilliant dislikes; and, above all, the very same predictability which unnerves the German intellectuals, who are hungry for some kind of elegant stimulation, but which has cured the German people of the addiction to political thrills and kicks that twelve years of nazism had brought upon a frazzled nation.

This is why that stiff, authoritarian, conservative, impeccable, and somewhat sanctimonious Dr. Adenauer was the greatest sweepstake Germany has ever won in one of its many periods of crisis. As never before Germany, in a rare coincidence of national destitution and an overpowering personality of curative effect, found the one statesman who had the correct answer to a national need. Germany, violated by lecherous rascals for twelve years, needed nothing so much as a righteous man of sane substance; and it found Konrad Adenauer. I do not know of a more fortunate coincidence in history. It may have been one of its brightest moments.

This is not to say that Dr. Adenauer has given Germany a faultless administration beyond doubts and above criticism. There have remained areas in Germany's public life that have never been completely cleansed. In particular there is considerable substance to the widely popularized complaint that former Nazis have found employment in sensitive parts of the administrative and judicial machinery of the new Germany; and that many a teacher in German elementary and higher schools cannot disguise his own Nazi education.

True, the situation is infinitely worse in Germany's Soviet zone where the ruling Communist party, *as a matter of policy,* pays for the allegiance of former Nazi leaders with political jobs. No fewer than twenty-nine members of the Soviet-German *Volkskammer,* the Communist "parliament," are former Nazis. Two communist members of the East German "parliament," Dr. Kurt Säuberlich and Dr. Heinz Funke, are former S.S. leaders. The East German minister of health, Luitpold Steidle, and his deputy, Dr. Farchmin, are former members of the Nazi party. So are the minister for chemical industries, Werner Winkler; the deputy minister for machine industry, Wunderlich; the chairman of the Research Council of the Board of Ministers, Professor Dr. Thiessen; the *Rektor* of the "Walter Ulbricht Academy for Law and Political Science," Professor Dr. Kroeger; the chairman of the *Volkskammer's* legislative committee, Siegfried Dallman; the chief justice of East Germany's Supreme Court, Kurt Schumann; the managing editor of the East German magazine, *Deutsche Aussenpolitik* ("German Foreign Policy"), Aust; the assistant editor in chief of the Communist party's central organ, *Neues Deutschland,* Dr. Günther Kertzscher, and the paper's correspondent in Bonn, Dengler; the military commentator on the East German official radio station, *Deutschlandsender,* Egbert von Frankenberg; the *Rektor* of the Technological Institute in Dresden, Pommer; the *Rektor* of the Electro-Technical Institute, Stamm.

In contrast to this cynically open alliance between the ruling Communists and former Nazi leaders, the penetration of West Germany's administrative and judicial machinery by former Nazis is casual, ineffective, and most certainly not intended by the Adenauer government. But it is a fact. And the regrettable sloppiness in selecting West Germany's governmental personnel cannot be validly excused by reference to East Germany's cynical policies.

There is, however, a strange contradiction in the attitudes of those impassioned crusaders who would impeach the Adenauer government each time a former Nazi is discovered somewhere in the governmental hierarchy. For they are, ordinarily, also the ideologues who never tire of pointing out that the German people, *as a whole,* participated in the Nazi binge. But if they are right in this, the unforgiving critics have no case against Adenauer. Evidently, if the German people *as such* was Nazi, it is theoretically and practically impossible to staff, only twelve years after the collapse of nazism, the enormous governmental machinery of a post-Nazi Germany with politically impeccable Germans. Adenauer's critics cannot have it both ways—they cannot claim a collective, congenital affinity of the German people to nazism *and* reproach Dr. Adenauer for slipshod leniency toward former Nazis.

In truth, Adenauer remains responsible for frequent bad judgment in matters of personnel policy, precisely because the German people is *not* congenitally Nazi. Admittedly, it would be difficult to find the required hundreds of thousands of professional men, of teachers, of lawyers, of public servants who, throughout the long period of totalitarian Nazi rule, were never touched by the forceful contagion; particularly difficult as the so-called educated groups, from which governmental servants must be recruited, are notoriously foolish and notoriously corrupt when exposed to totalitarian temptations. Just so, the task is difficult—not impossible. And the Adenauer government would have added a final touch of perfection to its extraordinary list of achievements if it had paid more discriminating attention to the record of all its employees.

Yet Germany's public opinion, far from being secretly manipulated by former Nazis in strategic position, is conspicuously sensitive to the slightest echo of an unmentionable past. And this official German sensitivity often grows grotesque.

In February 1958 the German minister for justice, Dr. Fritz Schäffer, made an uninformed remark on the German restitution payments. These payments—and by 1958 more than 2,250,000 claims of victims of Nazi persecution had been filed with the West German government—were getting, Dr. Schäffer said, out of proportion with other federal responsibilities, might result in inflationary pressures on the budget and, above all, were abused by German and foreign lawyers who were charging up to 50 per cent of the realized restitution payments as their professional fees. Having said so much, Dr. Schäffer sat down—and was immediately snowed under by an avalanche of public protests. For weeks the representative German press practically asked for his scalp; and when I left Germany, in November 1958, the case was a long way from being dismissed and Dr. Schäffer was still under some sort of cloud.

But what *was* the case? The minister, or so implied the respectable German press, had revived anti-semitism. Now there is no doubt, on the basis of the evidence offered, that Dr. Schäffer was in insufficient control of his facts—which, in a minister's public statements, is bad business. The restitution payments of the German government to victims of Nazi persecution—by no means only Jews—amounted in 1958 to several billion marks. This is a tidy sum, but it clearly remains within the grasp of a solvent German government; and of all continental currencies, the mark has shown the least inflationary tendencies. All other expert members of the Adenauer cabinet, contradicting Dr. Schäffer, have in the meantime testified to that effect. And they all agreed, with Dr. Schäffer's consensus, that the Restitution Law—a unique piece of legislation, about as unique as the gas chambers—remained an essential and rather cheap part in Germany's systematic endeavor to regain its status as a civilized nation.

But there was also consensus that many hundreds of lawyers, inside and outside of Germany, were high-pressuring old and helpless people, Nazi victims clearly entitled to restitution even without any clever legal help; and that these lawyers were doing it sometimes for scandalous fees up to and beyond 50 per cent of the restitution. This was the greatest bonanza German—and many American—lawyers had hit upon in a lifetime. One of them—who, in a clean-cut case of unethical incompatibility, was also the chairman of the Restitution Committee of the *Bundestag* in Bonn—confessed to "handling" thousands of such cases simultaneously; and competent experts have estimated that this one gentleman's fees must have exceeded, in a single year, the restitution receipts of five hundred victims of Nazi persecution. (Caught in the act, he resigned from his *Bundestag* job.) In short, at least one fourth of the several billion DM granted by the German Government to victims of Nazi persecution are being turned into a plush subsidy for a profession which has not been known lately to suffer from indigence.

Such were the facts in Dr. Schäffer's case. They did not help him a bit. He had digressed from a basic injunction on official German conduct: No German must so much as *touch* on a subject—and never mind his motivations—that may bear on Jews. I have nowhere seen a comparably effective social injunction on a topic of indubitable public interest. And I do not know of more convincing proof that the Germans must still be suffering from disturbed relations with the Jews.

In 1958, hardly thirteen years after the last Jew was burned in Belsen, there was, of course, still anti-semitism in Germany. At least one third of the adult Germans alive must have belonged to one or another Nazi organization that had no other "philosophical" basis than anti-semitism. Some of these Germans were indubitably cynics who belonged for reasons of personal advancement, i.e., without hating the Jews as much as they pretended. But most of them—say, 10 million Germans—must, in their own minds, have despised the Jews with *earnest* convictions. Yes, there simply must remain a deep layer of spasmic anti-semitism in the dark recesses of the German mind. And yet, during a year's contact with Germans I had to sharpen my ears beyond the normal duties of a reporter to hear the kind of anti-semitic talk I could hear, without even listening, every day in the smoking cars and the very best clubs of America. Nowhere in Europe or the United States have I seen so effective a social injunction against anti-semitic clichés and gestures as in the Germany of 1958.

I say "social" injunction because it surely is no mere compliance with the codified law. The Germans suppress their anti-semitic bias —which, on all logical grounds, cannot possibly be weaker among them than it is among Americans, Britons, and French—with a consistency and a discipline which I find disturbing. I, for one, object to what is loosely called "discrimination" against Negroes, or Irish, or Jews, because I deem it my inalienable right to call a Negro, or an Irishman, or a Jew, or anyone else, a rascal if he is one; but as a man who is controlled by manners, I cannot call him the name he deserves as long as he is *generically* suspect. The heat of racialism freezes tongues. That the German tongue is so conspicuously frozen amidst the global chatter about the Jews shows how seriously the Germans must still be afflicted with the pangs of racialism. Their silence is self-conscious. They do not trust themselves.

But could there be a more civilized evidence of an uncivilized state of mind? I have met Germans—and they were quite represen-

tative of an important minority—who seem compelled to spend the
rest of their lives with Jews only. They read, adore, befriend, and
love only Jews. It is an unmistakable case of racial discrimination
in reverse. And not in months of crisscrossing the country—not
even in Munich's stunningly vulgar *Hofbräuhaus*—have I met a
single German who was as vulgarly anti-semitic as the type of
people one meets, as a matter of course, every day in New York
or London or Paris.

I cannot believe that this is merely the result of a special German
aptitude for mimicry and mental discipline. True, the Germans
know that, in this matter, they are on a kind of probation before
the world; but no people, not even Germans, could voluntarily,
and so perfectly, comply with unenforceable social commands. And
as there surely must be an important residuum of anti-semitism
left in a nation that only a few years ago has coughed up the foulest
racialist pus, there must be an even more important factor at work
on the German mind.

That factor, I think, is a virulent outbreak of pragmatism among
the Germans—which, I am the first to admit, is an odd diagnosis.
For only a few years ago no one who knew the Germans and knows
Anglo-Saxon pragmatism would have thought it conceivable that
pragmatism could ever infect a single German, let alone the German
nation. For fateful centuries this has been a people of "ideal-
ists"—meaning, of course, not the compliment that is colloquially
implied but the technical essence of the term. The Germans, more
than any other modern nation, were moved and motivated throughout the last century by "ideas," by symbols rather than by measurable quantities and interests; and the vaguer these "ideas" were, the
more violently the Germans were motivated and moved. There
was a dense aura of "idealism" about every act of this people. They
were constantly stepping on their neighbors' feet, but only because
they were constantly staring at the flimsiest stars.

This time they have had it. For twelve years they lived an "idea"
with greater abandon and wilder vehemence than at any other time
of their history. For the sake of that "idea" they killed millions of
human creatures, destroyed famous cities, saw millions of their

own people killed, and their own famous cities destroyed. For the first time, even in German history, a people had taken an "idea" seriously enough to relapse into savagery. When it was all finished, the hangover was just as profound as the binge had been. What remained was an indescribably bad taste in a terribly dry mouth. When the Germans were again up on their feet, after years of crawling on their empty stomachs before the authorities of military occupation, they were allergic to the agent of their cataclysmic intoxication—"ideas."

This can change again, of course, but for the time being the Germans are the most pragmatic people on earth. They believe only in their five senses—and never mind the sixth. Nothing that cannot be measured is even worth talking about. Adenauer's lieutenants have not the slightest doubt that he owed his fantastic victory in the last elections to the crushing force of his slogan—"no experiments." Now nations have been in a conservative, even sluggish, mood before; and elections have been won by parties which, contrary to the usual chant of "progress," promised that there will be no change at all. But Germany's mood goes far beyond such self-satisfied caution. The mood that prevails in Germany, it seems to me, is an almost angry and sore antagonism against anything that, no matter how vaguely, smells of an "idea." And that, I contend, goes even for such seductive and easy-to-gulp anti-ideas as anti-semitism.

In the first place—and this is something "measurable"—the number of Jews in Germany is down to 30,000. It was difficult enough and it took a pretty long time to persuade 60 million Germans in the thirties that 600,000 Jews were exploiting them to the hilt; still, to the amazement of the world, which always had thought that Germans were strong enough to keep a minority of 1 per cent under control, Hitler did it. But now there are 30,000 Jews among 52 million Germans—about one twentieth of 1 per cent, precisely one Jew to 1,750 Germans (which would mean about 100,000 Jews in America); and so, as Hegel puts it, "quantity turns into quality." While a German, under the influence of an "idea," could have been persuaded that one Jew among 100 Germans is "a ferment of decomposition," it would take an "idea" of magic powers so far unknown to man to persuade a German that one Jew among 1,750 Germans "runs the show." Not even in Germany could an inferiority complex grow so malignant as to make the Germans clinically afraid of a 0.06 per cent minority. To put it crudely: too many Jews have been killed in Germany to leave the Germans even the smallest amount of anti-semitic narcotics.

This was put to a statistical test in 1950. At that time prosperity had hardly begun to fascinate the Germans. Millions of German refugees from the East had not yet been absorbed by an economy that was still just one step ahead of starvation. In short, what the economic determinist calls "the conditions" were unquestionably in favor of rabble-rousing. And there was also a German political party that undertook to do just that—in an undisguised bid to the anti-semitic bias. The *Sozialistische Reichs Partei,* a faithful replica of the Nazi party—so faithful, in fact, that it was outlawed by Germany's Supreme Court in 1952—entered the election campaign with considerable financial resources and effective speakers. And it gathered—under conditions of confusion, despair, and destitution—in North-Rhine-Westphalia, the largest of Germany's *Bundesländer,* 0.2 per cent; and in Schleswig-Holstein, a notoriously backward constituency, 1.6 per cent of the vote.

The following year, to be sure, the *S.R.P.* achieved a fluke of a success in Lower Saxony's elections for a diet—11 per cent of the vote. But by that time the party had fundamentally changed its program and its vocabulary. From its former emphasis on anti-semitism it had switched to a professed concern for the woes of the eastern refugees who, indeed, contributed most of the *S.R.P.* vote. At that time almost 33 per cent of Lower Saxony's voters were refugees, chiefly from the Sudeten territory; and there can be no doubt that in their blind distress they did not take another look but voted for the candidates who most recklessly promised to "solve" their problems.

At the time of their greatest hopes the only legitimate successors to nazism postwar Germany has ever seen gathered between 0.2 per cent (when they displayed anti-semitism) in North-Rhine-

Westphalia and 11 per cent (when they simulated a normal party of "interests") in Lower Saxony. The 0.2 per cent in Rhine-Westphalia seem to indicate, quite precisely, the number of unreformed, dedicated, and desperate Nazis in West Germany—probably around 50,000. The 11 per cent in Lower Saxony may indicate the dangerous grade of political confusion that still can be reached in a Germany on the edge of economic crisis. But those 11 per cent are not one iota worse than the normal magnitude of the "lunatic fringe" in mature and perfectly secure democracies. Which does not mean that "lunatic fringes" are harmless, even in well-balanced societies. There may come a point in time when the hysterical gyrations of a "lunatic fringe" can push the whole society into a pit of history. But, given a stable and self-assured course, a ballast of 11 per cent is by no means pernicious. And, at any rate, the record of the *Sozialistische Reichs Partei,* inasmuch as such phenomena can be measured at all, should lay the ghost of a rampant German anti-semitism.

And yet, anti-semitism remains a grave German problem, if only in a strangely inverted manner. For example, in April 1958 a German high-school teacher, one Studienrat Zind, was sentenced to a year in jail and the loss of his tenure as a public teacher for having shouted, in the wine cellar of his provincial town, a few ugly anti-semitic remarks. The extraordinary consequence was not the public prosecution of the vulgar man (though it is remarkable that West Germany—as far as I know, the only western country with such *codified* mores—prosecutes *expressions,* and not deeds, of racial hatred). Truly extraordinary was the *national* attention focused on a display of *provincial* idiocy: The respectable press of the whole country devoted not only the most extensive coverage but a plethora of editorials and flaming sermons to the conflict of a distorted, mediocre mind with the injunctions of ethics and the law of the country. On the other hand, at the trial in the town of Offenburg the local citizenry behaved quite differently: Studienrat Zind's neighbors who attended the trial seemed to sympathize with him and showed their feelings in unpleasant demonstrations outside the court building.

There exists, it seems, a delicate and perilous connection between the two phenomena—the unanimous national outcry *against*
and the local reaction *in favor of* Studienrat Zind; and this connection may be more significant for the state of Germany's psychic
health than many a solemn political event. For there arises the
intricate question whether the *legal* interdiction of human folly
does not increase rather than reduce the effectiveness of the
privately spewn poison. And there also arises the question whether
the decent principles that stand behind the public prosecution of
Studienrat Zind will forever remain compatible with the far less
decent fact of legal prosecution of *opinion,* even though it expresses
bias. In other words: How long can the West German Republic
maintain that the expression (*not* the application) of prejudice,
racial or otherwise, is punishable by *democratic* law? And how
long can a public opinion continue to function which, quite
evidently, reflects the feelings of a self-appointed elite rather than
the national mood?

These are precarious questions, supercharged with the unprecedented emotionalism that has been caused by the unprecedented
Nazi slaughter of 6 million Jews. It is still not possible in liberal
western society, it seems, to speak of Germans (or Jews) in the
dispassionate language of sanity. But while men have the right
to be emotional, history is not.

Germany will soon be socially determined by a generation that
remembers Hitler just about the same way contemporary Americans would be discussing the follies of prohibition; and it is less
than likely that such a Germany can be kept for long under a
law of siege. But it is precisely a law of siege to repeal, in this *one*
area of post-Hitler Germany, one of the fundamental presumptions
of civilized society: that private opinions, as long as they do not
lead or incite to illegal *conduct,* are exempt from public prosecution. And this obviously refers to private opinions which are
morally objectionable; for, clearly, *commendable* private opinions
would not even provoke the question of public prosecution. It is
always the *contemptible* prejudice that demands, and rightly
obtains, the contemptuous indifference of the civilized law. So long

as Germany is made to punish remarks that, alas, are par in exclusive clubs of New York and London, so long will Germany remain vulnerable as a democracy, unviable as a society, unhealthy as a nation.

This has nothing to do with the unquestionable need to encourage—and not only in Germany—*social* injunctions against indecent private conduct, lewd language, and vulgar idiocies. Studienrat Zind, by saying what he did say, lost any right to continue his services as a teacher of the young—not because his language offended the law but because it offended the ethics and the taste of civilized society. And it was, in fact, the cowardly behavior of Offenburg's school board that gave the case in the end its national notoriety: the board refused to discipline Zind "as long as he has not been sentenced by a public court." As usual, the lethargic stupidity of bureaucrats and the famous German "lack of civic courage" gave the highly questionable interference of state power the appearance of righteousness. Germany's metropolitan press, in celebrating the law's rather indefensible presumptions, seemed morally excused by the apathy of Zind's professional community. But the reverse is also true: Offenburg's school board and citizenry consider their apathy justified by the national outcry.

It seems crucial in Germany, more crucial than anywhere else in the West, to comprehend that one transgression feeds on the other. Perhaps a case could be made that the law of siege must not be reformed ahead of Germany's total ethical reform. But my own prejudice—which distrusts profoundly the alleged therapeutical effects of the law and the moralizing ambitions of government —advises me to the contrary. Social injunctions, it seems to me, have little chance to grow amid stiff legal stipulations. They grow in churches, not in courthouses—in man's soul afraid of the moral law, not in man's mind afraid of the jail warden.

German anti-semitism, in particular, will certainly survive as long as its expression requires "courage"; and there is a chance— only a slight chance, for man is absurd—that German anti-semitism will atrophy when it has become irrelevant, demonstrably stupid, socially despicable to express it. If Studienrat Zind's sympathizers in Offenburg had not felt that "they"—i.e., the government, the district attorneys, the income-tax collectors, the "sissyfied" editors of the metropolitan press, all the pillars of the establishment—had ganged up on the "bold and principled" Zind; if they had, on the contrary, felt that they were making themselves ludicrous and somewhat nauseating—they might have left the courtroom in silence and perhaps with a sense of catharsis. Except, of course, that there would not have been a trial, for the clumsy machinery of the law has no business in the sphere of moral and aesthetic decisions.

And it is equally true that Offenburg's tasteless *Bürger* had not the slightest intention of endorsing *materially* Studienrat Zind's convictions. All they were trying to drive home was their disgust with the insolent "outsiders" who dared to blacken the good name of Offenburg. And in this one weakness all German *Bürger* are alike: they do not want to be told that their prosperous and comfortable world is imperfect, that only yesterday murderous insanity reigned in the land, that felons and rascals and madmen still stalk through the night.

This is German "normalcy" again, this noisy, self-adoring parochialism. And if it is not attractive—well, "normalcy" hardly ever is. Some sensitive people in London are nostalgic for the time of ordeals, when the bombed world around them exploded and man could find his peace in work for others; and these sensitive Londoners loathe the "normalcy" of their dreary comforts. Yet only the preciously insolent would dare wish for his society the return of explosions, merely to please his need for the rare and the meaningful. "Normal" society may be unattractive, but it is healthy; and only the healthy society can ever hope to turn into the good society.

Germany, in short, is getting well again; and it has to thank for its complete convalescence—as complete, that is, as convalescence can be for a people that has not yet attained the *habit* of freedom—its Old Man, the sane patriarch who knew the exact German recipe: one part sternness, one part benevolence, and two parts immovable calm. With this concoction Dr. Adenauer has cured Germany. But Germany and the West will have to pay for such good luck when Adenauer is no more.

There is a legend at large that succession of leaders is an incomparably easier proposition in democracies than in dictatorships; that, in other words, the communist regime in the Soviet Union is truly shaken when a Lenin or a Stalin dies, but that the democratic regime in West Germany will hardly notice the passing even of an Adenauer. As usual with popular legends and most dicta of certified experts almost the opposite is true. (Almost only, for so unreliable are popular legends and "expertise" that one cannot even depend on the correctness of their exact opposites.)

A totalitarian regime such as the Soviet Union lives on its monolithic creed, on the authority of its sanctified scriptures, on an ingrained political style that permeates every public gesture and person, on a protocol that is just as rigid as the regime is illegitimate. When a Lenin or a Stalin dies, there might be a murderous brawl among the party hacks who all may have their private ambitions; but there will be no serious danger for the regime itself: its fate and even its policies are predestined by a formative ideology that is a much more compelling testament than the one left by the dead dictator.

In a democracy, on the contrary, there is no binding ideology— which, by definition, makes a society democratic. The effect of a true leader on a democratic society is therefore much more powerful than that of a dictator on a communist society: the democratic leader *sets* political style—the communist dictator only personifies the basically immovable style of his society. Political styles set in democracies are not rooted in omnipresent dogma, and not even in tradition, but in the true leader's personality, beliefs, and foibles.

When Franklin D. Roosevelt died, the United States was therefore actually in far greater trouble than was the Soviet Union at the death of Stalin—a fact that has been effectively blurred by the dramatic but irrelevant shenanigans, such as decapitations, that habitually accompany a change of guards in dictatorships.

Because Franklin D. Roosevelt was a "charismatic" democratic leader—a fact his serious opponents can much more clearly recognize than his passionate partisans—his people, when he died, were entirely unprepared for succession.

For more than twelve years the American people had entrusted this "charismatic" leader with their fate and fortune in a manner quite unknown in dictatorships—namely, voluntarily; which means: much more seriously than in dictatorships. A democratic people, once it has put policies into a trusted leader's hands, pays no more attention to them. For this is why it chose the leader in the first place: so that someone does what a democratic people are loath to do—namely, attend to government. If the leader gives the people the feeling that he has got what it takes—i.e., that he *is* a leader—then people trust him implicitly, take his advice unseen, leave the entire business of politics to him, and attend to theirs.

Though they may enjoy the *game* of politics, democratic people are, of course, fundamentally apolitical. For they distrust "ideologies" and are never tied together by one. The only thing that can "unify" a democratic people is a political leader of a certain magnitude. When he appears, "things get done." But when he dies, there is suddenly a weird vacuum. For while he lasted, people had enthusiastically forgotten how to think for themselves on public matters. And when he goes, they cannot relearn it fast enough, so there follows a perilous time of political paralysis, of spiritual nothingness.

The gap is truly perilous in a time of stormy weather. When Franklin D. Roosevelt died, the uncommonly common Truman era followed quite unavoidably. By "Truman era," of course, I do not mean the personal accidentals—the cast of characters, the flim-flam of refrigerators and mink-coat trimmings. They were avoidable. I mean the fatal mood of the era—the stubborn refusal to do any thinking at all on any crucial subject of policy.

The years from 1945 to 1950, even more than the years of Yalta and Teheran, were the years when the free world, "led" by the United States, tumbled into the night of defeat; when Potsdam marked the sellout of eastern Europe; when China was stolen by the Reds; when one country after another disappeared behind the Iron Curtain; when unimpeachable anti-Communists such as James Byrnes and Truman himself, comforted by General Marshall, worked day and night at persuading Europe's and Asia's reluctant friends of the United States to cooperate with their Communists. Those were the years when the United States *insisted* that the governments of China, France, Italy, and the local authorities of occupied Germany and Japan, include Communists. Those were the years when an American who dared do his own thinking on the subject of communism—the paramount subject of his era— was ostracized; and he was ostracized, not by governmental fiat, but by the prevailing mood of the nation. For Truman, Byrnes, and Marshall acted as they did from 1945 till 1950, not because of ill will, but because, in consensus with the American people, they stubbornly and angrily refused to rethink the policy set by the dead leader. And they refused to think, not because they were by nature sluggish, but because they were quite authentic representatives of a democracy that was still numb from having lost its "charismatic" leader. It takes a long time for a democratic people to recover from the childlike sense of security it had acquired with the ascendance of such a leader—and lost with his death.

I do not dare predict what will happen in Germany after Adenauer's death. But of one thing I am convinced to the point of predicting: a time of profound trouble will then begin for Germany. To predict this is as bold as to predict avalanches after heavy snowfalls in the Alps: it is to predict the unavoidable.

Just as it is impossible to foresee the detailed patterns the time of serious trouble will assume for Germany, just as clear are its structural stresses. It will be, of course, above all a crisis of leadership, a *true* crisis of succession. Like most strong-willed, long-lived, self-confident, "charismatic" politicians in democracies, Adenauer has put a hex on political talent around him. His type of democratic leader is utterly impatient with gifted men in his cabinet. It takes *time* to convince a man who is very much a person in his own rights and of his own convictions; but the "charismatic" leader never has time. So much must be done every day and by him. He needs obedient executives around him; all the necessary thinking he will do himself, before he falls asleep.

Of course there are moments when the fast aging leader is haunted by notions that even he must die—and what then? But there is a strange tendency in "charismatic" leaders, devout Catholics or not, to consider themselves somehow immortal after all, not subject to the normal tribulations of the human creature, under some special dispensation. So Churchill, with an almost devious and malicious stubbornness, rewarded mediocrity around him and trimmed talent. So Roosevelt created a governmental atmosphere in which self-respecting men withered, withdrew, or were cut down. And so Adenauer finally failed.

On April 7, 1959, he announced his intent to correct this failure. For, indubitably, Adenauer's surprising decision to assume in the fall of 1959 the West German Presidency, and to guide his hand-picked successor in the Chancellery from that elated position, is a rather shrewd attempt to reduce the pains of successorship.

As President, Adenauer will exert exactly as much authority as he already commands—certainly not the avuncular pseudo-authority the incumbent President, Professor Heuss, habitually assumed. Heuss, after all, was fully aware of the suffocating weight of his Chancellor, Dr. Konrad Adenauer; but President Adenauer will know that his successor in the Chancellery—as long as he is a member of the Christian Democratic party—will always submit to Adenauer's unchallengeable advice. What the West German Constitution has to say about the powers of the President is of secondary importance; and that Constitution, by the way, gives the President much more power than the proverbially modest Professor Heuss ever wanted for himself.

In some respects, Adenauer's impact on German policies might even grow after his withdrawal into the stratosphere of the presidential office: he will then be able to play a role entirely new to him—the role of "the man above parties." At any rate, the next West German Chancellor will have to please the new President at least as much as the *Bundestag:* Adenauer will pick his successor, and the man he chooses will owe him everything.

Until September 1959, Adenauer remains in direct command of West German policies; and after September 1959, his indirect command will be just as stern. In fact, this plan of reducing the tremors of successorship by changing political chairs may perhaps prove a trifle too shrewd: Adenauer's successor in the Chancellery may be too hampered by the Old Man's omnipresence to unfold his true faculties.

In Germany there was even in 1958 much talk—the kind of subterranean whisper that marks the uneasiness of people who discuss taboos—on Adenauer's successor. And most people agreed, with a sigh, that it would be Dr. Erhard—at first, and almost unavoidably. After all, he is Adenauer's best-known lieutenant; he is a Protestant (which, in a spirit of fair reasonableness, seems to improve his chances to succeed the Catholic Adenauer); he is safe, predictable, most certainly not a strong-willed politician (which, in juxtaposition to Adenauer, seems to make him strangely attractive, if only to other politicians). But there is always, as I said, a sigh in this prediction. For the knowing men know that Dr. Erhard has no real chance to *stay* Adenauer's successor. And *then* what? And *who?*

There is an informed rumor that Adenauer has picked his real successor, and that he is the relatively young Dr. Franz Etzel. Before he became minister of finances, Etzel did useful work as chairman of the *Bundestag's* Committee on Economic Policies and as the vice-president of the European *Montanunion.* He is indubitably an able and honest administrator. But what makes Dr. Adenauer think that Etzel can succeed him in any but a purely formal sense is inconceivable. There is solidity in this fifty-seven-year-old Prussian, but neither real greatness nor synthetic magnetism. He is inconspicuous enough to avoid, for a while, the annihilating brawl that would involve any strong-willed successor of Adenauer's in his own party. But neither can he win the kind of elections on which Adenauer thrived, nor can he force his leadership upon a governmental party which, after ten years of trying responsibility, is even now subject to stresses and strains of almost incompatible political tendencies. Etzel is neither a "charismatic" nor a parliamentary leader. Adenauer's alleged recommendation may get him the job for a while, but he will not be Adenauer's true successor. (And the same goes for Dr. Gerhard Schroeder, minister of the interior, who is sometimes mentioned as another crown prince.)

Who, then, will it be? There is, in terms of animal magnetism and personal push, only one visible candidate—Franz Josef Strauss, Adenauer's minister of defense. This young man (born in 1916) is indubitably the only genuine political talent that has grown under Adenauer's barren guidance. Strauss is able, driven by ambition, inexhaustible as a worker, intelligent, and even curious. But it would be most difficult to say what he stands for. For though he is the most articulate of Adenauer's lieutenants (he is far and above the most effective speaker Adenauer's party can send forward at gala occasions in the *Bundestag*), he only articulates what *Dr. Adenauer* stands for. Strauss himself, in his short and steep ascent to political power, has argued on just about all possible sides of the relevant issues (he was, for instance, only a few years ago an opponent of full German rearmament); and the truly disturbing fact is that none of his many enemies would take *any* position of his seriously.

For he is the kind of politician who will *first* find out which position pays politically and *then* he will take it. And each time he will argue with conviction, endurance, and aptitude. He is a friendly man and he can make friends; but he also makes the most dangerous kind of enemies—people who can take anything he says but who cannot stand him personally. He is witty, but there are in all his speeches irresolvable traces of Teutonic bathos—the kind of bathos the stern Dr. Adenauer is incapable of. Strauss, in his way affable, is almost exactly what the French mean when they speak, quite factually, of *boche*. There is heaviness in him, but little solidity. He has the gusto, the forcefulness, the ambitions of a "charismatic" leader—but not his substance, his serenity, his irreducible loyalty to one central idea. And yet, he may be Dr. Adenauer's final successor. If he is, Germany will soon be shaken by a kind of political partisanship it has not known in Adenauer's decade.

For if Strauss attains power, his own party may soon be torn apart by defiant objectors to a Strauss regime. The tendencies within the Christian Democratic Union–Christian Social Union toward a coalition with the Social Democrats—tendencies that Dr. Adenauer has suppressed at the risk even of losing control over his own party—will of necessity increase. And the Social Democratic party will have at last found in Strauss an antagonist who, for all his abilities, may be a sitting duck when the shooting starts. There is a consensus that Adenauer's stunning victories were entirely his own; that is, the C.D.U., as *party,* represents far less than a clear-cut majority of the German people. Were a Strauss to lead the C.D.U. into the next election, the opposition will have an excellent chance to conquer power.

And what the Social Democrats would do with power—the German Social Democrats who have the power instincts of masochists —is only too predictable: they would lose it. Not in succeeding elections to the C.D.U., but to the merciless and superior Soviet operators. This, at least, is what competent observers of the German political drama fear. And they do not mean to say that the Social Democrats are less patriotic or less anti-communist than the C.D.U. On the contrary, a German Social Democrat despises communist practices even more than any other German, simply because he has been more often their victim. But more effective than their experience is the Social Democrats' political nature—the feeble utopianism of incorrigible amateurs. And if Strauss were to assume command he would either open the governmental doors to Germany's Social Democracy—or he would have to take a most dangerous course of authoritarian scheming. In both cases, a time of serious trouble would set in for Germany.

These, at the moment, are the outlooks for Adenauer's succession. They are sadly disturbing—so disturbing, in fact, that an intelligent American policy should make use of the short time that is left to establish the foundations of a lasting and binding alliance with Germany; an alliance, that is, which excludes the possibilities of a German surrender while Adenauer, the guarantor of German resistance against the East, can still commit his nation.

CHAPTER THREE

Berlin: Political "Ersatz"

~~~~~~

THERE is an anemic and, seen from the perspectives of historic experience, un-German paucity about the political life of the new Germany. For this impetuous heart land of Europe was, for more than a century, the world's laboratory in developing political concepts. Nationalism, socialism, communism, anarchism, labor movement, anticlericalism, welfare statism, superman's contempt for the masses—since the beginning of the nineteenth century there was hardly a significant political idea that was not born in Germany or at least has not been tried there, with a radical determination, for the benefit of the world. Other nations may occasionally have had even more excited dreams than the Germans; but for more than a hundred years Germany was the field for the great political maneuvers, the radical social experiments, the uninhibited conflicts between opposing philosophies. The world's ambitious apprentices of the political trade, if they ever wanted to become masters, simply had to spend a few years in Germany: there was no school of comparable standing. This German century may have been confused, bloody, and even childish, but it surely was the century in which the whole world wanted to learn about its fate by studying German experiments. For that century Germany remained the classical country of "ideologies," of political extremism, of audacious experiments and radical conflicts.

But the new Germany lives in an unparalleled political tameness. Tensions? Clashes of political philosophies? The new Germany is thoroughly frightened by the mere idea. An American is used to a Tweedledum-Tweedledee two-party system that notoriously lacks emotional content and makes it quite impossible to define, with some kind of validity, the difference between a Democrat and a Republican. But compared with the under-chilled politics to which I was exposed in Germany for a year, the political life of the United States is downright explosive. What once was in Germany the clash of *Weltanschauungen* is nowadays the pitifully reduced tension between buyers and sellers, consumers and producers, debtors and creditors, business executives and labor executives. There is no other country in Europe whose citizens are less ready than in Germany to break each other's skulls over such trifles as convictions.

West Germany's political parties are not at all happy with this unexpected mutation of the German character. But what should they do? What *can* they do? The area of disagreement between the traditional German parties contracts more and more; and not because of a special readiness of the party leaders to achieve the great compromise (these leaders, on the contrary, keep trying to join battle), but simply because reasonable people could hardly disagree in the face of the new German reality: what one has to do, and not to do, is beyond doubt and, therefore, beyond debate.

The anemia of political life in the new Germany is, first of all, due to the fact that for ten years there *was* no political life. The total defeat of 1945 extinguished the last ideological spark; and under the conditions of military occupation it seemed utterly immaterial which ideological concept a German may have made his own. In a country that had lost its national sovereignty there could be no political sovereignty of an individual's choice. It so happened, rather paradoxically, that greater political talents developed under military occupation than any that could since be found. A man such as the late Dr. Schumacher, trembling with fury and passion,

was not only the most remarkable temperament the German Social
Democracy had known in generations but perhaps the greatest political figure to emerge in three decades of German history. Dr.
Schumacher's permanent explosion remained a quixotic adventure,
for the sober German reality of the occupation phase was impenetrable: the German problem then was not *how* but just *whether*
this people was going to live. And to the solution of this one problem the Germans themselves could contribute nothing. They were
the wards of a huge orphanage—and there is no politics in or-
phanages.

Quite abruptly, and altogether unexpectedly, prosperity followed
the occupation period. But there could be even less politics in
prosperity. Nobody is going to kill Santa Claus, and nobody could
possibly argue with German prosperity. What happened, and was
being done in Germany, was as simple and indisputable as the multiplication table. One had to work. One had to make money. One
had to eat, to forget, to luxuriate. And what else? Well, what else
was there?

This reduction of all otherwise conceivable alternatives was
further advanced by the new Germany's jurisprudence. Normally,
the world's appetites for extremism will be sucked into two channels: what is generally, though with some oversimplification, called
fascism and communism. Germany is the only western democracy
where the two extremes are simply *verboten*. In an otherwise
democratic new Germany both fascism and communism are a
matter of law enforcement, not of politics; and the country's public
opinion indubitably approves of such an unusual arrangement.

For, what the new German constitution has declared "unconstitutional"—namely, the existence of fascist or communist organizations—is certainly unlivable. The Germany that for one last time
survived a catastrophe such as 1945 decidedly cannot afford another fascist tremor; and the Germany that is constantly threatened
by the Soviet Union certainly must not permit the Communists to
race around in "the free market of ideas." Thus the two conventional channels of extremism are clogged in Germany for compelling reasons of self-preservation, and not primarily by actions

of the constitutional courts. The injunctions were as self-understood
as the ancient German habit of locking the doors at dusk. I haven't
met a single person in Germany who—moved, so to speak, by considerations of political aesthetics—would have regretted that clip-
ping of Germany's political spectrum. What can one do? Life in
Germany has indeed shrunk to such plainest simplicity.

Yet *Homo Germanicus* is still a member of the human race; and
so there must be among the Germans millions of individuals who,
congenitally, *are* Fascists or Communists. Thousands of them remain, indeed, illegally organized and move in a political under-
ground. But millions of Germans, who by instinct and preferences
are Fascists or Communists, keep swimming with the legal tide.
Yet the fact that they belong to, or follow, the respectable political
parties makes those parties even more cautious than they would
be out of their own volition. The immeasurably dangerous ballast,
submerged in the dark, could totally change their course if the
navigators did not steer with utmost precaution.

Both big German parties—the Christian Democratic Union and
the Social Democracy—must for the same reason resist the temptation to argue the vulnerable political past of many leaders of the
competing party. Each time Adenauer's crowd discovers in the
Social Democratic leadership a former Communist, the Social
Democrats can enumerate former Nazis who have made their home
in the Christian Democratic Union. Either party sits in a glass
house; and the presence of genuine converts and possible pene-
trators in *both* parties compels them to mind their polemical manners and to develop a very special aura of subdued politeness
against each other.

All in all, it is not quite understandable why a German nowadays
joins the Christian Democratic Union instead of the Social Democratic party, and vice versa. The programmatically stated differences
between the two big German parties are by far more serious than
their real differences. As to codified party program, the German
Social Democratic party is still "anti-religious" and "anti-capitalist,"
dedicated to class warfare and internationalism; and the Christian
Democratic Union describes itself, programmatically, still as Ger-

many's sole protector of the faith, as its sole pillar of free enterprise, as its only trustee of good traditional German nationalism. But these self-portraits have little resemblance to reality. Social Democratic leaders are professing, churchgoing Christians; German union leaders (most of them officially Socialists) are much more passionate promoters of free enterprise than many officers of the manufacturers' associations who lobby in Bonn for increased tariffs, statist interventions in the market, and various other pet ideas of planners. On the other hand, Adenauer is a far more convincing European than Ollenhauer, his party is far more genuinely serving the needs of European internationalization than the Social Democracy which, to me, seems to conserve the nationalist atavism of Germany. And one can find in Adenauer's camp much bolder advocates of social conflict than among the Social Democrats, who are never so embittered as when they notice and deplore a violation of the tepid "social peace." Why, then, does anyone in Germany today become a Social Democrat or a Christian Democrat?

The new German's motives, it seems to me, have more to do with family traditions than with the challenges of the day. The new German Social Democrat, if all is said and done, is nothing but the son of an old German Social Democrat; and the loyal Adenauer voter is the son of a man who—under Wilhelm II, Ebert, and Hindenburg—has loyally voted *"Bürgerlich"* (conservative). It is indeed fascinating to observe how (not only in Germany, but all over western Europe) the quantitative relations between "socialist" and "conservative" camps have hardly changed in fifty years. The German Social Democracy is under Adenauer roughly as strong as it was under Kaiser Wilhelm; the Austrian Social Democracy has remained for forty years a few per cent short of a majority; as far as ballots cast are concerned (though at the moment not in parliamentary representations), the left and the right in France have remained stationary since the beginning of the century. World wars were fought, revolutions took place, "ideologies" were torn to pieces on the barbed wire of reality, standards of living doubled, "capitalists" became protagonists of "planning," "socialists" proved efficient "free enterprisers," empires broke up, worlds trembled—but the son goes on voting the way his father did. I don't know of a better explanation of the political forces that account for the existence of Germany's Social Democracy and the Christian Democratic Union.

By that, of course, I do not mean to say that there is no longer any ideological enchantment or infection in Germany. There, as anywhere else in the world, the intellectual segments remain particularly excitable, unstable, always ready for a modish orientation, always in search of a strong dedication. But these intellectuals live outside the big parties; and the typical German form of their fermentation are nowadays the *Kreise*—vague "circles" without any special discipline and routine, but often quite influential. There exist such *Kreise* on all sides, and at their more or less secret sessions one can meet Germany's most vital intelligences. Also, they are indubitably the most effective tools of both outlawed extremisms. And the big parties reject them with genuine disgust; but one wonders whether this reluctance comes from a true recognition of the dangers involved, or merely from the party hack's conventional fear of intellectual stimulation.

In new Germany's glaring daylight "all cats are gray," and the new German *"Bürgerliche"* is in speech and deeds hardly distinguishable from the new German Social Democrat. They are all "reasonable," "moderate," "progressive," "modern." I have met fewer mavericks in Germany than in a notoriously "americanized" America. To the extent that one talks politics in Germany at all, one talks with the passion of a tranquillized side-line umpire. But once you've cut through the smooth surface, and looked at the gizzard, you know that an essential, painfully unequivocal test separates one type of German from another (and sometimes creates in one and the same German a bad case of schizophrenia). You just have to ask the question: Should Germany try to live with its communist neighbor in noncommittal neutrality, or should it accept the conflict, forced upon itself, with a courageous will to win?

This is the decision of German destiny. It is also a decision of the destiny of the world. All prosperity notwithstanding—it is inescapable. And the Soviets insist that even in 1959 all German choices be pre-empted in the one choice concerning Berlin. Most

Germans don't realize yet that this year will determine their history more decisively than 1870, 1918, 1933, and 1945. Yet soon they will begin to comprehend.

The communist regime in East Germany is a Quisling government, and there is no one on either side of the Iron Curtain who has any doubts about it. The people's uprising of 1953 has clarified once and for all that the "mass basis" of the East German Communists consists of, at the most, 10 per cent of the population, plus the Soviet troops stationed in East Germany. The government of West Germany, on the other hand, derives its legitimate authority from the indisputable fact that it is the government of Germany —the *only* government of the *only* Germany there is. Of all the cunning propaganda tricks of the Soviets, none was more skillful than the phrase of "the two Germanys." It has seduced the "realistic" opportunists in the whole world, and above all in West Germany, to camouflage the proposed capitulation as a "recognition of given facts." And now the Soviets deem the confusion of the West sufficiently advanced to enforce, with a "solution of the Berlin crisis," *their* solution of the entire German problem.

What, in truth, are the given facts? The central fact is that East Germany has never seceded from Germany. It simply was occupied, in 1945, by troops of the victorious Allies—just as every other part of Germany. The sections that are today known as "West Germany" were occupied by the United States, England, and France—East Germany by the Soviets. All four powers acted under joint responsibility (and, at least officially, under a joint command). In all contexts of the international law the Bonn government, once it began to exist and to perform, was recognized by all four powers as the legitimate successor to that German government against which the four powers were making war till June 1945. Three of the occupying powers (the United States, England, and France) ended the military occupation in the early fifties. The fourth—Soviet Russia—remained entrenched in its territory of occupation. And the "East German problem" consists in the illegal, arbitrary, and provocative extension of a war measure into an era of international peace.

The Ulbricht regime has not the slightest bearing on this problem of international law. The legitimate German government—and there is, of course, only one—has an unimpeachable claim on the legitimate successors of the Allied governments that ordered the military occupation of Germany: those who were responsible for the occupation remain responsible for the withdrawal of military forces from a Germany no longer at war with the Allies. And if the Soviet troops which, by the joint decisions of the four Allied governments, were delegated to occupy East Germany in 1945 are today involved in an act of mutiny against Allied orders, then it remains the business of the governments of the United States, Britain, and France to live up to their solemn commitments and get the mutinous Soviet troops out of Germany. In short, the "East German problem" simply consists in the behavior of the three western powers which, since 1949, hesitate to enforce their authority in the eastern parts of a Germany that was occupied under their joint responsibility. These are "the given facts." That a few thousand East Germans shine Soviet shoes for a consideration and serve them in various other respects has nothing to do with the *essential* facts of the situation.

Of those essential facts none was so absurd and unforgivable as the willingness of the three western Allied governments to accept Berlin, a city deeply *inside* the zone assigned to the Soviets for occupation, as "a joint occupation responsibility" of all four powers —without insisting that the supply lines of the western forces remain within the territory assigned to the western powers of occupation. An officer candidate who would consider such an arrangement acceptable would of course flunk the exams at any officers' school in the world. However, for reasons of his own, the Allied commander in chief, General Eisenhower, deemed these conditions acceptable; and West Berlin has thus remained, since 1945, the famous "western island" inside the Soviet zone of occupation. Again: the administrative problems of the city have nothing to do with the "Berlin question." The question consists exclusively in the joint responsibility of the three western governments for a foolishly accepted assignment that was part of the broad Soviet assignment. And if the mutinous Soviet troops create in Berlin difficulties for the western Allies, then it remains the duty of the United States, Britain, and France to enforce the authority of their governments.

Yet it is indubitably true that such unequivocal legal commitments do not always correspond to the political situation; that, in other words, to accept the obvious western responsibility for the situation in East Germany and West Berlin would mean to interfere with the current "peace policies" of the western powers.

A strong case could even be made for a thesis like this: As the western military responsibilities in East Germany could be enforced against mutinous Soviet forces only with warlike means, and as the West could not possibly want such a war in 1959, the western troops must be for the time being withdrawn from West Berlin. But in that case the western powers would of course have to be ready to take with them, and settle in the West, all those Berliners who trusted the word of the western governments and now would wish to withdraw from the Soviets—even if there should be 2 million of them. This would cost several billion dollars (certainly less than a war for West Berlin), but it would be clearly the moral responsibility of western governments who would be trying, in 1959, to escape the consequences of the unfathomable stupidity they committed in 1945.

As I said, even such a radical concession to the pacifist mood of the moment would be conceivable. Inconceivable (inconceivable, that is, within the coordinates of responsibly logical procedure) is the "solution" that is being seriously discussed in West Germany (and everywhere else): that the West at last acknowledge "the existence of the East German Democratic Republic" and finally start to negotiate with the Soviets, and with "the other Germany," the "reunification of the two Germanys."

What makes this position, so popular in the entire West, inconceivable to a responsible mind is its tacit presumption that there is between the interests of the West (which needs a united, strong, and westerly oriented Germany) and those of the Soviets (which need a military no-man's land in Central Europe) the indispensable common denominator that alone may justify negotiations. Behind the "realistic" demand "at last to recognize the existence of the East German Democratic Republic" simply hides the proposal to concede the Soviets a decisive hand in the German game.

For "the German Democratic Republic" is *German* territory occupied by Soviet troops; and to grant that "Democratic Republic" any kind of codetermination over German affairs—within a "German confederation" or even the vaguest "administrative cooperation"—clearly means to grant those rights to the Soviets. For no one would want to assert (and no one *has* asserted) that the Soviets, in suicidal good will, would *give up* positions of power in peaceful negotiations; in such negotiations nothing can be attained that the Soviets do not concede *voluntarily,* to suit their interests.

Therefore, to recognize the "German Democratic Republic" in any fashion at all would not just be a moral but an eminently practical capitulation. An illegally occupied part of Germany would, with one stroke of surrender, be turned into a communist fortification *inside* Germany. Obviously the Soviet troops would not be withdrawn from East Germany until at least the "demilitarization" of *all* Germany were granted. And this "demilitarization," under the geographical and psychological conditions of the case, would mean of necessity that a disarmed Germany must accept its dependence on its militarily overwhelming neighbor, the Soviet Union: there would be no other military power, or potent military alliance, left in Europe. This is why *any* kind of recognition of the Ulbricht regime inherently implies the surrender of *all* Germany to the East.

All this should be obvious. And the ghastly confusion of the western debate on "German reunification" indeed consists in the fact that no one denies the inexorable logic of such a development; and yet, that no one speaks of it. One speaks exclusively of things which have nothing to do with reality—of the Rapacki Plan, for example, of "disengagement," of "military thinning out" between Ruhr and Neisse, and of similar chimeras. The favorite political pun of the "realists" remains to point out the relative irrelevancy of any German armament: Is it not, assuming a rocket and missile war, utterly unimportant whether United States rockets (which must attain a range of several thousand miles) are fired a hundred miles nearer to, or farther from, the Soviet border?

Nothing in the German debate on this question has depressed me so much as the fact that the "realistic friends of peace" desire a situation in which the only available measure of defense is the total and global rocket war. For if such a war started, it would be irrelevant, indeed, whether United States rockets take off from Westphalia, the French coast, or Alaska and Florida. But once Germany is incapable of defending its sovereignty with its *own* force, then even the smallest offense against that sovereignty would have to be answered by the global conflagration (if not by total German surrender)—and literally within minutes after "a border incident," as the outcome of a rocket war will be determined by the undertakings of the first hour.

In other words, Germany's "demilitarization" has indeed no bearings on the *outcome* of a future rocket war. It only makes such a war *unavoidable*—that war, or the West's surrender. Whether or not Germany will be "neutralized," the "final conflict" would take place between the Soviet Union and the United States. But if the heart land of the Continent were ever militarily so denuded that it could never again repel even a "conventional" Soviet thrust, then it either cannot be defended at all or it can be defended only with the ultimate weapons and the ultimate war. Thus, the advocates of *any* kind of "neutralization" of Germany propose, in truth, that Germany's alternatives be reduced to this one decision—either to capitulate before any kind of Soviet thrust, or to provoke a global war that may destroy the human race.

True, what a rearmed Germany could do in such an *ultimate* war is most probably negligible. The essence of German rearmament and foreign policy remains, however, whether Germany can and should be made strong enough to crush an attack, localized on *Germany,* with *German* forces. In suggesting that Germany renounce that attainable size of power, the advocates of the Rapacki Plan and all related schemes propose to renounce German sovereignty and, by doing so, become the spokesmen for total rocket war or total capitulation. And how is it possible that this elementary fact is not even mentioned in the German debate? Simply because the German "realists" beat all world records in daydreaming, utopianism, and intellectual arbitrariness.

I lived in Paris and London in 1938, when Neville Chamberlain was trying to convince himself and the West that the sellout in Munich meant "peace in our time," that a common denominator between the West and Hitler could be found. But compared to the mental maturity of those Germans who deem "a negotiated compromise" with the Soviets and Ulbricht conceivable, Neville Chamberlain was a titan of forceful logic. For in 1938 it was intellectually still possible for the West to misinterpret Hitler's reach for the world as an overstated German desire for a "unified Great Germany" and so to hope that, after devouring Austria and the Sudeten territory, the Germans might find their appetite satiated. But it is neither logically nor psychologically understandable how, in 1959, a rational contemporary can still doubt that the communist claim to rule the whole world, and most certainly Central Europe, is meant in deadly earnest.

And, indeed, in my many conversations with Rapacki Germans I felt all the time that they were not even trying to fool themselves: to me, they did not seem to assert, actually, that their kind of solution *could* work—they only seemed to desire a situation in which Germany could capitulate "calmly and orderly," a situation in which they themselves would be politically, psychologically, and perhaps even morally entitled to surrender.

Nor have I met anyone in Germany who would not admit that Germany, unless the West *forced* the Soviets *militarily* to withdraw from East Germany (a highly unlikely case), would have to pay the Soviets a stiff price for "reunification." Those who know communism have no doubt that the price, shrewdly calculated, must be tantamount to the final sovietization of all Germany. But even the "optimists" admit that the Soviet *minimum* demand for withdrawing from East Germany would be the "demilitarization" of *all* Germany, its withdrawal from NATO, and the recognition of

Ulbricht's "Socialist Unity party" (that is, of the Communist party
of Germany) on the level of government.

The readiness to negotiate with the Soviets *at all* must include
the readiness to accept these minimum demands. Indeed, the German Social Democratic party is on record that it is determined to
pay for "reunification" with far-reaching limitations of the German
rearmament, with Germany's withdrawal from NATO, and with
conceding "certain transfer conditions" in the governmental setup
of East Germany. The German Social Democratic party speaks
indubitably for all Germans willing to "negotiate" the problem with
the Soviets; and *without* a willingness to pay the indisputable
minimum price, any readiness to "negotiate" would indeed be
merely childish.

There may be people in Germany who are seriously persuaded
that the Communist party could remain outlawed in West Germany,
even after it had been officially recognized in East Germany; but I
have not met any such German. However, I know many Germans
who remain serene even in the face of the inescapable necessity to
legalize, in all Germany, the Communist party after "reunification."
As the latest election in West Berlin proved, the Communists
would be getting in West Germany much less than 5 per cent of
the freely cast votes—and is this something to be afraid of? But the
time when communism was intellectually seductive is gone all over
the world, and has been gone for years; and yet, precisely during
those years of its declining intellectual attractiveness communism
has become a far greater political peril than it ever was before.

Never and nowhere, not even in the Russia of 1917, has communism risen to power democratically. Always and everywhere
communism has conquered power, as a determined minority, when
faced with a tired majority that was confused, "peace-loving," and
lukewarm. The Communist party of a "reunified" Germany, building on the trained cadres of a "recognized" Ulbricht regime, can
count on at least one million members. Emerging in West Germany
from years of outlawed poverty into the glories of a historic triumph,
it must rapidly penetrate the confused and bothered political
formations of the West German left. For it would not only be the

official pet of Germany's new teacher, the Soviet Union; it would not only be encouraged by a rare political victory to speed up its advance—it could, above all, no longer be tamed by a German government which, mortgaged by "agreements" with Ulbricht and the Soviets, would no longer be technically capable of administering, or even threatening with, military force.

For a German government that has been compelled to leave NATO could recover a posture "in the middle" just as little as a vehemently tossed seesaw could stop swinging from one end to the other. Forced by superior power to leave NATO, the German Government would be compelled, by the very same forces, to swing all the way into the Soviet orbit. It does not matter what Adenauer's successors would have in mind; whatever they might secretly desire, their actions would be determined by the towering fact that a "neutralized" Germany would no longer be capable of its own sovereign policy once it was marooned on an island of impotence amid an ocean of Soviet military power.

In such a case the United States would, of course, have withdrawn from any participation in German affairs; for without such a withdrawal no Soviet type of "reunification" could have happened in the first place. And NATO, of course, would have ceased to exist after Germany's withdrawal. Thus the Soviet Union would be, without the shadow of a doubt, the only militarily determining power on the Continent. And no German government could escape from the consequences. Whether and when the Communist party would enter such a German government is not very important. The decisive fact is that *any* government of such a "reunified" Germany would have to navigate according to the orders of the Soviets, for any other course would result either in Germany's suicide or in the global rocket war.

The truly decisive result of a "demilitarization" of Germany would be the immediate demise of NATO; or, to put the same thing in other and clearer words, the military retreat of the United States from the Continent. I do not know of a single military expert in Germany, or in France, or in Italy, who doubts that to Germany falls the central role in *any* system of European defense and par-

ticularly in the given (and evidently unchangeable) NATO structure. Even if it were not for the solemn German obligation to
supply NATO with the bulk of continental man power for decades
to come—no European nation (neither France, nor Italy, nor the
Benelux nations) can be expected to retain a permanent state of
preparedness against the Soviets, once Germany has escaped into
a state of "neutrality." And it is altogether inconceivable that, in
such a case, the United States would continue to hang on to its
precarious position on the outer fringes of Europe. Once a "reunified" Germany quits NATO, the concept of a European defense
against Soviet aggressions is extinguished.

Only he who cannot read, or refuses to understand what he is
reading, can overlook these consequences resulting from a "negotiated reunification" of Germany. They are neither speculations
nor interpretations. They are merely a condensation of whole
libraries of western and Soviet writings on strategy. The Communists
have hidden their aims and stratagems even less than had Hitler.
And the "realists" who, in the face of predictable, predicted, and
inescapable consequences of "a readiness to negotiate," rush into
the suicide of such "negotiations" have not even the puny moral
alibi of Neville Chamberlain and Edouard Daladier. For in 1938
one did not yet know what dynamic explosiveness animated nazism.
But twenty years later the dynamic explosiveness of communism
had already subdued a billion men. In 1938 the desire to conquer
the world was still merely the boast of a very poor writer, the
author of *Mein Kampf;* in 1959, the capacity of communism to
conquer and rule the world was an indisputable fact.

The directives for an adequate German (and American) foreign
policy, emerging from these inexorable circumstances of the German situation, will be discussed in the last two chapters of this
book. Here, in the context of a report on the vitality of the new
Germany, the phenomenon of intellectual anemia in all German
discussions on "reunification" commands attention. And the most
fascinating aspect of this phenomenon is the incompatibility of a
truly realistic calmness, which the Germans apply to the *internal*

problems of West Germany, and the well-nigh hysterical absurdity which shows in all German conversations on East Germany and "reunification."

The irrational, illogical, and often furious daydreaming that penetrates all these conversations seems to have two reasons. For one, the underlying nervousness may stem from the West German's troubled conscience: West Germany, in dishonorable truth, never cared much, during ten years of an exotic prosperity, about the Golgotha of 17 million East Germans; and when the tortured, in 1955, spontaneously arose, too many West Germans secretly prayed that "calmness and order" would soon be restored, so that there would be no temptation for West Germans to interfere in the East German misery. This kind of troubled conscience always renders the *Bürger* nervous and stupid. He will undergo the silliest contortion of spirit and mind, if only to find persuasive arguments in favor of his inferior conduct. In the case of East Germany, the West German *Bürger* (particularly when disguised as a Social Democrat) therefore insists that there *must* be a path toward "reunification in comfortable calmness and order," simply because there *ought* to be one.

For another reason, the West German responds with fatuous nervousness to the challenge of East Germany because of the profound confusion which has befallen the *entire* West. Like Americans, Britons, and Frenchmen, the Germans, too, will be to the last moment convinced that theirs is a *choice* between conflict and "coexistence" with communism. This ultimate knot of western confusion will also be more thoroughly discussed in a later chapter; but to submit a complete diagnosis, we must take here a fast look at the specifically German version of the general western contortion —the West German illusion that Germany can go far in satisfying Soviet wishes, and yet, in the case of "real danger," can still count on effective American protection.

This grotesque concept of a two-timing German policy, the dispensation of "a third force" in both directions, is partly due to a characteristic German cynicism that even the most decent German applies when he discusses policy. If you talk to the best mannered

German about the United States protection of Germany, for example, you will be unfailingly offended by the cynical smile he dis-
plays to show how well he knows that, whatever the United States
does, it does for no other reason but unmitigated selfishness; that,
in other words, the United States would protect Germany even if
it were engaged in a flirtation with the Soviet Union, simply because
American interests, in the last analysis, *must* insist on German
sovereignty. Therefore, why should the Germans pay, with their
own rearmament and with the distress of continued Soviet-German
tensions, for something that is coming to them anyhow and free
of charge?

True, the conduct of the United States has contributed to this
unpleasant misinterpretation of American "interests" in Europe.
American policy and especially United States propaganda in Europe
never knew how to persuade the Europeans that they must defend
themselves against communism, not to do America a favor, but
for their own good. Of course, it is admittedly important to the
defense of America to use military bases on the Continent. But it
is, from a technical point, increasingly *less* important: In "the final
analysis"—i.e., in the case of a rocket war—it very likely does
not really matter where the monsters will be fired.

And if one speaks of "selfish interests," one should be able to
comprehend that, say, for the people of the American Midwest it is
rather irrelevant if, in the defense of America, not only Moscow
but also Frankfurt and Paris are pulverized. It is above all a
European interest to see to it that the Continent ends up as neither
a jail nor as a crumbling moon landscape; and it is primarily a
German interest to avoid the sovietization as well as the material
atomization of Germany. Even if a Germany that was flirting with
the Soviets *would* be saved by America "in the last analysis" (and
I am not at all certain that it would be), the saving action would
of necessity consist of the more or less total destruction of a
Germany that, at the beginning of a conflagration, would be under
Soviet control. All this a superior and effective United States propaganda should have explained to the Germans; and it did not.

During my studies I have hardly met a German who would have

begun to understand that what is known as "American isolation-ism" (i.e., America's undying distrust of Europe and its hellish restlessness) remains, in spite of all signs of American participation in the affairs of the world, a powerful undercurrent in America's conscious and, above all, its subconscious mind. Except for a few thousand experts in European matters, no American is really convinced that fourteen years after the end of hostilities United States soldiers still ought to stay in Europe, as a kind of hostage. And if the Germans themselves were to ask for a withdrawal of these United States troops from German territory (one of the minimum demands of a "reunification" policy "negotiated" with the Soviets), then it would be grotesquely improbable that United States troops would return to Germany in our generation. The next evidence of United States military prowess to arrive in Germany will be in this case atomic rockets.

It would be in the mutual interest of both Germany and America if the United States propaganda in Germany at last started to tell the Germans that the concept of "Fortress America" has great popular possibilities in America and that it is bound to win if the Germans tried to escape into "neutrality." Indeed, it would not take much to convince Americans that Europeans in general, and Germans in particular, have no intention of quarreling with the Soviets; but once Americans are persuaded that the Germans have made a *deal* with the Soviets, then they are bound to pick up their marbles in Europe and withdraw behind the genuine or illusionary protection of a "Fortress America" with a speed that will surprise even German cynics.

No one understands the real possibilities of such an American turnabout better than the Soviets. Their policy—and the strategic goal of this policy has always been the American withdrawal from Europe, i.e., the "neutralization" of Germany—aims at this very American sensitivity; and the clever nuances of the Soviets' finger exercises *in re* "Berlin Crisis" remain a veritable lesson in the arts of psychological warfare.

The real—the *only*—intention of the Soviets was from the very beginning to maneuver the Allies into recognizing the Ulbricht regime: the recognition of "the other Germany's" existence is the jimmy with which the Soviets can demolish the entire European structure. For this very reason the Soviet propaganda (invaluably helped by the coarse naïveté of the western and, particularly, the German press) focused on the alleged Soviet demand that the Allies must withdraw their *troops* from West Berlin. But it does not make the slightest difference to the Soviets whether or not a few thousand isolated United States soldiers remain in West Berlin. Should the two world powers ever collide in earnest, the military value of our corporal's guard in West Berlin is assuredly zero. On the other hand, should the Soviets plan to continue their unnerving "peaceful" massaging of the United States (which seems to be their intention for unforeseeably long years), then it would vastly suit their schemes to leave America in a state of permanent nervous concern about the fate of a marooned United States garrison in West Berlin; for, or so the Soviets hope, in that case American public opinion is bound to explode in favor of a "compromise."

For all these reasons the Soviets launched the "Berlin Crisis" in disguise. Because their intention was to enforce the Allied recognition of the Ulbricht regime, the concern of the Allies was directed toward a banal irrelevancy—the "problem" of our military contingents in West Berlin. And after the West has trembled for half a year about the warlike threats of such a crisis, and yet has heroically insisted that western troops *must* remain in West Berlin, the Soviets will finally emerge as the great and lovable peacemakers. All right, they will say, the United States troops *will* stay in West Berlin; but their supply lines can no longer be administered in cooperation with the Soviet troops (which have been "withdrawn" from East Berlin and its environments)—they now, of course, must be administered in cooperation with Ulbricht and his "civil administration."

In this case the comically naïve press of the western nations will sigh with relief. War has been avoided! And the "Berlin Crisis" will have resulted in exactly what the Soviets wanted: the Allies will establish direct relations with the Ulbricht regime. The West will take some time to comprehend what it has conceded. And by

then everything will have begun to move according to the compel-
ing logic of surrender. The trick will have consisted in letting the
trembling West breathe with relief precisely at the moment it made
the decisive concession. It is a simple trick—simple as long as the
Soviets are allowed to count on the West's and Germany's readiness to play the stooge of history.

Germany's readiness to live up to such Soviet expectations is
even greater than that of America. This is partly explained (and
perhaps also excused) by the fact that Germany's skin is primarily involved; for in a mob that has been afflicted by an anxiety
neurosis he who is in direct proximity to the paralyzing phenomenon
will behave the least rationally. But I do not think that this is the
only reason. Perhaps even more important than the anxiety neurosis, which has disarmed the entire West with a pacifist fixation, is
the German tendency to quit history altogether.

Enjoying the pleasures of prosperity, the new Germany seems determined to forget world history in general and pathetic German
history in particular. In this sense Germany has much too thoroughly lost the war. Now it distrusts *any* kind of foreign policy—
simply because *every* kind of foreign policy constitutes a national
commitment; and commitments are dangerous. Germany would
want to be rich as the United States, but weak and neutral as
Monaco. And the policy of the nonpolitical has always been daydreaming. Because the new Germany resents foreign policy *per se,*
it is so anxious to play the stooge in the Soviet circus. Its rationale:
if one is only a good boy, and a patient negotiator, one day the
great love affair between East and West will start, West and East
will marry, and beget many prosperities.

I hasten to add that there are millions of Germans who *refuse* to
participate in such daydreaming, to yield to the hallucinations of
West Germany's "neutralist" press. The best known of these Germans, of course, is Dr. Konrad Adenauer, who has more influence
but also more enemies than any other politician in West Germany.
His nation's "public opinion" (i.e., its articulate "neutralist" press)
could forgive him anything, even that he has been intolerably right
for twelve years; but it is unwilling to forgive him his genuine real-

ism in *foreign* affairs: *"Der Alte"* has never hesitated, not for a single second, to recognize the communist intentions concerning West Germany for what they are; and whenever the Soviets started to lure him, he has proved rigidly unseducible.

There are, of course, millions of West Germans who love Adenauer primarily for this reason. But even his closest associates have no doubt that the imposing majority he has always rallied was never motivated by an enthusiastic approval of his *foreign* policy. On the contrary, the best experts on the currents in the German electorate agree that Adenauer won the last election *in spite* of his "rigid" rejection of "negotiations with the Soviets"— that, in other words, his "rigidity" is *not* backed by a majority of West Germany's voters. And this is my impression, too. Once the minority of genuine German realists is no longer led by Adenauer, then, I am afraid, the daydreaming "neutralists" will seduce the majority.

Much the more so as there is no other real difference of opinion in the lukewarm political life of West Germany; and thus, in the face of a growing boredom, the only recognizable conflict must gain in impact. Until now the daydreamers have lost one election after the other because, first, there was Adenauer and, second, there was a more or less identifiable United States policy that also rejected Soviet offers to "negotiate." The Germans consider themselves so much the object, and never the subject, of contemporary history that it would not occur to them to vote against a fact as capital as United States policy; and particularly, if it is also Adenauer's. But the geological formations of German politics are breaking up before our eyes.

There is, above all, the landslide in United States politics that almost buried the Republican party in November 1958 and has advanced a Democratic party which, in the United States Senate, is led by men who share, in foreign policy, the convictions of Fulbright, Mansfield, and Humphrey. All three senators are admirers of George F. Kennan and long-standing opponents of a Dulles policy that has always distrusted the "negotiability" of Soviet offers. Yet the triumvirate of Fulbright-Mansfield-Humphrey seems to determine the foreign policy of the United States Senate's Democratic majority. It is more than likely that the Soviets launched the "Berlin crisis" in immediate response to the Democratic landslide in the United States elections of 1958. Indeed, a United States Senate whose foreign policy is determined by Fulbright, Mansfield, and Humphrey must impress the Soviets as precisely the kind of playmate they would love to invite to a wild poker game.

In any case, West Germany's electorate is suddenly no longer certain that the United States will never allow a German "reconciliation" with the Soviets. Nor is Adenauer certain. But were he to lose his unfailing firmness in navigating West Germany's foreign policy, even a German opposition handicapped by the astonishing political clumsiness of Herr Ollenhauer would have excellent chances to high-pressure the country into "negotiations" with the Soviets.

And so the lukewarm German decade seems to be coming to an end. West Germany's political life in the new era will not necessarily be less puny, but it will be much more perilous. At last the Soviets seem to be in a position to take the German daydreamers by their dreams. Only fourteen years after it has been raped, Germany is getting ready for a new assignation with the Soviets. The outcome of the rendezvous is not a matter of surmise—it is known.

Whatever the outcome of the "Berlin crisis" will be, the Soviets have already attained a concession of unforeseeable impact on future developments in Europe. On March 11, 1959, President Eisenhower declared bluntly, unequivocally, and unashamedly: "We certainly are not going to fight a ground war in Europe." History will show, I am afraid, that with this one sentence President Eisenhower has dismantled NATO, dissolved all prospects of European self-confidence in defense preparations, and granted the Soviet Union its strategic main goal for the last fifteen years—the withdrawal of United States troops from the Continent.

For, in apodictically renouncing any United States readiness "to fight a ground war in Europe," Mr. Eisenhower has torn up the very concept of NATO. On American urging, articulated at that time most vigorously by General Dwight D. Eisenhower, the members of the Atlantic community were aroused, several years ago, to bury their defeatism and to rally, with the United States, behind a new plan for continental defense. During the first few postwar years, under the impression of its humiliating collapse before the Nazi war machine, and horrified by premonitions ignited by the Hiroshima bomb, an exhausted western Europe had virtually given up. What's the use? If the United States were ever to permit it, the Soviets could cut through to the Atlantic coast in a couple of weeks; and for the United States the only way of preventing them from taking that easy walk would be to drop atomic bombs all over Europe. Nothing within the power of European nations could affect this murderous dilemma: it's either piecemeal surrender to the Soviets or the nuclear holocaust.

And then came NATO. By 1950 the United States had finally sold western Europe a practical prospect of hope. The very gruesomeness of the new nuclear weapons makes the defense of western Europe not less but more feasible—provided the nations of western Europe pool their *conventional* forces and strengthen them to the point that the Soviet Union could no longer assume a *conventional* invasion to be a mere walk.

For once the Soviets could be persuaded that western Europe will resist long and effectively enough to let a *conventional* conflagration grow into an all-out nuclear war, the Soviets could not possibly take any risks with "limited" adventures. On the other hand, if no western conventional resistance was to be expected, those risks would be negligible. Precisely because the use of "the ultimate weapon" must have earth-shaking consequences, it will be used only on ultimate provocations; but, if no such provocation were forthcoming, if the Soviets were shrewdly to confine their future thrusts to "limited and localized" interventions, none of them in itself an adequate justification of the ultimate global nightmare, then western Europe would go bit by bit—in one "limited and localized" Soviet thrust after another. Therefore, or so went the NATO argument, western Europe must make those "limited and localized" adventures unfeasible. How? By being prepared for *conventional* ground wars. Once the Soviets are persuaded that no easy victory can be had in such a conventional "limited" ground war, and that a thrust of a greater magnitude would mean the certain nuclear all-out war, then western Europe is secure.

This, at any rate, was from the beginning the NATO rationale —until March 11, 1959. On that day President Eisenhower announced that there *will* be "no ground war in Europe." He has, in other words, served notice to the Soviets that United States troops will no longer be committed to defend the territory of NATO's members; rather, the United States will fight none but a nuclear war. To those who do not scare easily this means only one thing: if the Soviets mind their steps, and keep their provocations within tolerable limits, the United States will not fight at all. Certainly not on the European continent. For, on the Continent, one can fight *only* "ground wars." The American pledge not to fight ground wars in Europe, ever again, reduces European alternatives to the paralyzing dilemma of the late forties—either to surrender to the "little" attacks inside Europe or to turn the globe into atomic ashes.

As in all other areas of law enforcement, in international relations, too, the crime must fit the punishment. What would happen if the courts suddenly declared that they will pass no other verdicts than death sentences? Obviously, crimes would multiply. For no one will believe that larceny could possibly be punished by electrocution; therefore, the thief must be let off scot-free, once the judges refuse to sentence him to anything but death. Is it imaginable that the United States would start a nuclear war that must cause the destruction of a considerable part of the planet, just because, say, Herr Ulbricht's "custom guards" around Berlin interfere with the city's milk supply?

In other words, Eisenhower's refusal to "fight a ground war in Europe" will be interpreted by the Soviets, quite correctly, as formal notification that, so long as they carefully avoid the insufferable provocation, the United States will not engage in conventional military resistance to Soviet "limited" thrusts in Europe. It must be, secondly, interpreted as a pledge that United States troops will soon leave Europe altogether. For what, indeed, would they be doing there, once their commander in chief has solemnly pledged his country's abstention from any ground fighting in Europe?

These troops have been stationed in Europe, under NATO command, for one purpose only: to make unmistakably clear that the United States will lend NATO whatever military strength may be required to defeat a specific Soviet attack—from the employment of lowly jeeps and old-fashioned bazookas to the firing of gigantic nuclear missiles if necessary. Our troops were sent to Europe to disabuse the Soviets of one dangerous idea: that the United States was *"not* going to fight a ground war in Europe." Obviously, if the United States were now to fight no other but a nuclear war, it cannot possibly leave its own soldiers inside its nuclear target area.

Either the Eisenhower declaration stands—or our troops stay on the Continent. But the two things are absolutely incompatible. If the United States has made up its mind never again to fight a ground war in Europe, then it must, first of all, withdraw its troops from there. It is inconceivable that the American people will stand for the absurd confusion of policies that seems to be willing to forget all about 250,000 American soldiers in an abandoned territory. America is congenitally incapable of the "Kamikaze" insanity; and once its government decided that it is not going to come to the aid of the United States divisions in Europe, those divisions will have to be called home.

In that case no rational and responsible European government can remain a NATO member. Europe's western nations have accepted the burden of armament and the perils of a military posture because they could be finally convinced that the United States would participate in every necessary act of European defense. The solemn declaration of Eisenhower that the United States has now changed its mind, and will not participate in any European ground fighting, makes membership in NATO not only unviable but downright suicidal. For as there will be no ground fighting in Europe without the United States participating in it, a government that continues the expensive gestures of an inconceivable attitude would be committing hara-kiri. And Europeans, too, have no such habit.

Unless the United States government finds a way of repealing the President's declaration, and of repealing it most persuasively, one European government after another must reconsider its membership in NATO and commence a careful window shopping for an advantageous deal with the Soviets.

As far as Khrushchev is concerned, he has already achieved the most essential victory in the "Berlin crisis" on March 11, 1959. For, most assuredly, Khrushchev does not want a nuclear war. All he wants is that the United States stay out of "limited and localized" continental quarrels. He now has that pledge—and now he can proceed with the cautious, controlled, and masterful "little" nibbles that are his specialty. There is no hurry. He has all the time.

In February 1959, in the midst of the "Berlin crisis," the Adenauer government recalled its ambassador to Cairo and was all set to break off diplomatic relations with Egypt. And this was by no means an easy decision for West Germany to make. Even in 1956, when England and France were still practically at war with Nasser, West Germany most cautiously insisted on its intimate friendship with Egypt, and for very forceful reasons: Germany's export to the Near East, one of the mainstays of German prosperity, depends on Germany's prestige in Cairo. And so crucial are its prospects in the Near East that West Germany took chances on the good feelings of its closest NATO partners rather than weaken its Egyptian ties.

And yet, last February, when Nasser seemed to establish formal relations with the Ulbricht regime, Adenauer was ready to cut those ties. Nasser finally saved the day by announcing his resolution to consider the Bonn government the only legitimate representative of German sovereignty; his dealings with East Germany, he declared, would be confined to technicalities of commerce. Nasser acted as he did because nobody could doubt Adenauer's determination to stake West Germany's fate on its claim to sovereignty over all German territory.

In that he has no choice. Conceivably, the *de facto* recognition of the Ulbricht regime by the western powers must not immediately result in a sovietization of all Germany; but it is inconceivable that an Adenauer type of government (i.e., a German government committed to western alliances in foreign policy, and to liberal economic policies at home) can survive such a change of international climate.

The *de facto* recognition of the Ulbricht regime (Khrushchev's real objective in the "Berlin crisis") destroys the very fundament of the West German government because it annihilates that government's basic claim: that it is the legitimate government of *all* Germany. For the western powers, so much as to negotiate traffic technicalities with Ulbricht would of necessity mean to dispose of Adenauer. This may be difficult to grasp for an American. Indeed, an American can easily swallow that shyster lawyer's "argument," currently so fashionable, that the western powers would be dealing with the Ulbricht regime only in its capacity of "Soviet agents"—not as a government "in the conventional sense of the word." Yet to make this fine distinction one has to live awfully far from Germany. East or west of the Iron Curtain a German has only one acid test to consider: Will the western powers concede that there *are* "two Germanys"? If this is conceded (and never mind the technical amenities), then every single German will commence to come to terms with the Soviets.

Adenauer's political existence and all Allied policies for the last ten years have been based on this one central supposition: that the German territory still occupied by Soviet troops remains an inseparable part of Germany. True, to avoid an otherwise likely conflagration, Adenauer and the western powers were willing to deal rather patiently with the illegal Soviet occupation of German territory. But not for a moment have the western powers and the Adenauer government granted that East Germany has seceded from Germany—that a significant and governmentally acceptable segment of the German people has formed an independent government. And this, of course, has never happened. The Ulbricht regime consists of salaried camp followers of the Soviet troops.

If the western powers were now to recognize that regime, in any capacity at all, as a *de facto* government of a separate East Germany, they would have conceded (a) the partition of Germany and (b) the resulting need to bring about its "reunification" by some kind of "confederation" of the "two" governments. No legalistic weasel words could change one iota of this essential concession. And once that concession is made, the Adenauer regime must topple in West Germany.

East of the Iron Curtain the never-ending predicament of the Soviets is the indisputable fact that an overwhelming majority of the East Germans stubbornly refuses to accept the alleged legitimacy of the Ulbricht regime. This has been proved, not only by the immense uprising of 1953, but by the unceasing flight of East Germans to the West (almost 4 million of them have escaped since 1948—out of a total East German population of 17 million) and by the prevailing atmosphere of passive resistance. So long as the East Germans consider their territory illegally occupied, East Germany remains a dangerous sore of the Soviet empire. But once they have been shown that the West is getting ready to recognize the Ulbricht gang as a government, no matter in what legal phrasing, then all hopes of the captured East German people collapse, East Germany becomes a secure Soviet satellite, and the Ulbricht regime begins to perform as the Soviets' most important tool in the penetration of western Europe.

West of the Iron Curtain the reliability of West Germany as a partner of the western alliance depends on the German's unshakable conviction that his is the legitimate government of all Germany and, above all, that the West is going to protect those who resist communist penetration. Once this basic conviction is shaken, once the average German sees reasons to suspect that the western resoluteness has broken down, the notoriously cautious German citizen will of necessity "regroup."

Except for a small minority of deeply committed anti-Communists, the Germans have only one formative political motivation: never again to be on the losing side. The Communists have but slim prospects ever to persuade a significant part of the German people of their *philosophy;* but they will prove masters of Germany once they have succeeded in looking *invincible.* The West Germans hate the prospect of losing a next time even more than they hate communism. What made Adenauer the revered hero of German recovery was the unchallengeable fact that, to the Germans, he represented not only German respectability but also American security. And once the people of West Germany are allowed to doubt that his regime is irrevocably backed by the power of the United States, German allegiances must switch from Adenauer to the opposition that has always advocated a "cautious" course in regard to the Soviet Union and a "confederation" with sovietized East Germany.

This opposition—a coalition between the Social Democrats and the F.D.P.—has even in the last elections, in the hour of Adenauer's greatest triumphs, attained almost 45 per cent of the West German vote. Nor is this an accurate measure of the drawing power of "neutralist" ideas in West Germany. For, in truth, a not inconsiderable fraction of Adenauer's Christian Democratic Union is permeated by these ideas; only Adenauer's irresistible habit of success has so far prevented that "left" wing of his party from making common cause with the opposition. The moment that success habit is broken, and Adenauer's claim to representing German security in a firm alliance with the United States is repudiated, his own party will tremble. And even if the aged Adenauer were to survive such a turn of events physically, the next elections will most probably bring the opposition the few per cent it needs to assume power.

In short, with their decision on Berlin the western governments will pre-empt the decision on Germany, on Europe, on the West. The moment they declare their willingness to grant the Ulbricht regime governmental legitimacy, the western powers would have opened for communism the door to West Germany, to western Europe, to ultimate victory.

CHAPTER FOUR

The Cultural Life of a Convalescent

THE influence of the West's certified cultural giants on the disoriented German intellectuals, so anxious to conform with the wide world again, cannot be overrated. The Germans are going through a strange convalescence. This is a nation that must grow, and is growing immensely, without a valid reference to its own recent tradition. It is a nation with a case of deliberate amnesia: they must not recall what they all can remember. All, or almost all, Germans depend intellectually on their faculty to start anew.

Never before was there a nation so determined to renounce its own continuity. Every adult German, younger than sixty today, must forget, under the penalty of intellectual destruction, fifteen of his most formative years—the twelve years under Hitler and the first three years under military occupation and sheer nothingness. He must forget the events, the prevailing judgments of those years, their order of values, their central ideas. He must forget them; not just discard them but, indeed, forget them. It is a desperate psychological predicament. The German must remake his self; and on his flight from forbidden memories, in his unprecedented effort of resurrection in someone else's image, the intellectual heroes of the West are the German's only conceivable help: They

97

are the image after which the intellectual German must try to re-make himself.

What does the Germany that uneasily looks for spiritual vac-cination from abroad find in the West? While I was in Germany I was confounded by the eagerness and frequency with which young German artists referred to Picasso—not Picasso the artist, but Picasso the thinker. There are, in particular, certain remarks Picasso made to his busy Boswell, the art dealer Daniel-Henry Kahnweiler, in 1946; and Mr. Kahnweiler, who is also a prolific writer on art, took faithful notice of the master's every syllable and published, recently, these pronunciamentos of Pablo Picasso:

"Look at Michelangelo's 'Last Supper.' Is it executed? Naturally, it is not. It's just decoration. A lot in the museums is just decora-tion. Yesterday I was in the Louvre. The Assyrians, yes! But painting? It's exterior decoration. No one before us has really seriously painted. Certainly there has been [in the past], too, talent, even genius; but that does not matter. . . . You [Kahnweiler] should say the truth about the Louvre, for you know it. Prostitutes, very nice prostitutes, but nothing else. Cubism is the only real painting. . . . To do something, one must dirty one's hands. One must wallow in dirt. . . . Yes, it can be fun to sleep with a prostitute, but one has to be always aware of the fact that she is a prostitute."

He is talking of Michelangelo, Rembrandt, Goya, Renoir. It is one of the most remarkable statements ever heard about art but, offhand, I would have thought that it originated with a "sophisticated" adolescent—one of those bright boys who turn frightfully cynical at the age of seventeen—certainly not with the most famous contemporary artist when he was already in his sixties. Personally, like many intelligent people in the West, I can take Picasso or leave him; and what he says impresses me far less than what he paints. But it is different in Germany.

For the Germans, no matter how hard they try, cannot really escape their own intellectual traditions. They are, for instance, still Germans in the one quality that has been so graphically called *"ihr tierischer Ernst"* ("their animal-like earnestness"). By this is meant the German's fatal habit to take language literally and to *do* what others frivolously chat about. The German, congenitally a doer, is also an irreparable romantic who does not really know laughter. When the German laughs—and he laughs a great deal—it is always about a joke; that is, he predictably responds to a deliberate provocation. But the German hardly ever laughs "with no reason at all"—which is the real laughter, the liberating and healing laughter; the laughter, for instance, about one's ludicrous self.

In that one respect Picasso, too, is a German. But the kind of people who can *truly* laugh are invulnerable in Picasso's line of fire: They take one look at a sketch by Michelangelo and are shaken with laughter about the funny Picasso who has fooled several generations of the West, and about the enthusiasts who have allowed him to make a fool of himself. But it is tough on the eager Germans. I would not be surprised if a number of young German artists, talented and nice and filled with "animal-like earnestness," would on their next trip to Paris avoid the Louvre as if it really were Picasso's lewd house of assignation. That, in consequence, there would be no German painting of importance for years to come is irrelevant; the world can survive without German painters. But the West cannot survive without Germany. And Germany cannot survive in a downpour of cynical ashes. It is the one kind of fallout that is indubitably deadly.

There is, of course, not the slightest reason why Picasso, who so savagely wasted his divine talent as painter, should act more responsibly as talker; and Mr. Daniel-Henry Kahnweiler is entirely within his rights in publishing what this poor generation's Michelangelo had to say about his predecessor. If the aging Picasso erupts in asinine nihilism, no one is going to suggest censorship against a genius in his second adolescence. No, there is nothing that could be done to protect the eager young Germans from the flow of cynical western pus. They will have to go through that infection, I guess. But, as Picasso so elegantly put it, one at least has to be aware that one sleeps with a prostitute. And the West must be aware that its certified geniuses stimulate rootless German intellectuals into debauchery and nothingness.

They do not even find aesthetic stimuli in the West. Take, for another example, Mr. Kenneth Tynan, currently all the rage of "sophisticated" London and "knowing" New York, a young critic who corresponds in the province of criticism to the "angry young men" in what nowadays goes for creative British literature. Mr. Tynan, who performs weekly in *The New Yorker* and used to write in London's respectable *Observer,* is flatteringly read and quoted all over the Continent. He is the sort of critic who loves to substitute himself for the whole show: his cracks are supposed to enliven the drabness of a normal London or New York season, and his reviews are far more often discussed at the right dinner tables than the plays he reviews. To exemplify the kind of sayings that have made Mr. Tynan a howling success I have picked, at random, this gem:

No artist . . . should fear the charge of bad taste. Bad taste is that which offends against decorum, creates embarrassment, and speaks lightly of things considered holy . . . Good taste, in any society, is the taste he [the artist] is pledged to oppose.

Now this touching imitation of Oscar Wilde (who, at his best, was not exactly wise) was intended neither as witticism nor was it an exaggeration in a polemical rage. Mr. Tynan was philosophizing this time rather seriously. He did not go to the trouble of putting, in any sense, quotation marks around "good taste" and "bad taste." Nor did he indicate that he was spoofing the philistine's notions of propriety, beauty, and value. Mr. Tynan meant all he said (inasmuch as those "sophisticated" European wags are ever ready to mean anything at all). What Mr. Tynan here had to say was indeed, I am afraid, his aesthetic credo. It is certainly significant for the literary school he represents.

But do consider what he said: "No artist should fear the charge of bad taste." There is hardly anything else an artist should fear! No artist should fear the charge of burglary, of inadequate philosophical training, of criminal bankruptcy, bad economics, and impossible politics. But the charge of bad taste he must fear like the plague. For a sensitiveness of form, an irreducible, almost physical awareness of the nuances that separate authenticity from fraud, organic creation from synthetic imitation, art from *Kitsch,* is precisely what constitutes him as an artist. He is competent in no other area—neither as "thinker" nor as "seer." An artist is formed by taste; and hardly anything else.

Nor is it true, of course, that bad taste is what offends against decorum and creates embarrassment; though it is unquestionably correct that it is bad taste to speak lightly of things considered holy. In fact, the foolishly willful connotation of "decorum," "embarrassment," and "holiness" gives Mr. Tynan away: Freud caught up with him—his tongue slipped into self-revelation. Western "sophisticates" would forgive an artist anything, even good taste, as long as he "speaks lightly of things considered holy." One can, of course, speak of holy things—and one never can speak enough of them. But only the booby will speak *lightly* of them. And what makes him the retarded creature he is, it seems to me, is exactly his bad taste: he has no sense and no sensitiveness to distinguish among the nuances of which the higher life is made. Satan, for instance, shrewd as he may be, is such a booby: he lacks reverence.

I do not mean to say that there is something satanic in the thoroughly innocent Mr. Tynan; but he *does* cringe in the face of holiness. A generation has grown up in the West that considers holiness an anachronistic monstrosity, a repulsive psychic defect, an eczema of the soul. The world in which I grew up found nothing to be so sad, and so revolting, as the lack of reverence. It looked upon bad taste as precisely the modish routine that always complies with the decorum (decorum *was* bad taste); and it welcomed enthusiastically an artist who, because he had good taste, offended against decorum, even if he so created great embarrassment among the stodgy. "Decorum" was almost the exact negation of holiness; and far into the days of Chesterton the artist, because he—unlike the philistine—*never* could speak lightly of things man considers holy, was exactly the one to offend against decorum and to create incessant embarrassment among the unholy, decoration-loving, materialistic philistines.

Good taste, finally, was in *no* society the taste of the people whom the artist is pledged to oppose. Of course, Mr. Tynan's resources of irony are unfathomable, and in this one case he might have meant to imply quotation marks around "good taste"; but I doubt it. I am rather persuaded (by an overdose of attention I have been paying to the intellectual style of European intelligentsia) that Mr. Tynan *honestly* believes in the theoretical incompatibility between good taste and lovability; so that anything that strikes him as inoffensive to the traditional values of his society is, to him, neither art nor good taste nor even forgivable. To this ill-humored generation of somewhat lame *agents provocateurs* an artist is first and last an iconoclast; and it seems to them utterly irrelevant whether the artist can also *paint* icons. On the contrary, he would make himself unattractive by any evidence of serene creativeness. And it would be the ultimate in bad taste when such creativeness stems from reverence—the one unpardonable sin in the aesthetic credo of "sophisticates."

It is, I hope, immediately visible how these modish intellectual perversions have a bearing on the health of the Germans. As I said before, this nation is enormously handicapped by the weird circumstances of a convalescence the like of which has hardly been known in history. Germany cannot expect to settle down in the context of the West until and unless it succeeds in erasing fifteen recent years of its life experience—a clearly impossible task. And yet, no less will do. Every particle of the present German insecurity, imitativeness, disorientation is due to the urgency of an impossible task. Of course, you could live in Germany for years without finding anybody who could articulate this problem; and yet, it is ubiquitous, it permeates every layer of German society, and none more than the immense stratum of German *Gebildete,* the "educated" class of Germans who, with the one exception of France, form more decisively the will of their nation than do the intellectuals in any other European country.

This group of Germans has never before been more imitative,

and for very understandable reasons. With the desperate eagerness of the empty—or, rather, the emptied—they stare with
indiscriminating admiration at the intellectual conduct and value
preferences among their neighbors. Under these conditions the
Picassos and Sartres in France, the Faulkners and Arthur Millers
in America, the Osbornes and Tynans in Britain, are under a
heavy additional burden. In normally healthy societies it may be
unfair to artists and critics to hold them responsible for more than
their normal function—which is to be as exciting and amusing as
they happen to be. But this is an altogether unfair century; and
even if the western intellectuals were to reject the extracurricular
assignment of social responsibility (as they are indubitably doing),
it is still theirs.

The Picassos and Sartres, the Faulkners and Millers, the Osbornes and Tynans—whatever else they may be—are the only
effective "re-educators" of Germany (may God have mercy on the
Germans and us). What a more or less amusing critic writes in
The New Yorker and *The Observer* will finally—through that
essential process of social osmosis that lets values, acquired or
borrowed, sink into the fiber of a whole clumsy nation—determine
the fate of Germany, and thus the West, far more surely than the
acts of a British prime minister. It hurts me more than it will hurt
Mr. Tynan that I am inflating his ego. I have to. I have not made
him the star critic of *The New Yorker,* but I have studied the
peculiar German convalescence, and I must testify to the fateful
importance of the sort of cross-fertilization that reaches from
moderately frivolous salons in New York, London, and Paris to
the training grounds of the new German army.

In 1957 the German bookstores did the largest business in their
history. What books did the Germans buy for Christmas 1957?

Hamburg: Rampa's *Third Eye* (British); Montupet's *House
Vermorel* (French); Burgess' *Woman Without Talents* (British);
Frisch's *Homo Faber* (Swiss); Ceram's *Gods, Graves and Scholars*
(German). Thus two of these five writers were British, one French,
one Swiss, one German.

Frankfurt: Rampa's *Third Eye;* the Ceram book; Djilas' *New*

Class; Thornton Wilder's *The Ides of March.* One American, one Briton, one Yugoslav, one German.

Berlin: Ceram, Frisch, Djilas, Wilder. One American, one Swiss, one Yugoslav, one German.

Freiburg: Ceram, Djilas, Wilder, Frisch, Camus. One American, one Swiss, one Yugoslav, one Frenchman, one German.

Munich: Leading sellers were the expensively luxurious art books of publishers such as Skira, Hatje, and Schroll (average price: about $25.00—in German purchasing power about $50.00); also special Munich literature apropos the 800th anniversary of the town; finally Ceram (German).

Cologne: Gary's *Roots of Heaven* (French); Rampa; Djilas; Ceram; Frisch; Dudintzev's *Not by Bread Alone* (Russian). A Frenchman, a Briton, a Swiss, a German, a Yugoslav, a Russian.

Rhine and Ruhr (Essen, Dusseldorf, etc.): Ceram; Gary; Rampa; Faulkner; Camus; Pritzkoleit's *Who Owns Germany?*; Charles Morgan's *Challenge to Venus;* Mme X's *Madame Solario.* One American, two Britons, three Frenchmen, two Germans.

One fact sticks out from all data: German authors are entirely out of luck with the German public which, for Christmas 1957, bought almost exclusively translated foreign literature. The provincial nationalism of the German book market, so conspicuous in the twenties and thirties, is no more. The German public, if anything, now overdoes its cosmopolitan curiosity; evidently the foreign literature it is patronizing is not that much better than the admittedly poor German offering.

The German weekly, *Die Zeit,* publishes every month a carefully investigated best-seller list for all of Germany. For December 1957 it listed Djilas, Ceram, Montupet, Heyerdahl's *Aku-Aku,* Dudintzev. Thus the five national best sellers under the German Christmas tree of 1957 were a Yugoslav, a German, a Frenchman, a Norwegian, and a Russian. The *Zeit's* list of the books that had sold best, all over Germany, from July 1 to December 31, 1957, brought somewhat better news to German authors: among the best-selling writers of the last six months of 1957 were four living Germans, two dead ones, two Americans, two Frenchmen, two

Swiss, one Briton, one Russian. (Pritzkoleit, Hermann Hesse, Leonhardt, Erich Kuby, Bergengruen, Thomas Mann, Gottfried Benn, John Steinbeck, Thornton Wilder, Montupet, Camus, Frisch, Rampa, Dudintzev.) But, as the *Zeit's* Christmas survey showed in accord with all other available data, things were constantly getting worse for German authors: at the year's end there was a single German on the *Zeit's* list of Germany's five best-selling authors.

The situation is just as unequivocal on the German stage—and the German theater is probably a more formative cultural factor than the German book: Germany has remained the actors' dreamland, at least as far as steady employment is concerned. West Germany entertains 175 theaters for 52 million people. (Projected onto American conditions, this would amount to more than 500 theaters in the United States with 175 million people; but there were in America not even 100 professional companies playing in 1958, all road companies and sideshows included.)

Of these 175 German theaters 115 were subsidized by federal, state, or municipal government, and only 19 were privately owned. (There were 15 road companies, 11 open-air theaters, and 15 "specialty theaters" dedicated to folklore.) The 115 publicly owned theaters were heavily subsidized indeed. In 1957, the most prosperous year in the history of the German theater, they earned between them DM 80 million (about $19 million) and spent DM 240 million (about 58 million dollars). The deficit of 160 million DM (about 39 million dollars) was paid with tax money; which means that every adult German paid more than 5 DM a year to keep his theaters going (about $1.15). In American magnitudes this would mean the expenditure of at least $130 million a year of the taxpayer's money (in purchasing power very likely close to $250 million) for the support of a whole network of United States theaters.

Now in 1957 there were about 40,000 performances reported and tabulated by the *Deutscher Bühnenverein*—and it is an eloquent tabulation. Almost 4,000 performances staged American plays (*The Diary of Anne Frank* alone got 1,954 performances in less than ten months of 1957). The German classics reached, between them, about 6,000 performances (Lessing, 1,612; Schiller, 1,296; Goethe, 1,208; Gerhart Hauptmann, 1,184). Shakespeare was performed professionally 2,493 times—without doubt far more often than in the entire English-speaking world. Shaw was played 1,263 times. But all living playwrights who write in German (i.e., Germans, Austrians, and Swiss) got, between them, 2,849 performances—one out of fifteen evenings on the German stage. On the whole, more than one half of all 40,000 performances produced classics (dramatic and operatic) of all periods and nations. More than 40 per cent were reserved for imported foreign playwrights, and less than 10 per cent (including dead authors) for modern Germans.

By the way, Mozart held the operatic record with more than 2,000 performances in 1957, followed by Verdi's 1,910, Johann Strauss's 1,479, Puccini's 1,397, Lehár's 1,353, Offenbach's 919; then only followed Richard Wagner with 821 performances. In juxtaposition, a thorough survey by Mr. Frederic Cohen, conducted for the New York Metropolitan Opera and the Juilliard Foundation for the season 1953–54, indicates that there were about 1,500 operatic performances staged in the whole United States in that season—*including* those of amateur groups. And, says Mr. Cohen, "more than half of all performances were accompanied by one or two pianos replacing the orchestra."

These statistics, as statistics always do, can serve to prove almost anything. But one is certainly allowed to speculate on the sensational lack of nationalism on the German stage. On the other hand, one could also conclude that there must be but little creative vitality left among German playwrights if the German theater, so heavily subsidized by the taxpayer, cannot find enough produceable German plays to justify more than 7 per cent of all performances. Then, again, one could contemplate on the size, if not the depth, of German remorse in the face of 2,000 performances of *The Diary of Anne Frank* in less than ten months—almost as many as, during the whole year, were devoted to living German playwrights. Or one could appreciate the ratio of Mozart to Richard

Wagner—almost 3 to 1, on the breeding grounds of *Götterdäm-merung*—with a satisfaction that is even further strengthened by the pleasant thought that the delightful Offenbach, too, outdid Wagner. All this and much more could be said about German theatrical statistics.

In Vienna, by the way, they love the theater even more. The Viennese theaters sold 3,300,000 tickets in 1957—which is twice the size of Vienna's population. To match this achievement, New York's theaters would have to sell, in one year, about 15 million tickets (they sold, of course, in 1957 far less than one half of that quantity). The Austrian theaters received 176 million schillings' public subsidy (in purchasing power, about $12 million), paid by an adult population of about 4 million people—considerably more, per capita, than even the German theaters. (On the other hand, the Austrians spent in 1957 eight times as much on sweets, sixteen times as much on tobacco, and thirty times as much on wine and liquor; so that the Austrian pays—for every 100 schillings he spends on sweets, tobacco, wine, and liquor—less than two schillings for his theaters. Which really leaves one with no argument against the state-subsidized theater, except the principle of the thing.)

The movie industry, of course, provides the most popular German entertainment. More than 800 million customers paid in 1957 more than a billion DM at the cinema box offices—which means that every German over fourteen years of age visited a movie theater about twenty times in 1957 and spent for that privilege about 25 DM (in purchasing power, about $12). The Germans had a chance to see about 660 feature films that year, of which only 103 were German. More than twice as many came from Hollywood (226), 64 from France, 36 from Italy, 25 from Austria, and 85 films originated in the remaining provinces of the film-producing world (Britain, Scandinavia, the Soviet Empire, etc.). Of the DM billion spent at the box offices, the German movie industry received DM 172 million (more than the total subsidy to the German stage) and the foreign movie makers 190 million DM in rental fees, half of that take going to Hollywood.

The quality of the German film production fully justifies such an unfair disproportion. While there is an occasional German picture of merits, the average German film remains painfully inferior to the average product of almost any other country. Nine out of ten German pictures carry an unmistakable signature of banal sterility, a provincial sentimentalism, a cloying "humor," a sweetish inanity. The German movie industry—thirty or forty years ago, in the days of *Caligari, M, The Blue Angel,* famously bold in exploring the frontiers of picture making—is these days indubitably the most barren, most cowardly, most antiquated area of German enterprise.

In this, it seems to me, the German movie industry does as movie industries do everywhere: it crudely exaggerates but it does not set the prevailing cultural pattern. Provincialism, a dread to take *any* position, a horror of originality, a thoughtless preference for the sentimental cliché—all this pettiness unquestionably permeates *all* cultural life in Germany. Only that in Germany these cultural preferences are submerged under the veneer of elite tastes that, perhaps more than in any other European country, tend toward the *avant-garde.* Yet the German mass, in the darkness of the movie theater, shows what it really likes. The German movie industry only exaggerates the German mass preferences, and it does so for forceful reasons. Unlike a book or even a produced play, a movie is a major investment; and the considerable capital employed insists on safety. The safest cultural mode in this prosperous, strangely pragmatist, and yet still romantic, awkwardly convalescing Germany is to be irrelevant, sentimental, noncontroversial, *gemütlich* like a cretin.

The German movie industry flourishes and reconquers territory that seemed to have been lost to the foreign producers. The reason is by no means linguistic: all foreign films are shown in Germany in "dubbed" versions (and it is quite a fright to hear Alec Guinness speak a German of almost Saxonian timbre). The German movie industry, I am afraid, knows much more about German mass appetites than do the authors and publishers of literature. The German popular taste, contrary to the literary interest in foreign *avant-garde,* craves the maudlin *Kitsch*—as it always did, and not only in Germany.

It would be, on the whole, mockery if someone tried to impress a contemporary witness that the Germans have remained, or ever were, what they were fond to call themselves, *ein Volk der Dichter und Denker* ("a people of poets and thinkers"). What made the last few German generations notorious was certainly neither poetry nor thought. And yet, there has remained in the German's everyday life an element of devotion to beauty; and one finds examples of that trait in unexpected places.

For two arbitrarily selected days I have kept notes on what struck me as rather special broadcasts on one of ten important German radio stations. Here are my notes:

> *Sunday, February 23, 1957*: Mozart's Piano Concerto (KL 495); lecture on the British magazine, *Punch;* lecture by Prof. Karl Jasper, "My Way to Philosophy"; arias by Gluck, Mozart, Rameau, and Berlioz; Schubert's Seventh Symphony; Bach's Brandenburg Concerto No. 2; chamber music by Pergolesi, Vivaldi, and Abaco; Schubert's Third Symphony; Mozart's Violin Concerto in D major (KL 218); Poulenc's Symphonietta for String Orchestra; Haydn's Symphony No. 8; Dvořák's Symphony No. 4; excerpts from operas by Pfitzner and de Falla; Virtuosi di Roma playing Rossini's Sonata in E-flat major, Vivaldi's Concerto in F major, Concerti by Albinoni, Valentini, Corelli and Vivaldi; Bruckner's Symphony in D minor; Stravinsky's "Pulcinella"; Beethoven's Sonata for Piano and Violin in A major, op. 30; Schumann's Piano Quintet in E-flat major op. 47; Beethoven's Serenade in D major op. 25; Prokofiev's "Scherzo Humoristique"; Mozart's String Quartet (KL 157); Lessing's tragedy "Emilia Galotti"; modern music by Honegger, Poulenc, and Auric; works by Bach, Telemann, Pergolesi, Handel, and Stamitz; Mozart's Symphonia Concertante (KL 364); Maria Meneghini-Callas sings arias by Donizetti, Giordano, Massenet, and Puccini; Lieder by Mendelssohn and Loewe; Beethoven's Piano Sonatas in C major and C minor, op. 10; Dellapiccola's Concerto for Piano and Orchestra; Berlioz's "Symphonie Fantastique"; Concerti by J.

Chr. Bach; a-capella songs by Brahms; Stravinsky's "Petrou-
chka"; a radio play by André Breton.

Wednesday, February 26: Ravel's "Daphnis et Chloé"; a
radio play by John Steinbeck; Brahms' "Academic Ouverture";
a lecture on "Twenty-Five Years After the Reichstagsbrand";
Josephine Baker Sings; a dialogue on classical German poets;
Martinu's "Variations on a Theme by Rossini"; Beethoven's
Septet, op. 20; Mendelssohn's Quartet in D major; piano
music by Gabriel Fauré; Bach's Sonata in C major for violin
solo; Saint-Saëns' "Samson et Dalila"; a radio play about
August Strindberg; Boccherini's Cello Concerto in B major;
Haydn's Symphony No. 103; sonatas by Purcell, Handel, and
Vitali; Mozart's Violin Concerto in G major (KL 216);
Bartok's Second String Quartet; Reger's Sonata in A minor,
op. 116; Clifford Curzon plays de Falla; Mozart's "Haffner"
Symphony (KL 385); Bruno Walter conducts Brahms' First
Symphony; lecture on "The Contribution of Mathematics to
Culture"; Lotte Lehmann sings arias; Ravel's "Gaspard de
la nuit."

These radio programs, I repeat, I noted on two arbitrarily
selected days in February 1957. They were not the special type of
programs a special radio station such as New York's WQXR
broadcasts within the metropolitan radius of New York; they
could be received, each of them, in substantial parts of Germany
by any selective listener.

What does this prove? A cultural hunger or, at any rate, a
cultural readiness that could not be possibly matched in the United
States? I wonder. In the first place, one must keep in mind that
the German radio does not support itself in the American fashion;
it lives on enforceable monthly fees all owners of radio sets pay
to the public authority that runs the radio stations. Paradoxically,
such direct financing by the listeners weakens rather than strength-
ens their voice in determining the radio programs. The United
States radio, financed by the advertisers, must respond to the demands of the paying sponsor who, even though in highly debatable

fashion, finds out how well liked the sponsored program really is. The advertiser then sees to it that his program changes its level and its scope until it reaches the greatest audience (greatest, that is, in relation to the money he intends to spend on it). In short, the United States radio, precisely because it is subsidized by private advertisers, is compelled to satisfy either real or alleged mass tastes. Not so the German radio.

The individual German listener, although he pays for the entertainment himself, cannot influence programming, simply because his is only one of millions of scattered votes. It is exactly the situation of a very small stockowner in a huge corporation. A man who owns several per cent of General Motors stock can, if he smartly manages his chips, achieve considerable power in the company, even though he represents, say, only 5 per cent of the total stock: 5 per cent is a substantial fraction. But any one of the thousands who own a tiny particle of 1 per cent of General Motors stock is, for all practical purposes, disfranchised when it comes to determining company policy. This is the situation of the German radio listener. In Germany (as in all of Europe) the cultural level of the radio remains, for this very reason, considerably above what it would be if the management of the broadcasting stations had to respond directly to the appetites of its audiences.

To be sure, what the German radio gains culturally it loses politically. Because the public authorities in command of radio programming are political appointees, they will finesse and even suppress news and controversial subjects to please their masters—the governments in power. Neither in Europe nor in the United States is the radio listener the boss. Boss in the United States is the advertiser and in Europe the ruling party. In the United States, radio can take remarkable freedoms when it comes to public issues, but it will have to lower its cultural targets to please the sponsor who wants the largest possible audiences. In Europe, radio can retain a comparatively admirable cultural level, because it can shrug off mass approval; but the European radio will have to weasel on public issues whenever the ruling politicians raise their eyebrows.

In short, a broadcasting system that depends on public support can discard public demand; while a broadcasting system that lives from the sale of its programs to private advertisers must seek to please the largest audiences. Consequently, the mass-conscious privately owned radio cannot compete culturally with tax-subsidized, "aristocratic" broadcasting systems. Those who still believe that "the voice of the people is the voice of the Lord" may ponder this paradox. The realist is by no means surprised.

In Germany, at any rate, the radio is every day a source of pleasure for the discriminating taste (and an irritatingly inadequate source of news). But it is inadvisable to draw from this fact too far-reaching conclusions concerning the quality of popular German preferences. If one insists on comparing mass tastes in Germany and the United States, there are more dependable media. In both countries, for instance, records have become very big business; and because the consumer, when he buys a record for a considerable sum of money, surely discloses his cultural preferences, a comparison of German and American record sales would produce far more reliable results than a confrontation of radio programs which are, for all practical purposes, gratuitously received.

The German record business has grown in one year—from 1956 to 1957—by 40 per cent. Just so, German records are still much more expensive than American records; and this in spite of the fact that production costs are considerably lower in Germany. Now more than 60 per cent of all records sold in the United States in 1957 were those of "classical" music, and only 40 per cent were "pop" and jazz records. But 80 per cent of all records sold in Germany in 1957 were "pop" and jazz, only 20 per cent "classical" music—and this in the country which for generations has, somewhat arrogantly, identified "good music" with "German music."

Another acceptable check on the cultural habits of the German public may be a study of its behavior in the book market. There, too, "money talks": every purchase, because it involves a financial sacrifice, assumes a valid meaning. According to a diligently researched report of the Publishers' and Book-Sellers' Association of the Land Hesse, a whole third of Germany's adult population has never bought a book; and another third has bought books only as gifts for others, never for personal use. So that two thirds of Germany's adult population have never formed the habit of buying books. Even more. The emphasis of the statistical statement is on "never." Consequently, it does by no means follow that the remaining third buys books regularly; there are, among that last third, many millions of adult Germans who may have bought a couple of books in their lifetimes but hardly ever return to the bookstore. On the whole, this thoroughly literate Germany remains in a sadly median bracket of European book-sales statistics.

The ubiquitous reading matter in Germany is not the newspapers but the cheap picture magazines—*die Illustrierten*. There are dozens of them, published in every region of the country and by all kinds of publishers; but they are entirely indistinguishable in editorial policy, cultural ambition, and even make-up. Indiscriminately bought and inhaled, they are Germany's true horror and unforgivable shame. Not a single one of them begins to compare with *Life* in the United States or *Match* in Paris.

Technically unimpressive, they are editorially an infernal exercise in seeking the lowest common denominator of an audience —a level that no foe of Teutonism would ever have expected to exist in literate Germany. Garishly displayed on all newsstands of the country, these picture magazines seem to infect the whole nation with an idiotically distorted fifth-hand view of "reality"—a concoction of cheapest movie sentimentalism, whodunit sensationalism, adolescent eroticism, a pandering to all kinds of plain superstition, and, above all, a special type of *Illustrierten* fiction. These "novels," after appearing *seriatim* in the picture magazines, then fill the bookstalls of the nation in a second wave of invasion, attain a third life as most popular movies and, indubitably, are becoming the true national literature. It is as if the country were receding behind that haze—a nation doped by the most contemptible printed matter I have seen anywhere in the world.

And just as the German movie industry is gradually becoming an annex to the *Illustrierten,* just so one must fear for Germany's television. The danger is not yet acute because Germany is strangely behind in television developments. By August 1958 there were slightly more than 2 million television sets sold in all of Germany—which means that only one in six German families owns a TV set. (Every other family owns one in England, and even in France, where modern electronic appliances are still sheer luxury, television is far ahead of Germany.) The main reason is an inexplicably high price of German standard sets: to purchase one, a working man would have to spend about two months' wages.

But the final triumph of television as mass entertainment is, of course, just as unavoidable in Germany as anywhere else; and when it comes, I am afraid, it will be the final triumph of the *Illustrierten* mentality. These picture magazines have so disformed the German eye, so profoundly hurt all German sensitivity, that a visual medium such as television will have to carry this terrible mortgage. The prospects of the television era are dismal in the whole world; they are frightening in the Germany of the *Illustrierten.*

The German intellectuals, understandably enough, ignore television altogether. (Just as in America in the early fifties, it was in 1958 a matter of intellectual status in Germany not to own a television set.) All the rage of intellectuals in Germany is the Literary Cabaret that lives, or ought to live, on originality, wit, aggressiveness, and taste. I have never missed a Literary Cabaret when I visited a German city that possesses one. The German Literary Cabarets are not always an unadulterated joy; but they are always a reliable measure of the city's intellectual climate.

A German Literary Cabaret consists of a few young actors and actresses in a smoke-filled cellar, a pianist-composer, and one or several writers whose heavy burden it is to be original, witty, aggressive, and tasteful for two hours every other month or so. Such a Literary Cabaret, that is, plays to about two hundred persons an evening (some Cabarets can accommodate only a few dozen customers) and, thus, has reached its total potential clientele in a month or two. So that, to stay in business, it must, on the average, produce a new program four or six times a year.

The burden is altogether on the writers. For although the charm of young performers helps, the "material" is the thing—not the play, to be sure, because there *is* no play. No one goes to Literary Cabarets for the sake of dramatic experience. From a Literary Cabaret one expects abrasive smartness, political sophistication, topical hilarity, a cascade of allusions to the woes and fallacies of the day's communal life. In that sense, a Literary Cabaret is nothing but a dramatized Master of Ceremonies: it is a M. of C.'s continuous pelting of the topical events that counts—not the effectiveness of the actors. And one hardly ever hears from an *aficionado* of the Literary Cabaret the praise of a performance—the accent is always on the articulate crack.

A typical program of a German Literary Cabaret consists of about twenty single numbers—all of them basically "blackouts": somewhat crudely dramatized jokes with a burning sting at the end. Some are sung, some recited, some played out. The music is hardly ever tuneful and memorable. Its function is to regulate pace, rhythm, syncopation. The word is absolute king. And, with rare exceptions, it is not the writer's artfulness that matters. It is always the position taken, the jolt of criticism, the bite of aggressive, exposing, deflating thought. A Literary Cabaret, in short, is journalism —journalism that has an affair with the muses, but still journalism.

I have spent moments of enchantment in some German Literary Cabarets, but, on the whole, I have been depressed by a heavy-footed sameness. And for this, after many an evening in small German cabaret cellars, I do not blame the always excited and sometimes exciting young people who work there with attractive informality and a moving devotion. I do not even particularly blame the writers. Writers for Literary Cabarets are merely newspapermen with a knack for a tag line. They do not shape—they only *express* the intellectual climate of their audience. The oppressive lack of originality, wit, aggressiveness, and taste signifies, it seems to me, the state of the German intellectuals.

Throughout the winter of 1957–58 the German Literary Cabarets—*all* of them—had actually the same program. There were two or three blackouts on the revived German Army (usually some

songs or sketches that built up to the entirely predictable denoue-
ment that sinister forces of the past have taken hold of the tender
growth). Then there were, inescapably, some blackouts on the
Soviet Sputnik waiting somewhere in the outer space for its American colleague who (a) did not arrive at all or (b) was just as evil
as the Soviet brand. Then followed, invariably, some blackouts on
the unpleasantness of war, the blessing of peace, the atomic perils,
the need for mutual understanding and for summit conferences,
the need for coexistence, good will, and sunshine. Then (though
this was optional) came a few blackouts on the old, stubborn, and
—one would leave with that impression—just contrary Dr. Adenauer, who was simply too old to care, really, about the future of
mankind (the tacit assumption being that old men have some kind
of *Schadenfreude* about the tough luck of those who were able to
survive them). Then, unfailingly, followed some blackouts on the
cheapness of movie stars, the idiocy of parliamentary bodies, the
corruption of government in general. Then a few kisses blown into
the audience, and one was released until the next time.

Germany's Literary Cabarets are, in other words, the authentic
extension of the "high-class" German newspaper into the theater.
What they do with clownery and exaggeration these newspapers
do with the solid monotony of respectable German journalism.
Some of these newspapers, I hasten to add, are doing an admirable
professional job. The *Frankfurter Allgemeine Zeitung,* for example,
is in some personal, legal, and professional aspects the legitimate
successor to the late *Frankfurter Zeitung* (which, before Hitler,
was one of the glories of European journalism); page by page, and
day after day, one finds in the *Frankfurter Allgemeine Zeitung* a
competent coverage of world events, a sense of quality, a respect
for language, an erudition that is rare in contemporary journalism.
With a considerably smaller circulation, of course, and incomparably smaller treasures at its disposal, this paper reaches and in some
respects outdoes the level of the New York *Times.* Its literary department (*Feuilleton*) is mature, its economic supplement of almost scholarly perfection.

And yet, the paper's political philosophy, its *Weltanschauung,* is distressingly shallow. There is, in fact, none. But a German paper without a *Weltanschauung* is simply inconceivable; and so the *Frankfurter Allgemeine,* which happens to have none, assumes the protective coloring of the political philosophy that prevails among the German intellectuals: a somewhat coquettishly "skeptical" pragmatism, a somewhat cynical "neutralism," a somewhat nihilistic "leftism" that suspects government just because it is government and America just because it is America.

In this the *Frankfurter Allgemeine* is arch-typical for all leading German newspapers—the *Welt* of Hamburg, the *Süddeutsche Zeitung* of Munich, the *Tagesspiegel* of West Berlin. All three, again, are excellent professional jobs. And yet, they are drenched with the kind of tired sophistication intelligent youngsters assume at the peak of adolescence: everything is a racket, you know; munition makers are merchants of death; why doesn't everybody get together?; political parties are corrupt; peace is better than war; health is better than sickness; why can't everybody be nice? That kind of thing. One feels sorry for the erudite writers of those rather incredible editorials in the leading German newspapers. It is not only that they *should* know better—they *do* know better. But there is the trend. And it is not only the trend. It is also a heritage—and unfortunately an American heritage.

During the years of military occupation no German could publish or work for a newspaper without a United States Army license (or a British or French or Soviet Army license in regions occupied by America's Allies). The required screening system—weird in any case: a victorious army of occupation selecting the spokesmen for the vanquished!—could not have worked well under the best conceivable circumstances. While an army of occupation may be qualified to say who must *not* publish a newspaper, it is by definition disqualified to *select* the proper and authentic editors and publishers. But the circumstances that prevailed in the United States Army of Occupation from 1945 to 1949 were by no means the best conceivable; in fact, the political naïveté of the occupation authorities is responsible for most predicaments that confront the United States today in Germany.

And the worst of it all was the United States Army's cavalier approach to the innumerable fellow travelers who—officially in junior positions, actually doing all the important work—had permeated the Military Government. Many of them had once been Germans and, serving in the Army of Occupation with understandable zeal, seemed indispensable as true experts and incomparably devoted workers. Actually, with some exceptions, these former refugees were still partisans in German affairs. They may have been useful in technical functions—they were clearly in the wrong place wherever the United States Army had to *determine* German policy. And nowhere, it seems, had the dangerous influence of political refugee-partisans in German affairs more effect than in the synthetic fabrication of a German public opinion.

The Allied military control over German public opinion began with the "Law No. 191" of November 24, 1944, by which the military authorities of occupation restricted all means of communication within the occupied German territory to individuals specifically licensed by the several military governments. The orders were then amplified by legislation announced in May 1945—by which time the core of German licensed newspapers already existed. In 1946–47 a batch of new licenses was issued to would-be German publishers who looked appetizing to the curiously leftish young officers in actual command of the licensing United States authorities.

Ten years after the event a study of these doings remains a weird experience. From what I have learned in 1957 and 1958 in Germany, none of the formally responsible high United States officers could have been a communist sympathizer himself. But the people who did the office work for them, the corporals and sergeants and first lieutenants, they were usually the dedicated "ideologues" who had embarked upon a personal crusade against the defeated Germany—hardly ever provable members of the Communist party, but only too often the type the Communist party can easily manage by remote control.

Those who remember the strange days of America's alliance with Stalin, and also remember the intellectual terror a paper such as New York's *P.M.* wielded over Washington's bureaucracy, will recall the atmosphere of the American forties: when the fellow travelers had penetrated the Office of War Information, the State Department, the working staff of the United States Army of Occupation; when premature anti-Communists were treated like pathetic lepers; when Earl Browder introduced people to the White House, and the Office of Strategic Services was anxious to hire known Communists. One has to recall those days, their obtuseness and spooky confidence in Stalin's inherent virtues, the days of Ambassador Davies and his *Mission to Moscow,* to comprehend what was then being done in Germany.

In most areas of United States military intervention the German wounds have healed by now. The spontaneous workings of prosperity have corrected economic blunders. But the wounds are still open in the area of German public opinion. The German newspapers that had been created and staffed by the Allied Armies of Occupation in the late forties have remained just about the only articulate mechanism of German public opinion. By 1958 the German press was learned, impressive, well mannered; but it was synthetic. It was not a reflection of the German people's positions, preferences, attitudes, and, yes, prejudices. It has remained a creature of the forties.

On April 24, 1947, the Bavarian Diet took unanimous action against the licensed press that, at that time, was going wild. The Social Democratic speaker pictured Bavaria as "a jungle where no one is safe from being shot at by his political opponents." The speaker of the Free Democrats suggested that all "licenses" be investigated by a special committee of the Diet, to establish which party they really owe their allegiance to—the transparent implication being that one would not be surprised to find some "licensees" under communist discipline.

The same day the Diet of the Land Hessen also discussed the licensed press, and the speaker of the Christian Democratic Union accused the licensed press of "a one-sided political attitude." What attitude he had in mind became quite clear when, to defend the licensed press, the leader of the Communist faction, Emil Carlebach, rose to expound that "the nervousness of the governmental parties simply betrayed their bad conscience" and that they evidently wished "to destroy freedom of public debate." As it happened, Carlebach himself owned the license to publish the *Frankfurter Rundschau,* at that time the most important newspaper in Hessen.

On December 16, 1948, an official spokesman for the United States Military Government delivered a speech over all German radio stations in which he announced the Allied willingness to abolish the military control forced upon the German press. He declared specifically that "the Military Government is willing to renounce its right of licensing German newspapers" under certain conditions.

"In 1945," recalled the United States spokesman, "when the occupation started, the United States Military Government considered it one of its most important tasks to guarantee the German population an independent and free press. Paradoxically" (and it was very much to the speaker's credit that he noticed the joke right away) "paradoxically, however, it was the Military Government itself which at that time thought it necessary to introduce a certain temporary control. . . . Certainty had to be created that the available limited possibilities (of printing) were utilized in the best possible manner to secure Germany's transition to a democratic society. . . . This is why the Military Government created a system of licensing to put the newspapers in the hands of editors who would seriously undertake the task to supply the German people with news without prejudice and factually."

And then the United States Army spokesman presented the most astonishing stipulations under which the Military Government was "willing to abolish the system of licensing." In the first place, he announced, the existing licensed newspapers ("the independent newspapers," he called them euphemistically) must remain for at least eight years in possession of the printing plants they were then using as guests of the United States Military Government "at costs within reasonable limits."

As everybody understood right away—and as it, of course, turned out—this meant that the licensed newspapers would retain their monopoly-like position in German publishing. Once the United States Military Government granted them "reasonable" (which meant ludicrously low) printing costs for eight more years, i.e., until 1956, no newly established newspaper could hope to break their licensed colleagues' control over Germany's public opinion. For the subsequent eight years, their privileged competitors, in addition to their immense handicap as going concerns, were to enjoy contractual advantages no newcomer could begin to match. In that fashion the United States Military Government had not only given skillful leftist operators unique propaganda positions of unfathomable depth effectiveness, it had also created several enormous fortunes.

With a few exceptions, today's German publishers and newspaper owners are, not exactly self-made millionaires—for they all remain the creatures of strangely influential small fry in the United States Military Government—but decidedly first-generation tycoons. I know of a mighty German newspaper publisher who is today a millionaire and a public figure of conspicuous proportions just because, back in 1946, as a young man seeking some kind of military permit, he happened to stumble into the wrong room; and before he knew what magic wand was touching him, a bored United States officer, who had not yet filled his quota of newspaper licenses to be issued, threw one at him. In a few years—not to speak of political power—the slip of paper was worth a fortune.

To return to the embarrassed radio speech of December 16, 1948, the United States officer in charge of rationalization went on to discuss the kind of press legislation his Military Government demanded from the German *Länder*—there was at that time no Federal German Republic—as precondition for the lifting of the military control of publishing. Ironically, he emphasized that such legislation must make absolutely sure that "no *new* monopolies develop"—new, that is, on top of the monopolies the United States Military Government had granted, for years to come, to its journalistic wards. And the speaker made clear throughout his officious essay that the required legislation must be foolproof against any attempt of the legitimate German governments to counteract the press monopoly of the opposition.

Even so, the speaker found it necessary to reassure his licensed wards that "extreme reactionary elements will not be in a position (after the licensing system had been lifted) to publish newspapers." And, indeed, they never were since 1948. Now I am no more anxious to read an "extreme reactionary" German newspaper than the next man; nor am I sure that, under the mollifying conditions of the German prosperity, the traditionally vulgar German type of rabble-rousing would have paid off financially. But the point is that, beyond any doubt, what the spokesman of the United States Army understood in 1948 by an "extreme reactionary" German newspaper was dangerously close to what fellow travelers love to call "reactionary"—any kind of a genuinely conservative or uncorruptibly anti-communist attitude.

And it is equally doubtless that the United States Military Government, in a few years of a skillfully abused licensing system, has suffocated the freedom of the German press for decades: after ten years in unchallenged power, Dr. Adenauer in 1958 had still no important German newspaper to support his policies. This, I must add, is not entirely an American fault. The Adenauer government, though it shrewdly knows how to govern the German people with bland patriarchal benevolence, has incomprehensibly failed in its press policies. His immense social powers, not to speak of his governmental funds, should have made it possible for Dr. Adenauer to create, in ten years, a competitive German press that *agrees* with his policies. But the chancellor's party and his executive machinery have shown a curious lack of talent, even of interest, in molding public opinion. They stubbornly rely on Dr. Adenauer's personal gift to rally the voters at his will; what German conservatism will do once Adenauer is gone must not be mentioned in conservative German company. They all tremble when they think of it. And yet nothing is being done.

Five months after the United States Military Government had announced over the radio the end of its licensing orders, in May 1949, the chief of its Information Department, Colonel Textor, insisted that the publication of newspapers and magazines (also of books, movies, and records) was still under strict United States Army licensing regulations. That system was finally abolished not before the fall of 1949—almost a year after the solemn radio announcement of 1948. The British Military Government—obviously under the influence of the then reigning Labor party that is so famously dedicated to democratic freedoms—held out for a few more months, into 1950.

The Allies gave that licensed press not only legal aid. According to an official admission in July 1951, the United States Information Service had spent in 1950 (after the licensing system had been abolished) several million dollars in *direct subsidies* to the formerly licensed German press. A single newspaper, *Die Neue Zeitung,* had received $3 million in 1950. However, the formerly licensed press did not simply live on American alms. It was from the very beginning, in 1945, ably managed by trained propagandists and gifted businessmen.

To this day that formerly licensed press sets the tone of articulate German public opinion, mainly because it remains the best-edited press of the country. The winners in the great sweepstake of the forties, the original "licensees," proved, with few exceptions, to be clever men of great staying power. Papers such as the *Süddeutsche Zeitung* and *Die Welt* can compete with Europe's ablest newspapers in terms of news coverage, in pleasing make-up, and the facile tone of writing. What remains from the days of licensing is the editorial bias. As skeptical advisers could have told the United States Military Government in the forties—but who would have listened, in those days, to skeptical advisers?—the type of "anti-Fascists" who were then patronized by the license officers turned out, of necessity, to be the advocates of "coexistence" with the Soviets in the fifties and, in a pinch, congenital foes of American policies. This is partly due to the intellectual structure of ideologues who, in the forties, passed by the name of "anti-Fascists"; and partly it is the reaction to the rather questionable past of some of the Germans who, in the forties, won the confidence of the United States Army.

Hardly a month goes by nowadays without a prince of the Ger-

man press fighting desperately in the courts against accusations—
some of them well documented—that he was under Hitler just as
skillful a promoter of nazism. The licensed publisher of an important German newspaper, "neutralist" and more than slightly
leftish, is being accused of having worked in Martin Bormann's
office on sinister Nazi doings. And there is no better way to live
down such unpleasant memories than to assume, thirteen years
later, the posture of a friend of "disengagement" with the Soviet
Union, of a "progressive" Maecenas of everything that is "modern"
and "angry" in contemporary art.

The formerly licensed press, in short, has used its monopoly
privileges of 1945–50 to the hilt. It has secured its hold on the
German public with acumen and a shrewd business sense and,
remaining a faithful replica of the "anti-Fascist" image in which
it was built by the Military Government, it is today the most serious
obstacle to a German rally against communism.

In the spring of 1952, three years after the West Germans had
formally received the Allied permission to govern their own affairs,
the formerly licensed press was still in complete command of German public opinion. These publications, 159 in the *Bundesrepublik*,
had in 1952 a combined circulation of 8 million. And their power
could not be simply measured by the fact that they were regularly
reaching just about the total reading German population. Their
real strength was based on the unparalleled position of exclusive-
ness: no one but the formerly licensed publishers and editors
could speak, in print, to and for the Germans. Here, enforced by
the Allied Military governments, was a cockeyed press monopoly
granted the *opposition* against the legitimate government. And to
this day, I repeat, there is no German press to support Adenauer's
policies wholeheartedly—if one discards, as one must, parochial
papers.

So far, seemingly, this thoroughly abnormal situation has not yet
damaged the *Bundesrepublik:* no matter what the "respectable"
German press said, the voters kept on voting for Adenauer. But I
am afraid that Adenauer's extraordinary figure obstructs the view.
As long as he is alive, and no unforeseen predicaments arise, the

voters will keep voting for him, if only out of habit. No intelligent Christian Democratic politician doubts, however, that this is a private affair between Adenauer and the German electorate—by no means a deliberate choice of recognizable policies. Once Adenauer is gone, the German reality will emerge from behind the present mirage.

And it seems to me that this reality will be far more determined by the German press than many Germans care to admit today. Without the great patriarch, this people is without a leader again; which, to Germans, is a frightening spot to be in. And in such a situation articulate public opinion—the complex process of elite opinions penetrating the entire national body—will prove decisive. But the opinions of the German elite—those five or seven hundred thousand people who *are* the national mind—are being shaped by Germany's five or six leading newspapers. And these newspapers are what they are. The next two German chancellors, I am afraid, will be elected by the peculiar anonymous young men who, in the forties, diligently worked in the United States Military Government to "neutralize" Germany for the forthcoming conflict between East and West.

CHAPTER FIVE

The Young Zombies

THERE is also in Germany a generation of depraved-looking juveniles. They are called *die Halbstarken* ("the half-strong ones") and it is a rather apt phrase.

For even more than in the United States these displaced young persons are more pathetic than frightening. There is something very sickish about them, a paleness that spoils the good looks of youth, a clumsy insecurity that shows through all their bragging. The general tenor of the social workers and the publicists who discuss the phenomenon is not to take the infection too seriously; and it is indeed difficult to fear for Germany's future just because of these anemic youngsters with unbelievably long hair (if they are boys) and unbelievably short hair (if they are girls). Basically they are comical; and yet, the solemn sobriety of their pranks is disturbing, precisely because they seem to have no fun at all—which is the most conspicuous difference between today's *Halbstarken* and the "crazy mixed-up kids" of previous generations.

I vividly remember what hilarious fun it was, in the stormy twenties, to scandalize adult society. We did it with a genuine exuberance, with the kind of animal pleasure that must have been not only disarming but reassuring to sensible adults who may have occasionally worried about our capers. It is not quite that today. *Die Halbstarken* walk through the prosperous landscape of Germany with a diluted life sense, an unspirited and noticeably empty melancholia. And they *do* look like zombies. One is almost relieved when, occasionally, one of the *Halbstarken* commits a passionate act of violence, simply because one has begun to doubt whether there was any vitality left in them.

How the *Halbstarken* carry themselves in Germany has been ably described by the *Frankfurter Allgemeine* in a curious period piece published on April 2, 1958. It was a report on "the only appearance in Germany" of Mr. Johnnie Ray, America's fast-balding Elvis Presley of yesteryear. It took place in West Berlin's *Sportpalast,* seven thousand paying youngsters attending. After describing, with uncanny precision, the shaking gyrations of Mr. Ray, the reporter goes on telling of his audience:

> Once Johnnie had gone, it got hotter and hotter. The *Halbstarken* surged forwards, towards the stage; something had to happen. There was a streaming and screaming from the balconies towards the center, ushers were trying to keep the stage free, but the riot became louder. Girls in tight pants quaked and leaped on the benches, soon there flew the first bottles, the first chairs followed, and then there was a general crash throughout the hall. Now the furniture was being smashed to pieces, the air was thick with flying chairs, whole rows of seats fell apart, girls squeaked. Next to me three serious and collected youngsters smashed their bench. The ushers' efforts to restore order were submerged in the riotous noise, and finally there appeared, greeted with hisses, the police. Swinging their nightsticks rather symbolically, they slowly pushed the leather jackets and tight pants to the exits. The teenagers felt cheated. Mumbling groups gathered around the *Sportpalast.* Soon the many motorcycles took off. The other youngsters parted hesitatingly and with a vague feeling that, in separating from the mass, they were losing much of their magic, their threatening power.

I have quoted this perceptive report chiefly because of one sentence: "Next to me three serious and collected youngsters smashed their bench." Here, in a flash, are exactly the German *Halbstarken* as I remember them—serious and collected and inscrutably dumb.

Die Halbstarken, to be sure, comprise in Germany, as everywhere else, but a small part of their generation. But even numerically it is an important part—and of momentous importance symbolically. For among the majority of German youngsters, who have no run-ins with the police, or even with Mr. Ray, there are disturbingly many who feel much more represented by the leather jackets and the tight pants than they care to admit. The "bold ones" are not exceptional. They are, it seems to me, the uninhibited *typical* members of their generation.

Yet, as I said, the extreme cases are even numerically important. Amazingly enough, there are no relevant statistics available in Germany. Yet a few facts were collected in Vienna which, of course, is not a German city; but Vienna, if anything, has retained a softer melody of living than the big towns of West Germany, and it is, on the other hand, under just about the same cultural pressures and influences, so that facts established in Vienna seem to be quite telling in the context of West Germany, too, even if they might be prettifying the picture a bit.

In the informed estimate of the Viennese police, at least 10,000 youngsters belonged in 1957 to *Platten* (Vienna's organized gangs) and conducted themselves under *Platten* mores and discipline. Now Vienna is still a city of less than 2 million people, of whom no more than 180,000 can be in the age group from fourteen to eighteen. Of them, about 90,000 are boys. And every ninth of these boys belonged to *Platten!* (To match this dismal record New York would have to register about 55,000 boys as members of organized street gangs.) And here are the social results as they show in Vienna's crime statistics: In 1957, about 43 per cent of all burglaries were committed by teenagers; of people sentenced for sex crimes, 25 per cent were younger than eighteen; more than 20 per cent of all people sentenced for some crime or felony were teenagers.

To scrutinize what may be happening to this amazing young generation is as popular a parlor game in Germany as it is elsewhere—and just about as sterile. For no one knows. Even so, the more intelligent players at that game agree in Germany that the socioeconomic explanation of the phenomenon—poverty of the parents, slum conditions—must be discarded. In Germany this young generation started its bizarre conduct while *all* of Germany was going through the greatest economic uplift in its history—during the last ten years. Nor could the German teenagers of 1958 be excused, or even explained, with wartime and the immediately following experiences: those who were between fourteen and eighteen in 1958 were between two and six when Germany was immersed in stupor. And while it remains true that the impressions of early childhood are formative, it is exactly the orthodox psychoanalysts (mainly Dr. Anna Freud) who point out that major physical and social catastrophes, such as bombings and destitution in homelessness, are far less staggering to small children than adults assume— far less, at any rate, than seemingly minor tremors of social relations, such as fights among parents or a child's separation from its mother.

The Psychological Institute of the University of Hamburg, under Professor Curt Bondy, undertook an "investigation in depth" of 794 *Halbstarken* who had been arrested in nine German cities for rioting. This is perhaps the most serious study on juvenile delinquency to come out of Germany. Of its conclusions none seems to be more unequivocal than the defeat of "determinism," economic or otherwise. The investigated *Halbstarken* were by no means primarily children of lower-class families or broken-up homes; every element of German society, the whole scale up and down, was represented. Nor are the *Halbstarken* financially starved: on the average, the investigated *Halbstarken* earn or administer DM 235 a month—more than one half of the adult German's average income!

The Psychological Institute of the University of Hamburg, dismissing "determinism," submits an interesting theory of its own. As neither the much-cited "breakup of families" nor economic hardships seem to be the major factors in the delinquency "syndrome" of young people, the Institute suggested that we pay attention to the psychological tensions *within* the young people. And it arrives, for itself, at the conclusion that we do not have to wait for those ghastly "mutations" our nuclear scientists (and their dupes) predict from continued atomic tests. Serious "mutations" are *already* with us—owing not to radiation but to the *general* technological progress of which our scientists are so proud.

In particular, the changes in our style of living—comforts, nutrition, sports, mass entertainments—have pushed the young people of today *physically* by two years ahead of what, for centuries, has been assumed par. That is, pre-puberty of yesterday is puberty of today, yesterday's adolescence is today's maturity—but physically only. And because society, for hardly changeable reasons, must insist that children do not live like adults, those children boil over in weird protest. Or, rather, not even protest (for, characteristically, this new generation makes no conscious complaints against its social environment); it is numb dissatisfaction.

There is today, or so claims the Hamburg Institute, in this time of much faster living, a much wider and deeper no-man's land between childhood and adulthood than there ever was before. The child is no longer a child, physically, two or three years sooner than a generation ago—and yet, still not an adult before its early twenties. There are now about eight or ten years of awkward isolation outside the two "secure" states, childhood and adulthood. And during that apparently unbearable isolation the starved teenager needs self-assertion by the gang of his contemporaries, by a peculiar uniform (haircuts, leather jackets, tight pants), and, above all, by noisy association with masses of comrades in fate ("rumbles," general riots, rock 'n roll). Because he is so hopelessly isolated as an individual, he needs his type of mass. The mass audience of Mr. Ray's, or the mass of an utterly senseless riot, is the medium that enables the isolated young person to erupt in ecstasy. Kept out of the mass, he is listless—almost dead.

So there they grow up, whatever the reasons, those German youngsters, in a long-lasting period of material wealth, hardly scratched by the experiences of 1944-46; and yet seriously endangered. No discernible reason why it should be a lost generation —nor is there any certainty that it is. Many sound Germans (not at all the habitually "optimistic" type) reassure themselves that this young generation is no worse than their own and the one before; that all young people have silly difficulties in growing up, and take them out on their adult environment by getting ornery; that the Charleston was by no means more respectable in the twenties than the rock 'n roll is in the fifties; that the young girls with their hair cut half short were just as objectionable in the twenties as the young girls with disheveled "Italian" hair cuts are today; that the boys thirty years ago were no less criminally excitable than they are in 1959. Of course some of this one has heard before in the United States from experts who feel honor-bound to stick to the ancient cliché that there is no bad boy. Here are some characteristic statements by German professionals who are concerned with youth:

A journalist: "Our young men, more handsome and grown taller than their fathers, are quite normal, healthy, very self-satisfied. Every one of them is a walking 'policy of strength.' They have always, on principle, the right of way. Our young girls are demonstrative of their femininity, perhaps a bit too early and a bit too expert-like. These girls are twice as independent as those of an earlier generation, and certainly three times less naïve."

A high-school teacher: "When I wanted to discuss Eichendorff's poems, to celebrate the one hundredth anniversary of his death, the faces of my students grew bored. With their typical honesty they told me: 'Eichendorff's moon is not our moon. At night, we don't hear the horn of the mail carriage but, if we are lucky, the piep-piep of Sputnik.' Their dreams they get from the screen. Even during classes film magazines, film photos, and movie programs make their rounds surreptitiously. The stories of marriages, lives, and loves of the movie stars they know most precisely, but they know nothing of the saints whose life stories excited me when I was young."

An industrialist: "I've met apprentices who even before they started working wanted to know all about their old-age pension."

A stage director: "The young people don't seek spiritual adventure any more. They got lazy in the soft bed of our civilization. Words such as 'wonder,' 'fear,' 'despair' are unknown to them. They've proclaimed materialism in the East; but one lives it in the West, too."

A minister: "They are bored. When we were young, we were offered aims that required enthusiasm or passionate rejection—fatherland, humanism, class war. But in the young of today I don't see much excitement and no trace of revolution. Some say they merely are factual. That would be nice—if factuality did not turn into boredom."

A member of the Bundestag: "In 400 films shown in 1957 in the Bundesrepublik we could chalk up 310 murders, 104 robberies, 405 adulteries, 624 larcenies, 54 extortions, and 34 cases of arson."

A social worker: "Children entering school at six were, in 1955, almost two inches taller than the beginners of 1925. At the end of puberty they are today almost four inches taller than youngsters used to be forty years ago. Constitutionally, that type of fast-growing youngsters normally are supersensitive. Yet an aptitude investigation which they undertook from 1932 to 1937 in Lower Saxony had this very strange result: Grading 300,000 youngsters in 1932 they found 17.8 per cent to be above average, but in 1937 only 7.3 per cent."

Another social worker: "War, postwar times, prison camps, and starvation have created a *hubris* of making-up-for-it-all, a material craving that has swept the parents off their feet. All family life is infected by this greed. In that feverish atmosphere there are hardly those quiet regions left which a child needs if it is to grow up quietly. The young people accept the distorted measures. To them, to live means to own."

And so it goes. A German symposium on "youth today" produces just about the kind of observations, complaints, and self-delusions as those you would hear at a similar occasion in America. Is there here perhaps a key? Is it not possible that the common reason of the strange spiritual mutation that is taking hold of the world is the modern style of living which has triumphed in America sooner than anywhere else?

"Modernity" appears to have grown from a scientism that prefers "facts" to concepts, possessions to dreams, sobriety to "romanticism," power to love. That style, though it first was proposed in America, was checked in the birthland of pragmatism, for a long time, by countervailing forces indigenous to this country—a special concept of Puritan virtues, a stubborn rigidity of mores which were so powerful precisely because they were socially imposed rather than by law, a congenitally American sense of generosity. But all these moral fortifications did not help America; the modern style corroded them. And where they never existed, the breakdown came even faster. It might have taken longer for the *initial* infection to penetrate European societies whose conventional style was much more alien to scientism and "modernity" than is Puritanism; but once they *were* infected, these old societies were even worse shaken than America. Once even *Germans* get to be "factual" and sober— in a word: pragmatists—only God can help their youth. They can no more.

Germany's sober, "serious," and "collected" *Halbstarken* are, of course, first cousins of England's "angry young men." And Hemingway and Faulkner are, no doubt, the fathers of all the "angry young men" of Europe. But are not Hemingway and Faulkner themselves the children of the skeptical tiredness of a Europe that began at the *fin de siècle* a flirtation with death? William Faulkner, who somewhat coquettishly professes literary illiteracy, and Ernest Hemingway, who knows only too well what he does and why, have probably never read Nietzsche; and Baudelaire would simply embarrass those totally American Americans. Indeed, Faulkner's mighty life opus and Hemingway's somewhat monotonous loyalty to the only melody that has ever gone through his mind—the song of poised courage in the face of absurd pain—are as proverbially American as apple pie. And yet, it seems to me that the literary and cultural stream that is allegedly flooding Europe's greedy soil actually sprang in the Old World. The more closely I studied the malformations of European youth, and the more frequently I heard that it was all a response to American stimulation—jazz and flapper and "private eye" and violence and the Wild West and Truman Capote—the more was I impressed by the European traces of American "modernity."

The sensitive witness to America's last few decades can testify that this apparent center of modernism hobbles behind Europe's modish fads by about twenty years. I mean this literally. During the last sixty or seventy years there has hardly been a whim, a foolishness, a perverted stroke of genius in Europe that has not been revived—twenty years later, when Europe hardly recalled the spasm—in America where it then soon unfolded in subtropical fertility. It is as if, in spite of turbo-jet planes, ideas have to crawl the bottom of the Atlantic to get from Europe to America; so that, when they finally emerge in New York, the European witnesses of their first incarnation are long dead or, anyway, muted.

Psychoanalysis became fashionable in America at a time Europeans had become tired of even poking fun at it. Marxism took the salons along the eastern seaboard of America by frontal attack at a time when the intelligent young people of Europe only yawned at any mentioning of "surplus value" and the "expropriation of the expropriators." Franz Kafka boiled over in America exactly twenty years after the critics of Vienna and Prague had written him off as a neurotic young man of some strange traces of genius; and since 1946 one cannot thumb through an American literary magazine without encountering a veritably rhapsodical fascination with Kafka—a fascination that would have been decidedly bad form in Central European coffeehouses twenty years ago. I do not know of a single *idée fixe* that befell Europe—from Alfred Adler to Carl Jung, from the Blonde Beast to the Black Mass—which did not go, after it died in Europe, through a supercharged reincarnation in America; and always about twenty years later.

In particular, the cultural influence of America's literature on Europe—this embittered and desperately realistic tone of quiet despair—is for me (an American who was born and raised in Habsburgian Austria) a curiously violent offspring of the tiredness of a Hofmannsthal and even a Rilke. One would have to add to this a pinch of Dostoevskian spice, a touch of Strindberg, and a great deal of Nietzschean essences. But over and over again, though distorted to near-bestialism, Hofmannsthal and Schnitzler and Rilke—all the sweet pain of a time that enjoyed its own expiration. *Fin de siècle.*

Neither Hemingway nor Faulkner could feel concerned, and they would not even understand what I am talking about. Not only that they hardly know the names I have mentioned—the world I was referring to is more alien to them than the Congo. And yet, they come from that world—they and, most assuredly, their literary disciples whom, thinking of the *Halbstarken,* I would like to call "the half-angry." For what in the cases of Hemingway and Faulkner (whose genius is genuine) was the unconscious derivation from an anonymous *Zeitgeist* is in the cases of Tennessee Williams, Arthur Miller, or Truman Capote a hardly successful camouflage. They affect Europe—and they affect it immensely—because their effectiveness is European. Those half-angry, middle-aged men of literature, who during the last ten years—while prosperity engulfed the whole world, and everybody's neck grew fat—taught the European youth a precious revulsion against the wonders of living, are themselves the spoiled children of the Old World.

Inasmuch as these half-angry littérateurs are obsessed by anything at all—and I am afraid that they are rather underchilled, despite their overheated language—they are obsessed by sex. As far as I know, they are privately no sex monsters. But the writer, to create his own microcosmos, needs a superpersonal, an extrapersonal principle that could unify, commit, and redeem his creation. Once that principle was God. Then came the principle of superman who proves his mettle in the world and against it. But now, don't you know, "God is dead" and superman is dead and we live in the world of common man—and what can happen to common man? Sex, naturally.

Sex is the inarticulate's substitute for conversation. Unfortunately, it is much more difficult to be brilliant in that special form of dialogue than in normal conversation; and this is what makes the sex obsession of the half-angry so hopeless. The creatures of the half-angry writer are organically incapable of experiencing more than their bodies—and how little fun is there! The cramp, the mimicry, the stammer, the little shouts are always the same; and at the moment of climax the creature of the half-angry writer feels itself, quite correctly, a mere ant. Sex, in truth, is magic only for the sensitive and well-formed special persons who can play with the vocabulary, and with the colors of the cosmos, and with themselves. But the inarticulate cannot gulp a sensuous stimulus; he constantly chokes.

To the extent that the half-angry writers are whole artists they sense their trouble. Which is why they get ever deeper into the underbrush of perversion. That contemporary literature in general, and American literature in particular, reads as if it were an endless textbook for students of pathology is known; but I am not sure one knows *why* this is so.

The paradoxical reason, it seems to me, is the optimism of the half-angry writers. They just cannot get themselves to leave their creatures in the empty boredom of exhaustion; and because they know of no other sphere of human fulfillment, even of human self-identification, than the area of physiological reflexes, they keep experimenting with an endless chain of response to tickling sensation. Perhaps, they hope fervently, perhaps there is, after all, *some* sensuous specialty that makes all the fireworks rise up to the sky! Of course there is none. And the half-angry writers sense that their creatures are caught in a maze of meaninglessness.

Each new play by Tennessee Williams, the most gifted among the half-angry writers (whose every play is a major event on the German stage), begins with the tacit pledge to explore a new structure of the *humana comoedia*. All right, we have already met the half-mute moron who rapes his anemic sister-in-law (*A Streetcar Named Desire*). So the next time we are made to look into the gizzard of a young man who cannot touch his comely wife because he has a subconscious fixation on his boy friend (*Cat on a Hot Tin Roof*). The same old boredom? All right, then let us explore what it feels like to be torn to pieces and be eaten by cannibalistic children (one of Mr. Williams' latest plays). That, too, produces only nausea? Mr. Williams, a true American, never says die. He will walk from one case history to the next, with a saddened hope which never ends: that somewhere, sometime, somehow, he will run into an altogether maddening, altogether electrifying, altogether overwhelming perversity, an ultimate kick to which a man with an innocent faith in orgasm can finally surrender.

This type of poetry is heartsick. The *angina pectoris* of the half-angry writer is fear neither of pain nor of death; it is the fear of the ghastly discovery that there *is* no heart. The literature of three thousand years, and particularly tragedy, had never any doubt that life, in spite of all pain, remains sweet; that man, in spite of all his weaknesses, should faithfully plant trees; that God in heaven and a girl in his arms sanction him. But the human beings the half-angry writers have met, and make us meet, are not at all sure that they exist. God is dead—and who will sanction them?

Yet man cannot live without *knowing* that he is alive. He must assert his own existence. And the only proof of his being alive, of his identity (for he is no longer prepared for any other proof), is the more or less precise functioning of his organs. The heroes of the half-angry literature live from one little sex play, from one kick to the next, because they are not alive. Only when they do something all other creatures do, too, only then are they sure that they exist. And yet, this is precisely the moment when they do *not* know it. For how can one assert the uniqueness, the unequivocal identity of a human being through an act that is being reiterated billions of times—in the senseless reflexes of ants?

The great sorrow of the sensuous world is an inexorable law that rules pleasure: Pleasure, sought for pleasure's sake, must end in boring sadness. And that law destroys the literature of the half-angry, for they write (and I am speaking only of those among them who are artists) because they find the boredom that suffocates life intolerable. Thus they create. And what do they create? Creatures who are suffocated by boredom. Their game starts, each time, with a premonition of promise and adventure, but it ends, each time, with boredom. Why is it that the world of the half-angry writers is so gray and hopeless? I do not know. My world is colorful and full of a tragic serenity. Do I live in a time that is no longer? Do they live in a time that is not yet? I do not know. I only know that the world no longer blooms for the half-angry and the white clouds, for them, move no longer across a blue sky.

This is by no means a detour through the valleys of literary criticism. Contemporary American literature is quite probably the strongest single influence in shaping the intellectual profile of new Germany's youth. Its roots, as I pointed out, are European; but no serious observer of German society can overlook the fateful impact of contemporary American writing on the culture of this convalescing people. From the stage, the screen, the television sets, the novels, even from the angelic realm of music, the Half-angry Manifesto shouts at the German youth: "A specter is haunting Europe and America, the specter of boredom. . . . Half-angry of all countries, unite! You have nothing to lose but your yawn; you have an underworld to gain." The frightening fact is that the German youth responds to this jeer far more dependably than to any other western stimulation. And this is so, it seems to me, because this young generation sees around itself only one dedication—the dedication to prosperity.

The underlying presumption of European policies in general, and German policies in particular, is "precaution, precaution, and again precaution!" But it has always been the cry, "boldness, boldness, and again boldness!" that has made young people grow up with a happy eagerness to take over an exciting and meaningful society. The air of precaution is suffocating. It induces into the body politic fears and "existentialist" nausea and a horror of the inescapable vacuum. The satiated nothingness of public life makes youth riot. (Significantly, the most vicious of all youth riots occur in Sweden—the almost legendary country of prosperous comfort, of bread and circus and security for everybody, the country of the most orderly welfare state, of uninhibited sex, and the most honest materialism.)

It is clear, I trust, that I do not count myself among the opponents of Dr. Adenauer; on the contrary, with all I have said and shall say in this book I am testifying to his greatness. But he has failed—as America fails—in this last respect: his kind of policies, and ours, can never fill youth with a spirit of dedication. Yet without that spirit youth is of necessity delinquent. Without that spirit the West is doomed. In the end, the policy of precaution and nothing but precaution is *always* doomed. And though youth may be crude in most other respects, it has an unfailing sense for the future. The German youth, it seems to me, is not excited about the West's future. Is America's?

On January 30, 1958, the twenty-fifth anniversary of Hitler's ascent to power, an event of great significance took place in Munich, once called "the capital of the National Socialist Movement." In the overcrowded *auditorium maximum* and the adjacent halls of the Munich University more than 4,000 students killed a German tradition that had swayed German youth for 150 years— the tradition of the German student's unequivocal devotion to patriotism.

It was a formal plenary session of Munich's student citizenry. The University of Munich lists 15,000 students, out of 160,000 students in all of Germany; and never before had such a large and passionate student audience gathered at an official assembly. The students of Munich had been called together to decide whether the ancient academic motto, *dulce et decorum est pro patria mori* ("it is sweet and glorious to die for the fatherland"), should be replaced by a new *mortui viventes obligant* ("the dead commit the living"). That the meeting took place on the twenty-fifth anniversary of the Fatherland's darkest day was purely coincidental. But this is the kind of coincidence that forms a nation's metaphors.

Several months before, Horace's venerable expression of unquestioning patriotism, an educational cliché for innumerable generations of German youth, had been restored to one of the rebuilt parts of the badly bombed Munich University. There it stood again— *dulce et decorum est pro patria mori*—in a dignified lettering of iron, just as it had stayed engraved on German universities for years and years. But a few days later some students had confronted it with an anonymous poster which said: *Turpe et stupidum est pro amentia loqui* ("it is shameful and stupid to speak for lunacy").

The *Rektor* of the Munich University, Professor Egon Wiberg, sensed in this anonymous demonstration the makings of a great intellectual debate. He put the Horace quotation under cover and asked the Academic Senate—the University's governing body—for fast and final intervention.

The Academic Senate, on its part, invited the University's total citizenry, professors and students, to submit replacements for Horace's saying. The teachers suggested 490 Latin homilies, the students only three. *Rektor* Wiberg selected the one to be voted for or vetoed by the students—*mortui viventes obligant*. The elected representatives of the students, the *Allgemeine Studenten Ausschuss,* expressed their belief that the Horace saying was still good enough to formulate the sentiments of Munich's students. The *Ausschuss* was seconded by the traditionalist student organizations, the *Burschenschaften,* the *Turnvereine,* and the *Landsmannschaften.* But immediately a *Ring Freier Studentengruppen* ("Circle of Free Student Groups") formed to collect signatures to ask for a constitutional students' assembly that would decide the issue. When 1,000 such signatures were submitted, the assembly had to be called.

Udo Jansen, president of the *Allgemeine Studenten Ausschuss,* opened the procedures. Then Professor Wiberg took over and produced, in a soft and professorial manner, an appeal to elementary pacifism. It ended with the plea never to forget Sophie and Hans Scholl, the two Munich students whose almost gay martyrdom preceded the unsuccessful and yet most promising upheaval against Hitlerism, the conspiracy of July 20, 1944. In their memory, Wiberg closed, Munich's students should choose the motto, *mortui viventes obligant.*

What followed was as moving as it was depressing. Thousands of young Germans, in a helpless naïveté that was almost physically noticeable, tried to do right by throwing at one another the banalities precooked in the German press—pacifist banalities on one side, nationalist banalities on the other. Here were rather exceptional young men and women (less than 3 per cent of Germany's college-age youth reach the universities, as compared to the 34 per cent of college-age American youth who actually crowd the nation's colleges), desperately seeking the truth, but obediently willing to take for it the findings of routine journalism.

There was one moment of genuine drama. A Hungarian student, who was continuing in Munich the studies interrupted by his lost revolution of 1956 in Budapest, told the assembly how some of his friends, facing death before the Soviet firing squads, had scratched, with their fingernails, into the prison walls *dulce et decorum est pro patria mori*. There was a hush over the assembly. And yet, a few minutes after this interference of bloody history with academic debate the assembly voted, by more than 2 to 1, that the Munich University's motto be from now on *mortui viventes obligant*. Then, as if they wanted to bargain with greatness, the students also voted that the Academic Senate give the plaque with the renounced Horace saying to the Hungarian students, for safekeeping, until the day when it can be unveiled in the University of Budapest. Thus, the assembly of Munich's students seemed to decide, 2 to 1, that it is sweet and glorious to die for Hungary, but "shameful and stupid" to die for Germany.

But I am sure this was not what those seriously excited and excitingly serious students had in mind. An ordinary cloud of fear had taken possession of these uninformed young souls—the kind of fear, thoughtless and facile, that spreads over every page of Germany's civilized press: fear of nuclear holocausts, fear of conflict, fear of a mystical doomsday around the corner, fear of all the consequences that character and firmness may bring about. These young people voted against the past, not inasmuch as it was despicable, but inasmuch as it was the past; and they did so because their audible elders teach them to fear the future or, rather, to *yield* to it. The vote of the Munich students was a victory of the German press.

And yet, the *ohne mich* ("without me") kind of social atomization, the virulent attack of a naïve pragmatism that seemed to paralyze Germany in the early fifties—not, of course, as an economy but as a breathing nation—might be coming to an end. In July 1956, when the *Bundestag* discussed the building of a new

German army, the highlight of the great debate was the discussion of the new German's constitutional right to refuse armed service on religious and moral grounds. For the first time in German history, and indeed for the first time in the history of any continental nation, this right was granted, almost unanimously—which in itself may have been one of the truly meaningful signals that Germany has changed.

In 1956 the *Bundestag* had no doubt that a significant part of the German youth will make use of the new right; and the Social Democrats, engaged in a passionate crusade against any German rearmament, took the almost unanimous passing of the law that constituted the German's right to conscientious objection against military service as a symptom of the universal German groundswell against remilitarization. In 1956 there was consensus as to the trend: the *Bundestag,* quite consistently, anticipated such a massive rejection of military service on serious moral grounds that a special federal authority was conceived whose job it would be to find appropriate employment, in the national interest, of the innumerable young Germans who would qualify as conscientious objectors.

The test came the following year—the first year when a whole age class was called for military service. It was the class of 1937—young men of twenty, born two years before Hitler signed his treaty with Stalin and so plunged the world into World War II; who were eight years old when Hitler evaporated; who were twelve years old when the German "economic miracle" began; who were fourteen years old when Germany learned to understand, in the days of the Berlin blockade, that the Soviets meant business and wanted all of Germany.

The final figures on the decision of these young men were available in February 1958. Of the first 200,000 men of the class of 1937 called to military service, a total of 1,037 had filed a claim to be considered conscientious objectors—one out of two hundred. Of the first 437 claims, 262 were accepted by the draft boards, 114 were rejected, and 61 were not yet settled; of the following 600 claims, about 300 were believed to be acceptable. So that, in all, fewer than 600 of 200,000 young Germans can be thought to be

authentic conscientious objectors—three in a thousand. Under
these circumstances the Social Democratic opposition agreed with
the government to abstain from the formation of the planned *Amt
für Ersatzpflicht.*

This, God knows, does not mean that a new military romanticism is emerging in Germany. On the contrary, most Germans—
and certainly most young Germans—consider military service a
hateful nuisance. In many months of careful observation I have not
noticed in Germany any enthusiasm for, or pride in, the new German army. That 997 out of a thousand young Germans have no
conscientious objection to military service is a symptom, not for a
reawakened German joy in uniforms, but for a reawakening of
social responsibility. Young Germans still do not like barracks; but
they no longer have the hallucination that man can escape his fate
by shrugging his shoulders. The *ohne mich* obsession may be
dying out.

But I am not so sure of the trend when I look at the educated elite
of the German youth; and in Germany, more than anywhere else,
it will be this elite that will form the will of the nation. Germany's
intellectual community is just as conformist as any other, and the
young intellectuals are worse conformists than anybody else: if one
does not share the "proper" beliefs and attitudes of the *avant-garde,*
one simply does not belong.

What are these beliefs and attitudes in Germany? I should like
to submit a list, offered in good faith and not at all—as it may
seem on first sight—with ironical intent. If some of the tenets held
by the German intelligentsia, young and otherwise, move along
the borderlines of satire, this is not my doing; I am merely trying
to condense, in their essence, many thousands of words I have read
and hundreds of conversations I have listened to.

First: There must be no other war—never again. There is no
conceivable justification for another war—neither the defense of
so-called freedom, nor spiritual dogma, nor moral or national
integrity.

Two: The people's voice is God's voice. And yet, a parliamentary majority is suspect on the grounds of being a majority. In particular, Adenauer is somehow untouchable.

Three: Any member of the government's executive branch, by virtue of being one, carries the burden of proof: he is assumed to have been a Nazi until found innocent; and even then he may have been a Nazi.

Four: André Gide and Franz Kafka are considered greater prose writers than Walter Winchell and Elsa Maxwell; which assumption leads directly to a nobly reserved contempt for America, somehow balanced by unrestricted respect for Robert Oppenheimer, George F. Kennan, and the editorial writers of New York's liberal press.

Five: The assumption that Communists actually mean what they say, and really want to conquer the world, is considered uncouth. By contrast, the readiness to discover, from time to time, profound changes toward civilized conduct in communist nations is considered a measure of intellectual refinement.

Six: Though no self-respecting young German intellectual is a Communist, they all feel a binding duty "to keep the dialogue going," to uphold the "unity of the European spirit" beneath and above the fleeting political controversies of the day and, in general, to withhold judgment.

Seven: To belong, the young German intellectual must believe in the essentially unpolitical character of "culture" and arts. Which, by coincidence, permits him to see in Communists such as Bertold Brecht the quintessence of humanism and *avant-garde;* but in the occasional writer who opposes communism merely a politicized pamphleteer who, alas, has ceased to serve Europe.

Eight: The reunification of Germany is a laudable goal, but only if pursued in the way of a "confederation" between Bonn and Pankow. However, anybody who insists—with no better rationale than the old-fashioned argument of personal freedom and national integrity—on the restitution of usurped German territory is *ipso facto* assumed to be a potential neo-Nazi.

Nine: The cure for all conceivable conflicts between West and East is to "sit down and talk it over." However, to sit down and talk it over with former Nazis is neo-nazism; one can sit down and talk it over only with present Communists.

Ten: Monolithic societies are considered outside the pale. By definition, monolithic societies are Fascist or—though there is some uncertainty here—Americanized. Also by definition, Communist societies, since the advent of Gomulka, are thought flexible, potentially European, if not Christian, and, on the whole, not necessarily monolithic.

These tenets of the young German intelligentsia—and I repeat: I reported them without intentions of persiflage—are also the political credo of Germany's articulate public opinion. Let no one be misled by the recent election results! Dr. Adenauer's decisive successes are not only his personal successes, rather than votes of confidence in a coherent policy, but they also run contrary to the intellectual tides.

The self-pitying complaint of the German intellectuals—that they are alienated from "the" people—may be just as wrong as it is in all other modern societies (where the intellectuals, while they are noisily deploring their lack of social influence, are becoming the decisive factor of omnipotent government). And yet, it is true in Germany—as it is true in America—that "the masses" are normally responsive to conservative appeals; in their voting, that is, and as long as they are conscious of prosperity. But once the parliaments are elected, the conservative mass is immediately dispersed as effective force, the parliaments themselves respond to articulate public opinion rather than to their own constituencies, and the audible minorities rather than the numb electoral majority determine the national conduct.

Adenauer, with his unprecedented staying power, has created a false sense of security in Germany. Germans as well as many a foreign observer seem satisfied that some ingrained conservative sense of the German people protects the country against the kind of political and cultural "progressivism" that speaks, day after day, from the pulpit of the metropolitan German press. This façade will crack on the very day Adenauer dies. On that day, no matter what happens first on the level of political government, that press will emerge as the only compact rallying force of an otherwise atomized Germany. No matter how deeply rooted the political machinery of the country may be—and it is powerfully rooted in the forests and valleys of Bavaria for the C.D.U., in the factories of Rhineland-Westphalia for the Social Democrats—when Father dies, the Fatherland will be without a will of its own. And on that day the precious bias of the nation's youth, and the nation's elite, may take over.

CHAPTER SIX

The Atomic Scandal

ᗏᗏᗏᗏᗏᗏᗏᗏᗏᗏᗏᗏᗏᗏᗏᗏᗏᗏᗏᗏᗏᗏᗏᗏᗏᗏᗏᗏᗏᗏᗏᗏᗏᗏᗏᗏᗏ

GERMAN public opinion and German medical research are considered by the whole world as particularly fearful of radiation. Their anxiety is surpassed only by the Japanese and a few other Asiatic people."

This is from a scholarly report Professor Rajevski, director of Frankfurt's Max Planck Institute, delivered in September 1958 to the International Atomic Conference in Geneva. I can testify to the exactness of his finding. The air of weird superstition and latent panic that permeates the whole world since the days of Hiroshima has assumed in Germany a special density. During my year's stay in the German orbit no other question seemed to occupy the German mind with anything like the force of the nuclear fear.

It looked for several months as if the atomic obsession was to determine even routine politics. The Social Democratic party, assisted by the *F.D.P.*—a middle-of-the-road splinter group that for many years had served in coalition with Adenauer—focused the opposition's drive toward power on a plebiscite against "atomic death"; and had Germany's Supreme Court not found that such plebiscites are unconstitutional, the country would have been torn apart by a campaign of ghastly unreality: One half of the German people would have accused the other half of favoring atomic destruction over the blessings of prosperity. Had not its Supreme Court spared it the shame, Germany would have been the first nation in the adventurous history of mankind to vote on the question whether, as a Viennese humorist once put it, it is not "better to be rich and healthy—as no poor man can really enjoy his sickness."

To an outsider, all throughout 1957 and 1958 it looked as if the Germans, newly dedicated to pragmatism in all other spheres, had secretly saved their ancient talents for harboring outlandish suspicions and had put them all to work in the eerie fog of nuclear uncertainties. The obscene aspect of the fallacy, and not only in Germany, was the reckless participation of scientists in stirring up the moronic apprehensions of Caliban.

There have been waves of emotional mass disturbances before; and, in fact, a delight with hysteria has been validly diagnosed as one of the characteristics of "the mass" which, as one knows, is the effeminated appearance of a people. But there never was, to my knowledge, an outbreak of that hysteria sponsored and even evoked by the period's learned community of scientists.

The great intellectual scandal of our generation, I contend, is the conduct of our scientists, in particular our physicists, who at the very moment that they announced their claim to political relevancy, if not leadership, exposed the frightening irrelevancy and unreliability of their advice. A physicist, of course, cannot be indicted for lacking the qualities of a political leader; but he is reduced to contemptible futility if he does not employ, in his public conduct, the concepts and values of a physicist. And this is the demonstrable guilt of our nuclear physicists, in Germany as well as elsewhere.

With few exceptions, all German professors of physics and all authoritative spokesmen of German natural science have signed those innumerable "manifestoes" that originated the German nuclear panic. Their contentions—aside from the frivolous fact that natural scientists, *as natural scientists,* were organizing themselves as a political pressure group—were two unproved and, in fact, untrue "findings": One, the "fallout" radiation of past and current nuclear test explosions has created a considerable danger for the health of mankind; two, their continuation will endanger the survival of the race.

And, having firmly planted their feet on two demonstrably wrong premises, a large majority of Germany's natural scientists formulated two demands: One, Germany must not tolerate that its own new army be equipped with atomic weapons or that bases for atomic missiles be granted to the United States and NATO; two, further nuclear test explosions must cease all around the globe. In the course of a few months this temerity of German natural scientists resulted in a German mass panic.

As it happened, that mass panic stopped short of the political upheaval the German Social Democracy had hopefully expected in the spring of 1958. North-Rhine-Westphalia, the most densely populated of all German *Bundesländer,* was then to elect its diet, and the Social Democrats tried to make that election a substitute for the outlawed plebiscite. But, though the Social Democrats gained a couple of per cents, their ally, the *F.D.P.,* shrank miserably and Adenauer's C.D.U. won another victory. Had he lost—and Adenauer was fully aware of that perilous alternative—the victory of the "opponents of atomic death" would have, first, paralyzed and in a short while reversed Germany's foreign policy: nothing could have then prevented Germany from sinking into "neutralism."

Was Adenauer's victory in North-Rhine-Westphalia tantamount to Germany's rejection of atomic panic? I doubt it. What this election proved, it seems to me, is the remarkable inertia of the German electorate that, for Adenauer's and the prosperity's lifetime, remains weary of "experiments." In other words, no matter how hard the opposition tried to make "atomic death" the issue of that election, the only issue the German electorate was willing to acknowledge was the continuation of prosperity (and, thus, of Adenauer).

North-Rhine-Westphalia turned down, not the opponents of "atomic death," but the opponents of Dr. Adenauer—who, quite significantly, was most anxious to prove that he, too, wanted the cessation of all atomic test explosions and a general "atomic disarmament." He almost humiliated himself in this election campaign by stressing an "atomic pacifism" which his policy, thank God, never showed; and I think he knew what he was doing. He knew that even he, to stay in control of a potentially hysterical people, gradually irritated into near panic, had to "finesse."

No recent event contradicts Professor Rajevski's assertion that the Germans' "anxiety [of radiation] is surpassed only by the Japanese and a few other Asiatic people." But in their anxiety, it seems to me, the Germans represent the entire West. Because they (and the Japanese) have been physically more shattered by bombings than any other people on earth they may shake faster and more conspicuously than the rest. This is merely a matter of nervous conditions. True vigor is ultimately a matter of the mind. And the measure of the damage done to the German as well as to the western mind is the unfathomable confusion into which western public opinion has been thrown by the scandal of the age—the epileptic dances of the natural scientists.

The scandal is so unprecedented because these natural scientists, pledged to respect nothing but measurable facts, have seen to it that the facts remain unknown, are blurred by emotional outcries beyond recognition, are gradually considered altogether irrelevant. The "atomic debate" is being led, in Germany as well as everywhere else in the West, by natural scientists costumed as fiction writers and by fiction writers costumed as natural scientists. The confusion is total and, I contend, deliberate. This is why I propose to establish the known and knowledgeable facts first.

Hiroshima was the beginning of the West's final disarmament. The first atomic bomb was dropped by an American plane, but it scored, triumphantly, for the Soviet Union. On that day in 1945 the West's spine broke under the weight, not so much of a troubled conscience, but of a nightmarish fear. It was a faceless fear, for nobody knew what an atomic war will be like; but it was a tremendous fear—a fear without measure, a fear without the limitations of reasoning.

What reasoning there was came from the nuclear scientists who are a very special breed of men. I know some of them, and most of those I know I like greatly. There is usually a childlike simplicity about them, a singlemindedness that seems an indispensable prerequisite of patient research, and a somewhat banal kind of "idealism." Judging by the few I know, I would trust nuclear scientists with my last dollar: I might lose it, of course, but I would never feel cheated. They are that kind of men. But I would have always considered it inconceivable that nuclear scientists could be entrusted with the social function they have assumed since 1945—to form, in a measure still uncomprehended by the West, the political mind of the free world. And I would have thought this inconceivable for two forceful reasons.

One, the very structure of brain that makes a man a successful natural scientist disqualifies him as a social guide: he becomes a natural scientist because, basically, he has an irrepressible desire for orderly tabulation and an incorrigible prejudice that every problem is soluble. But anyone with this desire and that prejudice is bound to be a pathetic failure in the sphere of social relations—a sphere where a desire for orderly tabulation leads to intolerable regimentation and the assumption that all problems are soluble to cruel arrogance.

Two, the natural scientist is mentally conditioned by the circumstances of his research—by the fact, above all, that all experiments are permissible because all experiments can be repeated (i.e., undone). But anyone who advises or guides men in social adventures must, first and last, understand the fateful fact that, in human affairs, experiments can *not* be repeated or undone—that every intervention is unique, final, and the cause of inescapable following events.

And yet, behind the incoherent debates and gropings of western public opinion and, above all, behind the weirdly unspirited moves (or, rather, the catatonia) of western governments is always the feverish "reasoning" of our nuclear scientists. I say "feverish" because a true scientist will be the first to admit that, since 1945, the excursions of nuclear science into the sciences of human behavior were, all of them, without exception, nervous "hunches"—shots fired into the dark by fearful men against gigantic shadows. There exists not a single calm, reserved, and superior statement of nuclear scientists on the problems of "politics in the nuclear age." It would not occur to me to question the decent human urgency that made nuclear scientists draft whatever "manifestoes" they did release since 1945. But neither would it occur to me—or to anyone else who applies the binding rules of logic and remains committed to demonstrable fact—to consider those "manifestoes" as relevant documents.

On the contrary, in circumstances of sanity the type of public outcries that is currently ascribed to venerable amateurs such as Albert Schweitzer would be dismissed with silent mercy. For when a man whose greatness was always a true amateur's childlike loyalty to his many loves, and *never* a true scholar's dedication to demonstrable fact—when such a man suddenly leaps into public awareness with wild claims to an authority he could not possibly have, then human tact and genuine reverence for a lovable old man like Schweitzer should make us look compassionately the other way. But so totally deprived of any sense of intellectual measure and reserve have we become, under the nuclear scientists' attack on our nerves, that demonstrably uninformed statements by Albert Schweitzer could grow—at least in Germany—into some of the epoch's great documents, into a kind of scriptural text.

Schweitzer's statements have made more impression on the Germans than anything a qualified scientist has said on the subject. This, it seems to me, is only partly due to the veritable Schweitzer adulation one can find throughout Germany. (A public poll has established that Albert Schweitzer ranks first, far and above, among the world citizens whom Germans consider to be "the outstanding men of this age.") No educated or, for that matter, uneducated German would claim that Schweitzer can be trusted as an unchallengeable authority on any subject in particular; but the point is that he can be *trusted*. And he can be trusted especially when he, suddenly the "scientist," expresses some superstitious and, in fact, some primordial horror about the perils of science.

There are, without a doubt, prophetic elements in Schweitzer's amazing performance as a "seer"; and here, paradoxically, is the key to the surprising emergence of the natural scientist as political guide. Modern civilization has grown profoundly suspicious of modern science; but, having no other god, it would not dare express its suspicions—unless they are advanced by the scientists themselves. Now nuclear physics have become the area where modern science doubts itself; and so, in his desperate confusion about his own state, the nuclear physicist—otherwise, of all natural scientists, the least comprehensible person—has moved close to the heart of the human mass that is shaken with darkly inarticulate anxieties. If he is smart and lucky enough to speak through an Albert Schweitzer—a man whose specialty is the emotional generalities of "humanism"—the nuclear physicist attains the powers of popular prophecy.

In January 1958 the secretary general of the United Nations received a solemn document signed by 9,253 scientists of 44 nations, among them 36 Nobel Prize winners. Among the signers were 146 German professors of natural sciences—and there are not many more—among them the Nobel Prize winners Born, Heisenberg, Hahn, Alder, Butenandt, Kuhn, Windaus, and Domagk. The petition demanded the immediate cessation of atomic test explosions because, or so claimed the 9,253 scientists, each atomic test endangered the health of all people and will lead, through damaging effects on human genes, "to an increase of the number of seriously damaged children born in future generations." Besides, if atomic tests were to continue, "the menace of an atomic war will be increased that could be started by some irresponsible politician."

In short, the unprecedented political lobbying of the world's natural scientists, a deliberate attempt at high pressuring the United Nations into political action, summarized the arguments of all preceding "manifestoes" which—was it really a coincidence?—had mobilized substantial parts of the world against the conduct of the United States.

All these "manifestoes" have two arguments in common. One, they introduce—as arguments of natural scientists would—quantitative considerations into a purely moral decision. Wars, or so the nuclear scientists claim, have become "unthinkable" because nu-

clear weapons must multiply war casualties. Two, all pronounce-
ments of the pleading nuclear scientists are haunted by an untested
and rather inarticulate premonition: war or no war, continued
nuclear research may cause biological mutations of man in times to
come. And both apprehensions, the terror of anticipating a staggering magnitude of casualties in a future war, and the numb fear of
ghastly biological mutations, have conquered the public's subconscious mind.

I say "subconscious mind" because a number of polls in the
United States and in Europe have conclusively shown that the
public, as far as it knows its own mind, is moved by employment
apprehensions still more than by nuclear anxieties. And yet, in their
shapeless depths rather than in their conscious minds people, in
Germany and everywhere, are profoundly shaken by the new fears.
There is, since 1945, a spooky force at work on German public
opinion and public policies. The triumph of natural science in our
times has produced a situation unknown in Europe since the thir-
teenth century—a situation in which a superstitious mysticism,
emerging from the darkest recesses of the mind, threatens to determine conduct. This, it seems to me, will be the most fateful paradox
of the twentieth century: the break-through of science results in a
triumph of the subconscious over the mind.

Pacifism, surely an infantile disease of the intellect, has for the
first time in modern history been established as the most pertinent
factor in shaping, not only public opinion, but also public policies.
Statesmen, generals, and journalists, who from 1939 to 1945 did
not feel the slightest hesitation in recommending and insisting on
mass slaughter in a holy crusade against fascism and nazism, are
totally impressed nowadays by the two arguments of the nuclear
physicists—the quantitative argument of the magnitude of future
war casualties, and the shapeless argument of possible future biological mutations. But both arguments, disturbing as they are, appear to a mind trained in sane reasoning logically and morally
irrelevant.

To approve of a political conduct that results in the suffering of
a single human creature is just as serious and just as irreparable a

commitment as to approve of a conduct that results in the suffering of millions of people. The resistance against Hitler led directly to the death of millions of soldiers, to the mass terror of "petroleum-jelly bombs," the maiming of unnumbered children, the unimaginable suffering of unimaginable multitudes. And if this was the proper and just price the nations of this earth were morally entitled to pay for the deliverance from nazism—as the nuclear scientists themselves firmly believed during the last war, and continue to profess today—then I refuse to see the slightest *qualitative* difference between the situation of 1944 and that of 1959.

To resist evil, in spite of what such resistance means in quantitative terms of human suffering, is either right or it is wrong. If it is right, then I shall resist evil whether such resistance results in physical terror for "only" 100 million people or whether 200 million people will be maimed. The *number* of victims has nothing to do with the moral weight of my decision: If to resist evil at the cost of human suffering is wrong, then it would be wrong if "only" a single human creature were committed to involuntary suffering. This clarification, one should think, has been achieved at the latest by Dostoevski's Great Inquisitor; simpler souls may have been informed, even sooner, by the Gospel.

And those who insist on measuring moral problems, instead of weighing them, receive the identical information from logical speculation. As pain and suffering exist only in the experience of the creature that goes through pain and suffering, the sum total of *all* conceivable pain and suffering is all the pain and suffering *one* human creature can experience. There *is* no more. The whole world, all life, all pain, is born, and dies, with every single human creature. Nuclear physicists, trained for nothing but the taking of quantitative measurements, are perhaps incapable of comprehending this calculus of human experience; but anyone who has ever participated in the tragedy of man's existence must know its inexorable workings.

And what is one to make of the argument that mobilizes the primitive's fear of the unknown and the unprovable—his fear of biological mutations in times to come? Of these mutations I know nothing—which is no less than what the nuclear scientists know. But I do know of the spiritual, psychological, and physical consequences, some of them catastrophic, which were produced by past wars (especially the last one against nazism), by fire and pestilence and hunger and rape and utter destitution of countless millions of women and children. These consequences reach into the centuries and millennia, past and future. What of them? Was it, because of them, wrong to resist Genghis Khan, Islam, Hitler? If it was not, then the unknown consequences of nuclear warfare will not release me from making the morally right decision again—the right decision in resisting the evil of communism.

Even more. When advanced by *scientists,* the argument concerning the unknown biological consequences of nuclear radiation on unborn generations is particularly perverse. Have 9,253 natural scientists, among them 36 Nobel Prize winners, ever warned the world against the unknown consequences of modern drugs, vaccinations, synthetic food on unborn generations? Surely there must be such consequences, unwittingly produced by medicating doctors— by Dr. Albert Schweitzer, for example—in an unexceptionable spirit of charity and mercy (and scientific arrogance) to reduce pain and save lives. Has the world-wide community of natural scientists ever petitioned governments to stop the scientific interference with man's natural environment, those incessant experiments with the complex interrelations of insects, birds, plants, fertilizers, nutrition?

Have scientists ever engaged in a world-wide campaign to stop automobiles? But it is a statistical fact that automobiles are maiming, every year, hundreds of thousands of children all around the world—not unborn ones, but living and growing children. Those children are maimed—and more than 100,000 adults killed by automobiles every year—merely to speed up our petty business and our futile pleasures. Where is Albert Schweitzer's crusade against a contraption that not just mutates but *erases* unborn generations? I look with amazement at natural scientists who rush in murderous automobiles to meetings in which those potential killers protest against policies, proposed for the protection of a civilized world against expanding evil, because these policies may employ techniques which could possibly affect—in a manner completely unknown to science—unborn generations.

I, for one, shall never listen to scientists who do not, at the same time, protest against those unspeakable and unpronounceable chemicals that are being produced, by scientists, for the prettification of faces, the alleged improvement of the soil, for all those innumerable interferences with the majestic course of nature and decay.

It is the natural scientist who tries to persuade me that, no matter what chances I may be taking with the health and happiness of future generations, my postulated belief in "progress" must give me faith in the good services of science. I am asked, in other words, to commit the future—and to do it in total ignorance—whenever *physical* appetites, pleasures, and entertainments are concerned. No one has ever heard of natural scientists who worry in public over the physical and spiritual dangers 50 million radiating TV sets may mean to unborn generations. But those men who assert the need to resist communism, with whatever force is required to resist it effectively and victoriously, are excluded by the arrogant nuclear scientists from the human race. You are a progressive participant in the adventure of civilization, so long as you kill and maim children with automobiles, with DDT, with vaccinations, and sundry other drugs; but you are beneath the state of man when you propose to employ nuclear weapons rather than submit to communism.

It is about time to dismiss the accusers and the accusation. It is about time to demand facts from the incessant and ubiquitous busybodies of our day, the natural scientists who have turned politicians and propagandists, the frightened men who whisper in everybody's ear irresponsible professional gossip, the degenerate Prometheans who first reached for the fire, and then, driven to hysteria by its light, accuse everybody else of the vilest intentions and dirtiest motives. It is not true that the facts are unknown. Albert Schweitzer, to be sure, may have never looked at them. But the facts of radiation are established, as far as humanly possible, and they are unequivocal.

The unit of measuring radiation is called "roentgen." If a person is exposed to a thousand roentgens at once, he will almost certainly die within thirty days. But a thousand roentgens of radiation spread over a lifetime produce no apparent biological consequences. All atomic explosions, from 1944 till 1958, have produced a per-capita radiation of 0.004 roentgen. It is the unchallenged finding of responsible scientific calculation that a contemporary's *lifetime* exposure to radiation caused by all atomic explosions from 1944 to 1958 (except, of course, the immediate victims of the atomic bombs dropped in 1945 over Japan) cannot exceed, on the average, *five roentgens*. I repeat: *a thousand* roentgens spread over a lifetime produce no apparent biological consequences; but the radiation to which a person is exposed in his lifetime due to all atomic explosions is *less than five roentgens*—one half of 1 per cent of the lifetime radiation that is considered safe.

Yet there is reasonable suspicion that *any* amount of radiation, even the smallest one, may increase a person's vulnerability to bone cancer and leukemia. The most pessimistic statistical estimate, calculated under the watchful eyes of the world community of nuclear scientists, contends that, roughly, per one "megaton" of fission energy exploded, 200 persons all around the world may get leukemia or bone cancer—200 persons, that is, who would not otherwise have contracted the dreaded diseases. All atomic explosions, from 1944 to 1958, have involved about 50 megatons of nuclear energy. Thus, according to the most pessimistic estimates, 10,000 persons may so have contracted bone cancer or leukemia, to erupt during their lifetime. By "lifetime" the statisticians mean the next thirty years.

But during the next thirty years about 6,000,000 people will *normally* die of bone cancer or leukemia; in these 6,000,000 cases there will be no connection whatsoever with radiation caused by atomic explosions. All atomic explosions, from 1944 to 1958, may have added 10,000 cases to the next thirty years' "normal" 6,000,-000 cases of bone cancer or leukemia—about 300 cases a year all around the globe. This is less than one third of 1 per cent of the *annual* deaths caused by automobiles. I repeat: one third of 1 per cent. During the next thirty years, 10,000 people may die because of radiation caused by all atomic explosions from 1944 to 1958; but during the next thirty years at least 3,000,000 people will be killed by automobile accidents.

The human body, all around the globe, is constantly exposed to radiation effects caused by cosmic rays that reach the earth. A person living at sea level absorbs every year about 0.035 roentgen of cosmic radiation—about *nine times* the annual radiation effect of all atomic explosions. The effect of cosmic radiation on persons living at 5,000 feet—in the extremely healthy city of Denver, for instance—rises to 0.05 roentgen a year—*twelve times* the annual radiation effect of all atomic explosions. Nor are cosmic rays the only carriers of natural radiation. The total radiation from all natural sources amounts to 0.15 roentgen per capita and year. In other words: the average inhabitant of this planet absorbs 0.15 roentgen of natural radiation every year—*thirty-six times* the annual radiation due to all atomic explosions from 1944 to 1958.

But it is by no means established that radiation *really* causes bone cancer or leukemia. In fact, there is considerable evidence to the contrary. Cosmic radiation, as stated before, increases with altitude; so that a person absorbs 0.035 roentgen of cosmic rays at sea level, but 0.05 roentgen at 5,000 feet. One would therefore assume that the frequency of bone cancer and leukemia must be higher in Denver (altitude 5,000 feet) than in New Orleans and San Francisco (both at sea level).

The opposite is true. According to official medical statistics, there were per year and per 1,000,000 inhabitants 24 cases of bone cancer and 64 cases of leukemia in Denver—but 28 cases of bone cancer and 69 cases of leukemia in New Orleans, and 29 cases of bone cancer and 103(!) cases of leukemia in San Francisco. "One possible explanation for the lower incidence of bone cancer and leukemia in Denver," suggest Dr. Edward Teller and Dr. Albert L. Latter in their book, *Our Nuclear Future* (Criterion Books, New York, 1958), "is that disruptive processes like radiation are not necessarily harmful in small enough dosages. Cell deterioration and regrowth go on all the time in living creatures. A slight acceleration of these processes could conceivably be beneficial to the organism. One should not forget that while radiation can cause cancer, it has been used in massive doses to retard and sometimes even to cure cancer."

The ordinary drinking water is an even more prolific source of radiation than the cosmos. The radium deposited in the human body from drinking water reaches 0.55 roentgen a year—*150 times* the annual radiation due to all atomic explosions from 1944 to 1958. "The difference between living in a brick house and living in a wood house could give rise to ten times as much radiation as we are currently getting from fallout," report Professor Teller and Dr. Latter. From a wrist watch with a luminous dial a person receives *ten times* as much radiation as from all atomic explosions. From all known radiation sources, cosmic and earth bound, an average person receives, every year, *a hundred times* as much radiation as from all atomic explosions from 1944 to 1958.

A special and, for the moral maturity of our natural scientists, significant case is radiation due to the medical application of X rays. The average person receives, per year, about 0.1 roentgen of radiation from doctors, in examinations and treatments. This is *twenty-five times* the annual amount due to atomic explosions from 1944 to 1958. "In some cases," submit Professor Teller and Dr. Latter, "medical X rays have intensities which are noticeably harmful. Yet this damage is practically always of little consequence compared to the advantage from correct recognition of any trouble that the X ray discloses."

The scientist, in other words, normally weighs a potential harm against a potential benefit; and, having found the attainable good greater than the possible harm, he then acts—according to a choice for which he was informed by his moral judgment. And this, of course, is exactly the situation of the contemporary statesman: he has to consider the possible damage caused by the consequences of further atomic explosions and the quality of the values—freedom, human dignity, private happiness, religion—he would be securing by a continuation of atomic tests. But the same natural scientist who grants any doctor the right to endanger a person whose health he intends to protect, the same natural scientist *denies* that right to the protectors of our whole civilization, even though the danger of continued atomic tests is a small fraction of the risks any doctor takes in treating a patient.

There exists a tabulation of the risks a person incurs by choosing different courses of conduct. This tabulation, worked out by Dr. Hardin Jones on the basis of most carefully checked statistical data (and, in the last line, completed by Professor Teller and Dr. Latter), gives an exact measure of the intellectual fraud our learned community of natural scientists is committing on the world:

	Reduced Life Expectancy
	by
Being 10 per cent overweight	1.5 years
Smoking one pack of cigarettes a day	9 years
Living in the city instead of the country	5 years
Remaining unmarried	5 years
Having a sedentary job	5 years
Being of the male sex	3 years
Automobile accidents	1 year
One roentgen of radiation	5 to 10 days
Lifetime radiation at present level of atomic explosions	1 to 2 days

Germany trembles under the impact of the protests her natural scientists file, day after day, against the further testing of atomic weapons which all competent strategists of the West deem indispensable for the defense of the West against communism. And how great is the risk which, according to those natural scientists, we must not take, even if that choice may mean the end of our civilization? One twentieth of 1 per cent of the risk a person accepts by smoking one pack of cigarettes per day. One third of 1 per cent of the risk he incurs by overeating. One tenth of 1 per cent of the risk a person accepts by living in the city rather than in the country.

It is, in other words, a fraction of the risk every human being gladly incurs *a dozen times every day,* just to feel alive, or to pursue his frivolous pleasures, or to earn his livelihood. How dare, in the face of these incontrovertible facts, the natural scientists claim our attention? I wonder—and I realize that this question is irrelevant. For the truly serious phenomenon is not the irresponsibility of the natural scientists. The oppressive phenomenon of the age is the public's readiness to fall for the fraud—its savage anxiety, the quivering urge to avoid pain, that is at the bottom of the scandalous "atomic debate."

If the facts make monkeys of the natural scientists in the matter of radiation danger, they can do even less for them in the area of their second argument—the dangers of biological mutations. For as the "background radiation"—natural (environmental) as opposed to atomic-explosion radiation—has a hundred times more effect than man-induced radiation, the "normal" biological mutations obviously must exceed those "future" mutations by at least a hundred times. In other words, those sickening predictions of children to be born with three arms or no ears are a fraud. If radiation can indeed interfere with the genes, it has already done so for the last several millions of years, generation after generation, with a force infinitely greater than any radiation force man could possibly produce.

And yet, the human race rather likes itself the way it emerged from millions of years of mutation effects. Of course, there is no way of telling whether or not the powers of an Aristotle or, for that matter, of a Schweitzer happen to be a mutation effect of radiation; the point is that, on the basis of several millions of years of mutations due to radiation effects, we have no reason to expect "damage" to the race by adding 1 per cent to the radiation forces that have been *normally* at work on earth *for millions of years.*

All atomic explosions from 1944 to 1958 are responsible for, at the most, 0.002 roentgen per year to the human reproductive cells, the carriers of the genes. Per generation, this adds up to 0.05 roentgen of radiation effects on the reproductive cells, accumulated over a lifetime; but over a period of one generation the "background radiation" effects on the reproductive cells amount to five roentgens. Which—always assuming, without any scientific proof, that an increase of radiation effects causes additional mutations in direct proportion—means that all atomic explosions from 1944 to 1958 can, at the most, have added 0.1 per cent to the number of mutations that have occurred or will occur in the present generation—one "man-made" to 1,000 "natural" mutations.

And considering the blissfully small number of "natural" mutations, the danger of man-induced mutations can be dismissed: It is one tenth of 1 per cent—just about as big as the chances my parents took on having a three-armed baby. (The people of Peru, because of the high altitudes of their country, have for the past few thousand years lived under a many times greater impact of cosmic rays than any radiation that could be conceivably produced by atomic explosions. Yet neither among the people nor among any other living species have there been any recorded cases of special biological mutations.)

These are the established, the unequivocal facts of the alleged dilemma. At the same time the Congress for Medical Therapy gathered in Karlsruhe, Germany, in September 1958 to receive learned reports on the effects of air pollution, particularly of the carbon monoxide that permeates the air of automobile-plagued German cities. A man dies if he breathes air that contains 0.2 per cent of carbon monoxide; but on days of heavy automobile traffic, the air of German cities contains nowadays 0.03 per cent of carbon monoxide. The German city population, in other words, breathes an air that has been contaminated, by the automobile, to the incredible high mark of more than 15 per cent of the deadly dosage. This is not a layman's estimate. This has been established by the collective authority of Germany's doctors.

All atomic explosions from 1944 to 1958 have added less than one half of 1 per cent to the lifetime radiation exposure that is considered safe for man; they have added one fiftieth of 1 per cent of the lifetime radiation exposure that is considered deadly. But the air pollution caused in German cities by exhaust gas from automobiles already exceeds 15 per cent of the deadly dosage. The danger from the exhaust of his car is 750 times more serious to the German citizen than the danger from all radiation due to atomic explosions. Yet he dreams of new automobiles, bigger and better ones; and his sleep is disturbed only by nightmares of atomic radiation, by the fraudulent panic his press creates day after day, and by the embarrassingly shrill outcries of the venerable Albert Schweitzer.

The "atomic debate," I repeat, is the greatest intellectual scandal of the age. The world has allowed natural scientists, who are secretly shaken by devastating self-doubts, to play a prank of cruel deception—a prank that may determine the conflict between communism and the free world.

For the defense of the West depends on the availability of nuclear weapons. That the Soviet Union may match, someday, the West's atomic potentials is not decisive. Decisive remains that the West, by possessing nuclear weapons, can make a conflagration so utterly devastating that the Soviets may recoil from aggression. Since 1948, since the West began to recover from its wartime illusions about the nature of communism, the total concept of western defense was based on its possession of nuclear weapons. In particular, the central prerequisite, the intellectual foundation of the whole NATO concept, was, and remains, that the West shall stay atomically armed.

Because the West possesses nuclear weapons, it was satisfied with building a mere skeleton of an army to secure, not Europe as such, but the European atomic bases against a Soviet onslaught. No sane military mind has ever ascribed to NATO a more ambitious job. The contributing NATO powers, including the United States, have programmed for 1961 a total force of 30 battle-ready NATO divisions—to confront 82 Soviet divisions currently poised against the West, plus more than 400 Soviet divisions that can be set going within a month after the outbreak of hostilities. At the moment, and all throughout 1959, about 20 NATO divisions are actually deployed against such overwhelming Soviet superiority in troops—

a superiority at a ratio of 4 to 1 in battle-ready manpower, of 24 to 1 a month after a conflagration starts.

This, under normal circumstances, would be of course considered the survival chances of a maniac suicide. And yet, sound NATO strategists are prepared to take these chances—for one, and *only* one, forceful reason: As NATO would remain equipped with atomic weapons, and its army would merely serve as a protective shield for the West's atomic bases, the man-power proportions on both sides do not really matter. The military establishment of the West can be considered adequate once it is big enough to hold these bases against any surprise attack. The rest would be up to the United States Strategic Air Command that has been created to deliver the nuclear bombs over Soviet territory.

Now what would happen if the Soviets suddenly accepted Mr. Eisenhower's honest offer—extorted from the United States Government by the world-wide movement against "atomic death," by the massive conspiracy of the world's nuclear scientists—that both sides disarm atomically, under mutual disarmament controls? And it is entirely feasible that the Soviets one day will grasp the ultimate advantage which an atomic disarmament, even under *effective* mutual inspection, would give them. In the past the Soviets have shown a ritualistic horror in regard to foreign controls on their territory; and western diplomats got used to reckoning with that Soviet repugnance as an unchangeable fact of international life. But it is not. The post-Stalin leaders of Soviet communism have given abundant evidence that they are capable of taking another look at practically anything.

One day they *must* discover the promises of mutual atomic disarmament, in counterbalance to traditional Soviet revulsions against foreign observers on Soviet soil. And once they discover that the presence of a few United States control commissions in the Soviet Union (even if they were not impeded in motion and observation) is as nothing compared to the gigantic change in the international balance of power an honest atomic disarmament must unfailingly produce, the whole western position cracks. For to overlook their fantastic strategic advantage, in the case of mutual atomic disarmament, the Soviet leaders would have to be blind to reality. And we have no reason to presume that they are.

The Soviets' acceptance of Eisenhower's disarmament proposals would of necessity result in Europe's surrender to the Soviets. As long as *both* sides possess atomic weapons, the likelihood of atomic consequences precludes a frontal Soviet attack. For even though the immensely superior Soviet army could crush the 20 to 30 NATO divisions in a few weeks, the continuous atomic counterattack would have in the meantime rendered the occupied territory uninhabitable; would have destroyed the supply lines between the Red Army and the Soviet Union; and would have, above all, turned decisive Soviet regions into atomic ashes. Therefore, simply because it cannot pay, a Soviet attack has not yet materialized— and, as far as humanly foreseeable, will not materialize as long as the West remains atomically armed.

But once there are *no* dangers of a devastating atomic reprisal, once *both* sides have effectively dismantled their atomic establishments under working mutual controls, then Europe sinks *unavoidably* under the gigantic weight of a "conventional" Soviet army that outnumbers the West, first, 4 to 1 and, a month later, 24 to 1.

Even more. A responsible European government, *any* responsible European government (i.e., not at all a "neutralist" or a procommunist type of government), would have to come to fast terms with the Soviet Union *before* the military avalanche came down on their country. An individual can heroically decide to die for a hopeless cause—a nation must not. A nation, once resistance has become intellectually inconceivable (because theoretically hopeless), *must* surrender. And a mutually guaranteed atomic disarmament of both sides makes West European resistance against a Soviet attack theoretically hopeless and, therefore, intellectually inconceivable.

True, if the western nations are so anxious to be freed of their atomic apprehensions, they should be willing to pay the price; and the price can be exactly stated: it would have to be the willingness of the western nations to expand, in exchange for atomic disarmament, their "conventional" armament at least *seven times over*. To be precise: The western nations would have to keep, *from now on till the end of communist time,* a minimum of 90 to 100 battle-ready divisions in Europe, in fighting posture, *plus* a minimum of another 200 divisions to reach the battlefield one month after the fight began. In other words, the Red Army *can* be checked in Europe, even after an effective atomic disarmament, provided the NATO nations are willing to increase their current "conventional" military establishments *immediately* from five to fifteen times their present size.

But democracies cannot shoulder that kind of permanent mobilization, for whole generations, and yet remain democracies. Neither free economies nor free cultures can survive, *in peacetime* and for generations, the sort of total mobilization the Soviet Union thrives on. Nor is this all. Behind the Soviet Union, the enormous figure of Red China is rising to military power. The 82 battle-ready and the 400 reserve divisions of the Soviet Union may be augmented, in a few years of communist planning in China (a country of 600 million people), to 200 or 300 battle-ready and 800 to 1,200 reserve divisions. Should that ever happen, the western countries would be no match, even if they were mobilized to the hilt permanently and without further concern about the nature of their society. The essence of the problem is inescapably clear: The West has chances to survive *only* if it employs its strongest *technological* potentials. This means atomic power. If the West were ever to renounce the use of nuclear weapons, it must surrender. Its man power is no match.

This is the inherent logic of the case. The natural scientists who recommend the renunciation of atomic weapons are still committed, as scientists, to reason within the bounds of inherent logic. Those who do, and still insist on their recommendation, have honestly arrived at the conclusion that the West must surrender to communism. And there are in Germany respectable people who, though they hate communism, frankly advocate Germany's surrender to the Soviets, if the only alternative is the employment of atomic weapons.

I do not agree with these men; in fact, I consider them foes of their and my civilization. Yet I consider them *honest* foes. But for the irresolute, incoherent opponents of "atomic death"—those ludicrous men who would "rather be rich and healthy than poor and sick"—I feel nothing but contempt. These Germans are trying a con game against history. They will fail, of course; and, in losing their freedom, they will have lost even their claim to be free. They deserve nothing but our contempt and the Soviet boot on their necks.

CHAPTER SEVEN

The Nature of Communism

THE West's undoing is its craving for peace. And perhaps it will prove impossible for a Christian civilization to live through an age that has made the readiness to fight one war after another the precondition of survival. If so, the West is doomed. For the preposterous essence of the West's conflict with communism—so preposterous that hardly anyone dares face the fact—is that communism *thrives* on peace, *wants* peace, *triumphs* in peace. No distress in history can compare with this. The evil spreads lustily in the very state all western religions have taught us to deem blessed and to pray for—peace.

Yet the West, to survive at all, must be *believably* willing to wage war.

To be merely *prepared* for war will not be enough: as long as communism can reasonably assume that, short of an "ultimate" provocation (which a coolly maneuvering Kremlin will of course painstakingly avoid), even a militarily potent West would not resort to its dreadfully potent nuclear weapons, so long the advance of communism will proceed in spite of western technical readiness.

Nor would even *willingness* to fight suffice: judging by the

West's uninterrupted record of past revulsion from conflict, communism may make the fatal mistake of misjudging a sudden western resolution as a mere bluff; and thus, quite unwittingly, stumble into the very provocation that may release the dreaded world-wide destruction.

It seems imperative that the West become *believably* willing to fight a war if there is no other way to stop and turn back the advance of communism (to carry a big stick *and* to talk loudly), so that not even the contemptuous leaders of world communism can doubt any longer that the West is in earnest. There is no other hope to avoid an absurd—because utterly hopeless—war with which even a pacifist America would finally respond, in a last youthful outbreak of rage, to insufferable communist expansion.

How could the biblical promise have become so perverted that decency suffocates in peace and evil thrives on it? But it seems to me that not *peace* has been corrupted but *our concept* of peace. A tired age, given to inferior pleasures and an abstruse overestimation of physiology, speaks of peace when it merely means a state of relative painlessness; while nobler centuries, when they prayed for peace, were praying for an elated state of human brotherhood.

And it is one of the shameful paradoxes of this age that the atheistic Communists have retained a dedicated comprehension of peace, even though in a perverted negation, which the devout pretenders of faith have lost. To the Communists, what we call "peace" is a phase of their permanent war against the western concept of man—a phase during which, for a fleeting moment in history, political weapons may prove more effective in establishing the communist concept of brotherhood than the employment of armored divisions and intercontinental missiles. But what they want —and they want it with a fervor the lukewarm cannot even sense— remains to them incomparably more important than what we call peace. This is why they are winning. For those who want something *more* fervently than peace must always win over those who want painlessness above everything else.

Forty-one years ago a ludicrously small group of Russian revolutionaries in exile took advantage of a historical fluke and grabbed power in Moscow. The historical fluke, itself quite accidental and avoidable, has since grown into one of those formative experiences of mankind that separate one millennium from the next. In my lifetime the somewhat pathetic Bolshevik establishment in Moscow and St. Petersburg of 1917 has expanded into an empire of a magnitude and an explosiveness without comparison in history. One billion human beings are directly or indirectly ruled by communism; another billion has been "neutralized" into impotence; and the remaining 500 million free men live in panic.

Whatever the West undertook to check the frightening expansion of communism throughout these forty-one years has always gone wrong. Is this sorcery, is it a curse? Is it a continuous ghastly accident that, for forty-one years, western policies keep failing? But had we just erred, the laws of probability would require that, over such a long period of time, the white balls of chance match the black balls of defeat. Yet there was, since 1917, not a single significant period of western victories over communism; constantly shaken by its own recurring internal fevers, it also kept constantly spreading around the world.

Is it, as the Marxians claim, "the meaning of history" that communism must inherit the earth? But every human mind, once it has emerged from immaturity, is convinced that history has no such meaning; that communism is not the product of either "inexorable laws of history" or of "inescapable tensions within capitalism"; that communism is winning because of our own weaknesses rather than its inherent strength. And underneath the air of serenity all western officialdom likes to put on, there is a consensus of minds: the West has failed in forty-one years because the West has never understood the nature of communism.

The intellectual acumen, the toil of perpetual rationalization, the research efforts of communism, are putting to shame every enterprise that is being undertaken on our side to study communism. And the reason for this disproportion is obvious. The West tends to live on a capital of political wisdom that has been accumulated in a magnificent past. Perhaps not the most creative but certainly the wisest men of western civilization were those who, almost with a tired resignation, and always with a civilized skepticism, understood that there was no new idea to be thought, simply because "everything under the sun" had already been noticed by a great past. Goethe, at the height of his perception, advised: *"Was du ererbt von deinen Vätern, erwirb es, um es zu besitzen"* ("What you have inherited from your fathers, take hold of it so that you may own it"). Our world has been pre-empted by our ancestors, who knew everything; and the mark of the mature man, in the West, is to realize his position of debt. This is the mood of western civilization. This is the prevailing attitude even of scientists (once they have grown up). It certainly is the temper of our great religions.

Communism has been the fundamental break with the unchangeably conservative spirit of western civilization. And the failure, even refusal, to recognize this momentous fact explains to me the impotence of anti-communism. The anti-Communists—and the learned scholars among them more than anybody else—are satisfied with the official communist rationale: that communism is the application of certain utopian ideas certain men such as Marx, Engels, and Lenin have put on paper between 1840 and 1920. The scientific research of anti-communism begins and ends with a critical exegesis of these scriptures. But there could be no more disastrous mistake. The immense force that flows from the center of the communist formation does not spring from the scheming thoughts of accidental men.

It is what it is—namely, a historical hurricane of unparalleled sweep—because communism came into our world as the conclusive, the final synthesis of all heretical tendencies that have pervaded western civilization for many centuries. Communism is the culminating *hubris* of Promethean man who reaches out for the world and means to remake creation. It is scientism gone political.

Anti-Communists who hope to reduce communism by belittling it are cruelly mistaken. Communism *wants* to be belittled. Just as the devil gets men when they no longer believe in his existence, just so communism profits immeasurably from the self-conceit of its opponents who make it appear as a fallacious obsession of perverts and fools. Communism is neither an obsession nor fallacious. It is an ultimate challenge in history, one of the great tremors in human experience that compel man to revaluate his total civilization—an event of formative magnitude.

This, it seems to me, is why for the last forty-one years communism has attracted the emotional allegiance of the world's insecure and doubting intellectuals—even of those who, quite honestly, in their conscious minds oppose it. We like to ridicule these intellectuals, and nothing is easier. But underneath all derision there remains a tense curiosity: Why is it that the congenitally sensitive, the professionally learned, the nervously creative in all the world, since 1917, fall so much heavier for communism than any other segment of our society?

It is because communism is a mutation of the *mind,* a *spiritual* venture, the synthesis of several centuries of all the heretical but *intellectual* unrest in history. The intellectuals are fascinated by communism because its fascination *is* intellectual. Never and nowhere, of course, did the workers—the appointed bearers of history's communist charisma—form the nucleus of a Communist party and they really have no business to: The "masses" are as little the apostles, the teachers, and the disciples of communism as they have been the apostles of religious crusades, the teachers of the Reformation, the disciples of Enlightenment.

In communism, all the bold insolences of the human mind—insolences that kept accumulating, seductively, for hundreds of years —have achieved a unity of purpose and the *élan* of action. Man (and that means "man, thinking") is on the move to control nature, his own emotions, matter, mind, fate, birth, death, God. In communism—and this is why two out of three nuclear physicists have at one time or another felt its pull—in communism "the absurd and magnificent simplificators," the modern scientists, hear a social response to their absurd and magnificent simplifications. In communism the disturbed—and thus creative—artists see a social reflection of their own revolt, growing for centuries, against what they are by compulsion driven to consider the chains of "conventional objective aesthetics" (even though the Kremlin is stacked with atrociously conventional art). In communism the sensitive, the learned, the nervously creative find a common denominator of all Promethean cravings that have plagued, for centuries, the tense nerves, the tormented ambitions, the dissatisfied minds.

To recognize communism as the final phase of scientism, rather than a special system of social power, is crucial. Our civilization could never have been endangered by the crude proposition to replace public opinion with secret police, free unions with labor camps, ballots with bullets. Were communism really nothing but a system of controlled social violence, our world would have proved invulnerable; and communism would have drowned, a short while after it came into accidental power in Russia, in a flood of universal revulsion. But communism, in forty-one years, has grown from a slightly funny conspiracy of Russian intellectuals, pompous and unattractive exiles, into an ultimate challenge to western civilization. Such triumphs, achieved at such fantastic pace, do not accrue to a mere clique of Machiavellian operators. This global upheaval of unprecedented magnitude must have causes of comparable seriousness; for man's destiny is not governed by clumsiness and moronic farce. The true, the serious cause of communism's career will be visible to those who have the courage to look beyond the banal: scientism, for centuries rising underneath western civilization, at last achieves in communism social effectiveness.

Only when this clarification has been gained, the reality of the last four decades begins to make sense. It becomes clear, for instance, why the humanly decent liberal of our time—a genuine product of the nineteenth century—is so pathetically disarmed by communism. When that liberal swears that he finds communism in power detestable, he is sincere. And yet, he will each time, regardless of his preceding experiences, permit communism to mobilize his, the liberal's, potentials in the service of whatever happens to be communism's cause at the moment. Why? Because—audible to those who are attuned to the wave length of scientism—the leitmotiv of communism keeps floating above all repulsive statics of the moment, above all the noise of purges and the cries of the tortured: Man is about to conquer his fate, to control creation, to

manage all life, and God, through applied science! Given the omnipotence of science, everything seems so delectably manageable,
corrigible, perfectible. It is this heretical readiness of modern
man to put his trust in science that constitutes the persuasiveness
and the power of communism.

And this is also the element of truth within the fundamental
communist stratagem of popular front. No matter how profoundly
the upright liberal and the decent socialist deny that the end justifies the means—they all, in their hearts, do believe in the same
ends: that man will remake creation, that science will redeem man.
The Promethean heresy has formed them all; and the popular front
is the logical outgrowth of this common heritage. The communist
end is the ultimate triumph of the same scientism that has shaped
the "optimistic" world view of the eighteenth and the nineteenth
centuries—the centuries that have begotten the upright liberals and
the decent socialists. Their desperate and absolutely sincere efforts
to escape the communist embrace are as moving as they are
futile. In the end, communism will get them; for communism is the
only potent and the only legitimate administrator of the heretical
heritage of centuries.

The West's incapacity to comprehend the nature of communism
shows in the pet argument of its ideologues: that communism cannot begin to match the efficiency and the wealth of capitalist production. And, indeed, it cannot. It is quite—though by no means
entirely—safe to predict that the Soviet Union will not for a long
time match America's record of having reduced the physical squalor
of labor and having raised the body comforts of the individual
above the dreams of a few decades ago. And what does this prove?
It proves a lot to those who happen to agree with the dedication
of *capitalist* productivity—and nothing at all to those who happen
to agree with the dedication of *communism*.

If a man is motivated by a desire to augment the comforts and
the self-determination of the individual, he will not be a Communist to begin with; nor will be anybody who is seriously impressed
by productivity records. The point is—and so few defenders of
capitalism grasp that point—that *any* social system can perform

satisfactorily *within the motivational coordinates of that system.* If capitalism could not increase the wealth and the comforts of the individual, it would be doomed; for in that case it would not have fulfilled its essential promise. Communism would be doomed if it failed, not to increase the individual's wealth and comforts, but to increase and widen its own power. For these are the motivational coordinates of communism—to develop the power of the monolithic state to control the fate of individuals, to develop the powers of scientism "to control nature." Its inability to produce consumer goods in maximum quantities and at minimum prices will make communism collapse? This is like saying that the wolf's inability to fly will result in the extinction of the breed.

Communism would tend to destroy itself, a victim of self-produced contradictions, only if communism were compelled to *reduce* the powers of its political machine; and, above all, if it were constantly compelled to *give up* territory it had already conquered. But this, surely, is not what the West's habitual prophets of communist doom have in mind. Not even by the widest possible stretch of their imagination could George F. Kennan and Walter Lippmann claim that there has been, since 1917, a *trace* of such a contraction in communism's record; or that there is a trace of rational justification in expecting such contraction in the future. What Kennan and Lippmann mean to say is, on the contrary, that communism will die because it cannot perform as capitalism does.

Yet communism evolves according to its own rules of growth, and it invades every area of western weakness. It all started with Lenin's awkward *coup d'état* on November 7, 1917; and a single company of soldiers could have stamped out the fire—if the Kerenski government had had a reliable company of soldiers left and the decisiveness to use it. One year later—and it is a measure of Winston Churchill's clairvoyance that he knew it even then, in 1918, as the only statesman in the West—a competently deployed regiment would have overthrown a slightly hardened Bolshevik government. (Lenin, by the way, knew it, too.) In 1922, after the Bolsheviks had burned their fingers in Poland, a division intelligently employed in the still fluid vastness of the Soviet Union would have sufficed to overthrow Lenin. In 1943 even a German army led by a maniac would have conquered the Soviet Union, had not the West given Stalin—for perfectly justifiable reasons of self-defense—decisive military aid. In 1945 the victorious Allied armies in Europe would have compelled communism to comply with western demands had not the uneducated pacifism of our generals made "the winning of the war against Hitler" its *only* objective. By 1945, at any rate, it would already have taken gigantic armies to force communism into retreat, contraction, and final defeat. Next time it will take the total powers of the entire free world.

The point is the constantly rising magnitude of power needed to defeat communism: the investment grows in geometrical proportions to the time lost since the preceding chance was wasted. This, too, is in the nature of communism: yesterday's crisis becomes a source of its additional strength today—and for the perfectly natural reason that, like any other system of pragmatic power, every crisis withstood adds immensely to its self-assuredness. In this respect, too, the West has never comprehended the nature of communism. It always felt that communism, somehow, remains an improvisation of blundering fools—while it is in truth a social system that has made practicality and competence the yardsticks of performance. Indeed, because it *is* scientism triumphant, communism is, much more genuinely than free society, tied to practicality and competence. In a free society man may still dream even foolish dreams and, no matter what the rationale of capitalism may proclaim, competence remains one of the lesser values in a free society. But there is no higher test in communism than effectiveness.

And, above all, the West has never understood that communism, which is determined to conquer the world, is also determined to avoid war. This, by an incorrigible quirk of the western mind, is considered incompatible: the two determinations are thought to be mutually exclusive. In truth, the two determinations are interdependent and inseparable: *in order to* conquer the world, communism is determined to avoid war. But this truth is so openly displayed that it remains invisible like Edgar Allan Poe's celebrated purloined letter. Western commentators, statesmen, and preachers will forever debate war and peace, armament and disarmament, conflagration or coexistence. The West is obsessed with the only peril it feels viscerally—the peril of war. And this is the root of western futility.

Ever since Hiroshima, the horror of cosmic destruction has paralyzed the nerves, the appetites, and the brains of the West. That mushroom proved poisonous for its growers. During the years the United States remained in monopolistic possession of atomic power, the years of the "Baruch Plan," the United States was terrorized by its own seeming omnipotence into a state of obsessive humility: the very fact that it held in its hands the ghastly atomic bomb made it rigidly motionless. For while a youngster does not mind an occasional brawl, a sensible giant, armed with nothing but the ultimate punch, recoils from so much as touching anybody.

And then the United States suddenly realized that it had no longer an atomic monopoly; at which moment paralyzing humility turned into paralyzing fright. The question was no longer whether an omnipotent United States could *afford* to move; now the question was whether it could *dare* to. War, in Eisenhower's word, became "unthinkable." Yet, for this very reason, war became the tortured, the eternal, the omnipresent preoccupation of the West: for the last ten years the West has thought of nothing but the "unthinkable." And it occurred to no one to ask whether war was indeed the decisive problem.

Is it? War, the avoidance of war, armament, coexistence—are these the problems?

The answer, again, is tied to a correct comprehension of the nature of communism. Never since 1917 has the West ceased to interpret the methods as well as the goals of communism in its own, in western, terms. The most celebrated commentators of the West (Mr. Lippmann, for instance) have always tried to describe the ambitions of Soviet foreign policy in a "historical continuum." This school of western interpreters, employed and honored by the West for comprehending communism, has never conceded that, with communism, something unprecedented, altogether alien to western experience, has entered history.

The Lippmann school was, on the contrary, always busy with recalling historical precedents: how *this* Soviet move was comparable to *that* Czarist maneuver of 1856; how *that* apparent goal of Soviet policy dovetailed with *this* ancient ambition of Russian czars (for instance, the ubiquitous reference to the age-old Russian dream of warm-water ports); how the would-be architects of a balance of power in 1959 might learn from the experience of balance-of-power architects at the Congress of Vienna in 1815; how the diaries of the ambassadors our grandfathers had sent to Moscow still read as if they were written today by C.I.A. agents. It is always the same basic axiom, the same intent: communism has to be shown, not as an altogether alien phenomenon, but as a political growth that can be treated with the routine of the past, the expertise of diplomacy, the learning of the genteel historian. In other words, by Mr. Lippmann.

The active politicians were by no means more realistic than the mere commentators. All responsible politicians of the period (with, perhaps, the sole exception of Winston Churchill) proceeded from the assumption that the Soviet leaders, after all, were politicians themselves. Which in the minds, the philosophy, the language of western politicians simply meant that everybody is seeking a deal, a compromise, job security, comfort; or else, he may be seeking a fracas. But in any case the Soviet politicians—"when all is said and done," or, "in the last analysis"—are "just like us." Every single mistake Wilson, Roosevelt, Truman, and Eisenhower have committed is due to this inextricable conviction of western politicians: that Communists, too, are politicians.

Mr. James Byrnes, who is a deeply conservative gentleman, was as Secretary of State not one iota better or wiser than Mr. Dean Acheson. In the crucial postwar years, when the world was molded after the Soviet image, this impeccable conservative and unimpeachable patriot was much more influential in shaping that world than his President, Harry S. Truman. And any future historian, though it may hurt him to arrive at this conclusion, will find that the foreign policy of Mr. Byrnes was the beginning and prototype of the final decline of the West.

He did not know what it was all about? But this is precisely the point. Indeed, Mr. Byrnes did not know what it was all about. His entire experience at home—and it was a long and honorable experience—had conditioned him: Mr. Byrnes, who never in his life had suffered from uncertainties, was certain he was dealing with politicians. He had learned that a politician must sit down with his opponents around that famous table and fight, tooth and claw, for a bargain. Politics, to him, was the art of compromise—nothing else. He, the county judge who had risen high in the world, knew every bit there was to know about county politics. That fellow Molotov—and no one was going to fool Judge Byrnes—was exactly like that ornery fellow Jones he had had to wrestle in South Carolina, way back in 1908; and Judge Byrnes, by golly, knew how to handle Jones. And so there went eastern Europe; and then chunks of Asia; and then Central Europe; and a lot of other "real estate." Molotov, you see, was *not* like Jones; but how was Judge Byrnes to know?

If it were useful to focus on a central reason for the creeping malaise of the West, one could choose this: that the West, particularly its Anglo-Saxon epitome, has an uncontrollable animosity against abstract concepts. But communism cannot be understood in any other symbol language. The Anglo-Saxon compulsion to interpret everything by precedent accounts for much of the goodness and humanity of life in the Anglo-Saxon world; but it also accounts, I am afraid, for its suicidal behavior. The world has never been really moved by precedent. It has always been moved by abstract concepts. Never was history what *happened* to people; it was always what the flame of ideas made them *do*.

The Anglo-Saxon world could afford, for a few centuries, to abhor abstractions simply because it was so securely *built* on some very noble ones—abstractions accumulated over preceding centuries. And then, for a moment in history—and perhaps it was a peculiarly pleasant, livable moment—the Anglo-Saxon civilization could act as if nothing mattered but reality and precedent. But it was caught short when the next big tremor came in history. Confronted with a generic idea system as magnetic as communism, the precedent is a joke and the "realist" a dunce. This system, above anything else, must be understood—not as replica of the West, but in its own conceptual terms.

To be sure, these terms are not those of the communist textbooks. The communist homilies of self-interpretation—"dictatorship of the proletariat," "internationalism," "the withering of the state"— may be subjectively honest, and the Communists may still believe that they believe in them; but they are, in truth, irrelevant. Communism, in relevant truth, is a tremendous drive to unify the whole world under the management of applied science.

Unless this is understood, nothing is understood about communism. Its essence is modern man's craving "to control nature," including himself. The more juvenile, ambitious, "backward" a nation, the more tempted it will be by the promise of communism; by the same token, the more juvenile, ambitious, "progressive" an individual's mind, the less can he resist. This has nothing to do with formal membership in the Communist party or even conscious sympathies with communism. Mr. Nehru, for instance—whose contributions to the communization of the world cannot be overrated —is an honest Socialist and despises several communist dogmas as well as all of India's Communist party. Mr. George F. Kennan, whose part in weakening the western position is second to none in the United States, is altogether an honest foe of communism. What makes them both, Nehru and Kennan, nonetheless perform to the demonstrable profit of communism, is their invincible ignorance about the nature of man: they honestly believe that man, if only he put his whole trust in science, could approach perfection. And once you believe that, you are caught in quicksand. Nehru and Kennan are of course no Communists; but they have no sufficient reason *not* to be Communists. And so, unwittingly and unwillingly, they will serve what they subjectively consider to be their enemy.

I remember a cartoon that was published in 1920 in the leftist press all around the world. A huge General Foch—at that time the symbol of "imperialist" might—asks a tiny Lenin: "And with what armies do you propose to win?" And Lenin answers: "With yours." This, indeed, has always been the essence of communist strategy.

It explains, in a nutshell, why communism hopes to conquer the world by *avoiding* war.

Communism, the extreme form of scientism, is "progressive" to the point of banality, "optimistic" to the point of childishness, sold on the future to the point of trance. "Progressive," "optimistic," future-bent, communism would of course also accept war if its final triumph *depended* on war. But there is overwhelming evidence that the world's *repugnance* against war assures the triumph of communism. While the world was still at war with Hitler, communism trembled; but when the world returned to its idea of peace, the Soviet Union began to grow from a nation of 200 million to a world empire of a billion people, in twelve years of peace. Consequently, the communist strategy is to preserve peace—but to preserve it in such a fashion that the West (in order to "avoid" a war which the Soviet Union wants even less than the West) remains willing to pay the Soviet Union most heavily for what the Soviet Union most desires itself.

This strategic goal communism is achieving with an accuracy unmatched in history. Since 1946 the West thinks of nothing and speaks of nothing but "the avoidance of war" with the Soviet Union. Yet the survival of the West, the defeat of communism, requires a western strategy that, by confronting the Soviet Union with steadily increasing pressure, including the possibility of conflagration, would roll back communism.

Because communism *is* scientism—"progressive," "optimistic," future-bent—it has not the slightest taste for *Weltuntergang:* very much unlike Hitler, Khrushchev would not know what *Götterdämmerung* is about. Communists have never felt the secret ecstasies of Black Masses and they feel no temptation of death. Communists crave a *predictable* world, as all scientists do, and they know that military conflagrations are unpredictable. A world *afraid* of war (and this is predictable) will yield; but a world *at war* may erase itself—may erase communism in power and all communist claims on the future.

If the Communists can help it, there will be no war—not because Communists respect the sanctity of human life (they feel about human life the way botanists feel about the life of plants), but because they respect the promissory notes they believe to be holding on history. Unlike Hitler, who would have insisted on the romantic splendor of war even if the whole world would have meekly surrendered to him, communism—the epitome of nineteenth-century rationalism, materialism, progressivism, secularism, scientism—has not the slightest romantic desire for war's glories. It hopes to get the world *without* war. It sees in a general war its only historical risk.

From this follows that the only rational strategy of the West would be to keep communism constantly *confronted* with that risk. There is no other conceivable method of impressing communism. In its forty-one years of imperial policies, communism has each time reliably responded to a serious danger of conflagration—from Lenin's near capitulation at Brest Litovsk in 1918 to the NEP that followed the communist defeat in Poland; to the treaty Stalin signed with Hitler in 1939 to keep the Soviet Union safely out of Hitler's path; to the hasty Soviet retreat in Iran, a few years ago, when it looked as if the Anglo-American forces meant business in that area. Paradoxically, communism is under far less compulsion to "save face" than a democracy: it depends far less on domestic public opinion (which may turn against a free government that has "lost face") and, above all, it has a perfect rationale for retreat.

Those who firmly believe that history, in the end, must honor its own "mandate," can withdraw with much greater elasticity and far less shattered self-confidence than those who suspect that history consists of unrepeatable chances. As long as the Communists retain the innermost center of their power—Russia proper—there are no limits to the withdrawals they would be willing to undertake if the only other alternative would be a war they must lose.

Again, the forty-one years of Bolshevik history present consistent evidence. When world revolution seemed to have been halted in Germany, in 1923, Lenin reversed his policy and executed an almost complete communist withdrawal from Europe for several years. When Hitler proved his determination to wage war, Stalin was willing to prefer the most inconceivable humiliations to making a stand; and, in fact, he remained throughout the war constantly ready to sign a separate deal with Nazi Germany. From 1941 to 1945, the United States government, on the basis of reliable secret reports, lived constantly with the nightmare of a sudden Soviet-Nazi understanding. (What prevented it was not Stalin's conscience but Hitler's stubborn romanticism.)

This, then, is the crucial nexus of world strategy which the West has not even begun to understand: (1) Communism is determined to avoid a general war at all costs, short of surrendering its innermost center of power, Russia; (2) communism will keep the world "on the brink" of war so long as the West's horror of war yields dividends; (3) communism is conditioned by its own tradition to withdraw, with a perfect rationale, each time it encounters *believaable* western determination to wage war; (4) communism, if it does *not* encounter that determination, advances with the inexorable and merciless certainty of a force that pervades any vacuum.

This, of course, does not mean that communism would not start a military invasion the moment it has been proved (at least to the satisfaction of the Communists) that the opponent has no power or no intention to resist. From the attack in Poland in 1920—which the Bolsheviks *themselves* proudly called "Red Imperialism"—to the desecration of dead Poland in 1939 and the attack on Finland in 1940, to the intervention in Hungary in 1956 (once it was clear that the United States would *not* intervene), the communist record is unequivocal: Every indefensible or undefended area of the world will be invaded by the Soviets. But the opponent's believable determination, not only to defend himself, but to press against the outlying Soviet positions, will be elastically evaded.

This type of strategy would not have achieved the staggering successes that communism can show for the last decade had not a peculiar axiom taken possession of the western mind: that "armament races" of necessity lead to wars. It is one of the clichés that are never analyzed, never proved, never disproved. Snow is white; twice two makes four; armament races lead to wars. But they do not—demonstrably. There is no armament race in history that has ever led to a war. On the contrary, most wars of the last several centuries broke out because one side was informed, or assumed, that the other side was *not* adequately armed.

This is true of all Napoleonic wars, of the Prussian war against Denmark in 1864, of the Prussian war against Austria-Hungary in 1866, of the Prussian war against France in 1870, of the Balkan wars in the first decade of this century, of World War I and World War II. Every one of these wars broke out, according to mountains of documentation, because one side thought the other inadequately armed; because, in other words, there had been *no* armament race. There is not a single known case of a war that started *because* of an armament race; but there are several recorded cases of war intentions that aborted because the other side was arming to the hilt.

In the face of such an unequivocal record, the West remains terrified by "armament races." The better educated a western citizen, the more he trembles: recent public polls in the United States, Great Britain, and Germany agree that college graduates outtremble graduates of public school by almost 2 to 1. The men of Yale, Harvard, Oxford, Cambridge, Heidelberg, and Göttingen are every bit as opposed to the armament of the West as the illiterates of Asia and Africa (who, at least, have the excuse that they had heard nothing about European history).

The addiction of the educated West to inane and disproved catch phrases has nothing to do with the morally informed and coherent position of non-violence. Those who knowingly prefer the martyrdom of surrender to the pain of armed resistance against communism are wrong, I think. But they are intellectually and morally respectable—so long, that is, as they do not claim that man can have both, non-violence *and* comforts. Gandhi was never that cheap. Even though he was recommending non-violence against a highly civilized foe—one who finally preferred his own surrender to the effective use of his vastly superior force—Gandhi knew and preached that he who renounces violence must be prepared to *suffer* for his principle. Gandhi, even in an easy struggle with Christian England, never promised the pleasures of peaceful victory. He promised nothing but the discipline of jail, the pangs of hunger, the school of fasts, the sorrow of pain.

Gandhi would have despised the most audible spokesmen of contemporary western pacifism who argue from these two positions: (1) While it was moral and reasonable to resist and to overthrow nazism by getting more than 50 million people killed and more than 100 million people maimed, it would be immoral and unreasonable to prevail over communism by getting *much* more than 50 million people killed and *much* more than a 100 million people maimed. (2) While it was moral and reasonable to fight nazism with "jelly bombs," "blockbusters," and the mass burning of civilians in "saturation raids," it would be immoral and unreasonable to fight communism with nuclear weapons. This kind of dialectics, so significant for Mr. Nehru, the western intellectual who succeeded India's great religious leader, would have been hateful to Gandhi.

In truth, as always in climactic moments of history, an elementary moral decision will determine our conduct. Two morally tenable positions seek to persuade the West—a determination to fight evil, and a determination to suffer rather than to use violence. But these two determined groups of men are, between them, a small minority within western society. The overwhelming majority—in Germany no less than in the United States—still try to avoid *any* decision. They pride themselves on being the "non-neurotic," the well-adjusted kind of people; and adjustment to life, it seems, is nowadays the insistence on the pleasures of the moment, Pollyanna's serene ignorance of tomorrow's troubles.

And perhaps this is just as well. The human race would have worried itself off the planet long ago had not the normal person devoted but a casual moment's thought to the "big issues" of his day. But the normal person's talent for satisfaction with fleeting bliss is one thing—his decay into lukewarm corruption quite another. Surely not everybody who fails to see the urgency of decision is one of the lukewarm who, as the Apocalypse promised, "will be spewn out of His mouth." In this age of mass communications man is so appallingly under-informed (because he is so appallingly over-entertained) that he can justly claim invincible and therefore pardonable ignorance. But no such claim will be granted the small elite who, in this mass age more than in any openly aristocratic period of the past, constitutes the working organism of public opinion.

I am speaking of the 2 or 3 million men and women in America, the 600 thousand people in Germany, whose business it is to guide the nation, to think for it, to worry about a future which massman is congenitally unable to perceive. This modern elite is neither appointed nor predestined by birth. It is an elite: it unmistakably performs an elite's functions. It sets the tastes, formalizes the manners, prejudges the trends, shapes the notions, articulates the ideas, determines the emotional climate, pressures the policies of a nation. It is, in fact, the tightest-woven, the most powerful elite of all history. You are never formally initiated to this elite; but you know perfectly well whether or not you belong.

When this elite will have to give a final account of itself (and the day may come soon), it will be deeply shocked by the long list of its failures. And the worst will be its irresponsibility—an irresponsibility which begins with the characteristic denial of being what it is: an elite. When nobility was the openly privileged segment of western society, neither the nobleman nor his inferior could have doubted, or even questioned, who the elite was. Anonymity was not among the nobleman's privileges. It emerged in our time and it falsifies the personal data of responsibility. Today's elite can deny its identity. This is its constant temptation, this its ultimate sin.

The intellectual who belittles his specific weight in society; the college professor who coquettishly complains about his lack of social effectiveness; the businessman who makes blistering remarks about "labor-controlled politics"; the labor leader who chants his ritualistic laments about "business-controlled politics"; the artist who with masochistic delight points to his utter irrelevance; the minister who deplores society's rejection of church guidance—they all merely offer alibis for the constant dereliction of the elite to which they all belong. Our society is putty in their hands. They rule. Through thousands of tiny channels, over thousands of invisible transmission belts, the images and values and judgments of this elite guide the otherwise shapeless and undirected mass. To claim its own unimportance is the final measure of this modern elite's irresponsibility.

What the elite says today, in the curious conformism that characterizes tightly coherent groups, is *vox populi* tomorrow. But time has shrunk faster than space, and no man can hide—neither in ignorance nor in anonymity. A few short years may be left for Germany, for the United States, for the West, to arrive at a responsible decision. Communism has advanced beyond the pace of any known conqueror. Communism is in earnest; but is, for instance, the Reverend Dr. John C. Bennett? To him I dedicate my next chapter.

CHAPTER EIGHT

Pious Undoing

~~~~~~

THE Eighth Assembly of the Congregational Council, gathered in Hartford, Connecticut, was especially distinguished; for the main speaker was to be the Reverend Dr. John C. Bennett, dean of faculty at Union Theological Seminary in New York, which for the last twenty years has enjoyed a world-wide reputation as the center of Dr. Reinhold Niebuhr's profound re-examination of the Protestant posture in time and society. Niebuhr's neo-orthodoxy remains a majestic witness to the great spiritual reconsideration which, vehemently responding to the eruption of bestialism in the thirties, looked for a while just as significant for the fate of man as did, on the other side, nazism and communism. And when Dr. Niebuhr retired from active leadership of Union Theological Seminary, Dr. John C. Bennett seemed altogether worthy of the tremendous successorship.

What, then, did Dr. John C. Bennett have to say to the Eighth Assembly of the International Congregational Council in July 1958? He spoke of his generation's main concern, communism. And this is what he said:

"The churches should be sophisticated about communism . . . They should not take so rigid an attitude that they cannot see that second-generation Communists in Russia may become concerned chiefly about building their own country, that they may become less fanatical believers in their ideology, and less of a threat to their neighbors." The time has come for the churches, concluded Dr. Bennett, to modify their views about survival, communism, and the cold war. In a subsequent press interview—and one must keep in mind that Dr. Bennett is today perhaps the decisive intellectual authority of American Protestantism—he interpreted his broad statements at the Assembly. Two developments, he suggested specifically, make a re-examination of the churches' "inflexible attitude toward communism" imperative.

First, there was "the arrival of the missile age." And second, Dr. Bennett was impressed by the Soviet Union's "apparent change of emphasis from ideological fanaticism to a genuine self-improvement." What is awaiting us, Dr. Bennett continued, is a period of coexistence, interaction, and competition—all of which "will modify the West and the Soviet Union in as yet unknown ways." "We need a shift, and not a reversal, in priorities," said Dr. Bennett. "We should put the prevention of general war ahead of the defeat of communist power, and a real acceptance of coexistence ahead of a victory in the cold war." In such an ambiguous situation, the churches stand "as a bridge between the universal and the particular."

Not in years, and not even in Germany, have I seen a more devastating summary of all the defeatist accents that prevail in the western position. This was no glad-handing politician, no professional Pollyanna, no reckless demagogue who speaks after the mouth of dumb masses. This was one of the most learned theologians of world Protestantism, the successor to Professor Reinhold Niebuhr in an almost apostolic mission to restore, for a vulgarly "optimistic" age, the Christian sense of tragedy. This was one of the few voices in Christendom that were really "called."

We must consider Dr. Bennett's thesis as seriously as befits the speaker; and let us not stop too long to review that gamy Madison Avenue tone in the opening fanfare—"the churches should be *sophisticated* about communism." (In another context, a critic of this age may secure some gruesome results from assessing the phenomenon of a dean of faculty at Union Theological Seminary who applies the jargon of cigarette advertising—"sophisticated"— to the most meaningful moral decision of his time.) Dr. Bennett is an authoritative spokesman for the Federal Council of Christian Churches in America—not just the mightiest structure in American Protestantism, but without much doubt one of the three or four most powerful political lobbies in the nation.

For the last several decades the Federal Council of Christian Churches, a kind of holding company that combines the many denominations of American Protestantism into a unified center of immense power, has sought to minimize the differences between those denominations by stressing the elements of common accept- ance. And in this noble endeavor two ways would have been possi- ble: The Federal Council could have emphasized the unifying fervor of dedication to the common first principles of the Christian creed and the mystical source of them all; or the Federal Council could have stressed the modish aberration they all were afflicted by —a consuming concern of the churches with various aspects of social reform ("the social gospel"). The Federal Council chose the latter course.

It would take a magnificent memory to recall an occasion when the Federal Council turned its attention to the true problems of religious concern: the subjects of Christian dogma, of man's inner relations to his God. But the records are filled to the brim with a documentation of the Federal Council's unending fascination with economics (viewed usually with unmistakable New Deal bias), with problems of labor and race, and, above all, with the concerns of United States foreign policy. All these problems, indubitably, bear on man's religious nature and need informed religious advice—just as it would not hurt the President's Advisory Board on Economics, or labor unions, or foreign-policy committees, to seek for the guid- ance of religious thought. However, it would not occur to anybody to expect such secular task forces to perform as organs of churches. And yet the Federal Council has consistently performed as a body of secular dedications.

In particular, the Federal Council, for the last fifteen years, has acted as the clearinghouse of American pacifism. Though all churches (with a few non-conformist exceptions) have solved the problem of Christianity's position to just wars many centuries ago, the clergy of all denominations seem to suffer from that ancient problem in every generation anew. And there was hardly a generation so profoundly bothered by it as ours. It seems that with the emergence of communism as a militarily potent world power the deep pacifist concern of many churchmen has merged with their special kind of "troubled conscience"—the incessant disturbance of certain clerics with the "social injustice" allegedly inherent in the capitalist system. And this mixture—the pacifist temptation and the social irritation with "inequality" and "inequity"—proves every time explosive.

The Federal Council, at any rate, has strangely succeeded in dispersing American Protestantism as an army available for the war against the communist antichrist. There are, of course, innumerable millions of United States Protestants who qualify as impeccable anti-Communists. But in so forming their political dedications they have most certainly not responded to mobilizing efforts of their churches; on the contrary, they could easily feel reprimanded, gently but unmistakably, by their articulate church hierarchy.

The Federal Council, especially, for the last fifteen years has been in constant danger of petrifying into a pacifist lobby that would more often than not (although, of course, unwittingly) seem to support the position of Soviet policy in every conflict with United States policy. Fortunately, for the United States as well as for the Federal Council, John Foster Dulles, long before he became Secretary of State, has done backbreaking work in educating the Federal Council on problems of foreign policy; and, thanks to him, the Federal Council has refrained from endorsing surrender in preference to war. But there are most influential members of the highest committees within the Federal Council who take issue with Dulles and advocate undiluted pacifism. One of them seems to be the Reverend Dr. Bennett. And this is why his programmatic statement of policy merits the concerned attention I propose to give it.

Who, I should like to ask, did the research for Dr. Bennett's momentous speech? Who supplied him with evidence that the second-generation Communists *are* becoming "less fanatical believers in their ideology and less of a threat to the freedom of their neighbors"?

For surely the eminent Dr. Bennett could not have said what he did say so short a time after the Hungarian mass slaughter *without* overwhelming evidence. Surely Dr. Bennett means to say that the churches must change their "rigid attitude toward communism" because *communism* was changing before our eyes. Surely, since he did speak, he spoke of what he believed was *reality*, not just an exercise of speculative imagination. And so I ask again: where was Dr. Bennett's evidence?

He did not feel duty-bound to present any. The churchman postulated. Worse even. He did not have the gracefulness, not to say humility, to concede that the opposite thesis was just as admissible as his; that, in other words, he was merely thinking aloud and tentatively. He prescribed. He prescribed apodictically. He announced *the* correct Christian position. Still worse. If a theologian of Dr. Bennett's prestige calls on the churches "to modify their views about survival, communism, and the cold war"—no less—he is under the irreducible obligation to submit *theological* grounds on which such a crucial modification is to be demanded. For surely he did not mean to say that the allegedly outdated views of the church—those that "have to be modified" in 1958—were conceived on *non*-theological grounds. No agnostic would dare such brazen offense of Dr. Bennett's church. The Reverend Dr. Bennett must have at least tacitly stipulated that there is a theologically definable need for the desired modification. What could it be?

The allegedly outdated view of the Christian churches—quite simply that communism was antichrist—could be abandoned on only one of two grounds: either some new insight has proved this assumption to be false; or communism has recently changed its innermost nature. The flow of Dr. Bennett's argument seems to indicate that he was not ready to challenge the theological soundness of the traditional Christian position. Rather, he intended to say that communism, whatever it may have been in the past, was *now* changing its nature. And at precisely this point shows the fatal irresponsibility of his position.

The operative phrase in Dr. Bennett's argument is the Soviet Union's "apparent change from ideological fanaticism to a genuine self-improvement." Yet what is "apparent" about it? Not a single known fact supports this contention. On the contrary, Khrushchev has said in six months more often than Stalin had said in six years that communism was going to "bury capitalism."

Does Khrushchev's anxiety to raise living standards in the Soviet Union indicate "genuine self-improvement"? Since the earliest days of Lenin, through the years of NEP and Stalin's interminable Five-Year Plans, the Soviet regime has never stopped to promote, if only in utopian promise, the living standards of its people. A totalitarian regime, even more than a democratic government, is in constant need of an enthusiastic optimism of its regimented people that can come only from the popular impression—genuine or fabricated—that "things are getting better every day in every way." With the exception of the few years when Hitler's armies tore into Russia, there was not a single year of bolshevism in power that the Soviets did not claim, often enough with considerable fact to back them up, an important measure of self-improvement.

What do churchmen such as Dr. Bennett think communism is? A concept of asceticism, flagellation, sacrifice? From its very inception (and this is precisely why the churches very soon understood its challenge) communism was the most consistently Promethean, the most uninhibited cry for material "self-improvement." It derives its magnetic powers mostly from the utopian scientism which sees no limits to material abundance a "scientifically" regimented society will produce for everybody. To say that communism ever *changes* "to a genuine self-improvement" is like saying that atheism changes to a genuine denial of God.

What most spiritual operators of western public opinion cannot grasp is that, in communism, a concern for "genuine self-improvement" *and* a fanatical belief in a rigid ideology inseparably go together. The more genuinely a Communist desires material self-improvement, the more fanatically does he hang on to communism. For, to him, productivity depends on the precise execution of "scientific" orders issued by the planning command; so that, to produce more wealth, not less but *more* regimentation is required.

There is no theologian in two thousand years of Christianity who does not agree that man's *hubris* will always be fatally nourished by the material successes of his striving and that ultimately nothing but "failure in this world" lets man find the way to his Father's house. In non-theological terms, there is consensus among all students of human behavior that—short of the intervention of grace —man will not correct his errors so long as, by committing them, he prospers.

The Communists have pressed into the forty-one years of their governmental career more imperial success than has ever been recorded for an equal period in history. From 1945 to 1959 they have conquered 7,000 new slaves every hour of the day, every day of the year, every year. They have marched from one political, territorial, scientific, armament, propaganda triumph to an even greater one. They have seen the free world constantly fumble, hesitate, fail. And in the teeth of this unprecedented communist experience the Reverend Dr. Bennett expects—nay, diagnoses—that communism is "changing."

Were the Communists to change, in spite of their triumphs, this would be so new under the sun, so provocatively unexpected by Christian and every other theology, so contrary to anything psychologists keep teaching in all licensed schools of the land, that the Reverend Dr. Bennett should have felt a scholar's need to elaborate on the spectacular phenomenon. He did not. Instead, he presented his discovery as an indisputable, generally granted fact. I say: There is every reason on earth to make a Communist today an even more fanatical believer in his ideology than he ever was before. The Reverend Dr. Bennett says: There is the Communists' "apparent change of emphasis from ideological fanaticism to a genuine self-improvement." The difference between us: I offer evidence— Dr. Bennett does not.

But while he was silent on proof, he was most eloquent on motivation; his *own* motivation, that is. He said what he said, not because it was demonstrably true, but because he wanted to offer
a prescription: "We should put the prevention of general war ahead
of the defeat of communist power, and a real acceptance of coexistence ahead of victory in the cold war." And with this prescription the Reverend Dr. Bennett spoke indeed for the official West.

The proposal of coexistence and "a priority of peace over the
defeat of communism" is not arrived at by normal processes of in-
ductive reasoning (processes that start with observable fact and
end in an evaluation of probabilities). Seldom has the human mind
functioned so contrary to scientific rules as in the age of scientism.
It now starts with some violent spasm of the will (or, rather, its
failure), with emotional preferences; and *then* it stuffs the intellectual vacuum with irrelevant or false evidence. The Reverend
Dr. Bennett knew, before he began his analysis, what he was going
to recommend to the faithful—coexistence. And, having decided
beforehand on his prescription, he *then* adjusted his diagnosis ac-
cordingly: Because, to him, coexistence looked viable, it had to be
presented as possible.

Dr. Bennett's contortion act represents the *Zeitgeist*—in Germany as well as elsewhere—because of its honest naïveté, its disre-
gard for all rules of investigation, its desperate "optimism," and its
pious inanity. From Eisenhower to Kennan, from the daydreams of
Germany's "neutralist" press to the passionately illogical editorials
of the *Manchester Guardian*—it is always, to the last wrinkle, Dr.
Bennett's style of reasoning: the desirable is the possible, the hallucinations evidence, the daydreams objective data.

An especially meaningful monstrosity is the sentence " we should
put the prevention of general war ahead of the defeat of communist
power." What is here being put ahead of the *defeat* of communist
power is the *victory* of communist power: once the prevention of
general war is accepted as a goal superior to the prevention of communist victory, nothing on earth could prevent that victory. By
shifting from "a victory in the cold war" to "a real acceptance of

coexistence" we do not just change priorities; we *reverse our intents*. In the one case the emphasis is on the preservation of our way of life—for example, of Dr. Bennett's professed faith; in the other it is on the act of living itself.

"A real acceptance of coexistence" is of course not just the renunciation of western victory in the cold war but a knowing acceptance of western defeat. The cold war was conceived—not by the West, but by the Communists—as a very real, very serious, very final war. What we call "cold war" is a strategic concept of world revolution based on the Communists' confidence that they can conquer the West without firing a shot. The Communists are engaged in their version of a religious war. And for the first time in human history the attacked religion not only refuses to fight but refuses to acknowledge the *reality* of that attack. Even worse. Important religious leaders of the West advise their flock to put "a real acceptance of coexistence"—with antichrist—*ahead* of a defense of their faith. And in this apocalyptic situation such church leaders do not even have the visceral courage to profess what they are doing—namely, advise capitulation for the sake of sensual existence. Instead, they drape their advice with the vestments of spiritual service.

If surrender in "peace" is preferred to the defeat of communism, then "the prevention of general war" is indeed not only possible but it just cannot be missed. For as surely as the laws of logic remain in control of observed reality, such a "shift in priorities" makes the victory of communist power unavoidable and secures with that victory the ultimate peace of immobile slaves for those who have surrendered for the sake of such a peace. Communist power, if not defeated, conquers; and, having conquered, it "pacifies." The only *dependable* way of preventing general war is to allow communist victory. There is no other.

We seem to have entered an age in which churchmen are not just wary but downright contemptuous of dedication. No, let no one misunderstand what the Reverend Dr. Bennett means by "fanaticism." What frightens churchmen like him, I am afraid, is not *what* the Communist believes in; on the contrary, a tone of envious admiration for the Communist's utopianism sneaks into many a churchman's discussion of "social justice." What frightens them is the *intensity* of the Communist's belief: the emotional depth of the communist persuasion smells positively of dedication. Yet genteel churchmen are what they love to call "sophisticated." They are, above all, well mannered and "tolerant." Which, taken together, means that they underwrite the behaviorist code of this generation: you may believe in whatever you choose to believe—as long as you keep lukewarm about it.

And there is indeed no other obstacle to "coexistence" than the fact that the Communists are unsophisticated, ill-mannered, and intolerant enough to be "fanatical." The Communists, in more precise language, are in earnest about their faith. And that is deemed deplorable by some churchmen; no civilized person, you see, should be. Civilized persons are "tolerant." Communists are "crusaders"—and there is no dirtier word in the language of "tolerant" churchmen. The Communists believe that they have seen the light; they will not rest until everybody else shares their elation. And that is the kind of fanaticism no "tolerant" churchman can tolerate.

A future historian of the twentieth century may very well explain the finality of the western crisis with this momentous change in spiritual thermodynamics. The established religion dropped from the level of fire and heat and light to the level of "tolerance"; while all the congenitally dedicated people were told to rally behind the devil. The dignitaries of many a church have disarmed their souls a long time ago; and it would be most rewarding to confront their exhausted "moderation" with the vigor of an Asiatic prophet of non-violence such as Gandhi.

For Gandhi, non-violence—certainly the only consistent form of pacifism—was never the underchilled minuet of neatness that pacifism is in the West. Gandhi, in leading his faithful onto the path of non-violence, was driving them straight toward expected and desired suffering. He promised, not comfort, but redemption—not coexistence, but victory. He was not lukewarm. He was burning. And in burning he gave light. He proposed not the kind of compromise by which each side would observe five of the Ten Commandments and so live forever in peace with the other. He was seeking the triumph of good over evil, as he saw it. He may have been wrong; but he was a religious man—though never a dean of faculty at a theological seminary.

What churchmen such as Dr. Bennett try to couch in careless theological terms is of course President Eisenhower's pacifist policy.

Yet for the Germans, who have their very special experience with soldiers turned statesmen, he has remained the general. There is, for German ears, always a militaristic overtone in everything President Eisenhower says. Germans will never grasp, I am afraid, that in a democracy such as America it takes a famous soldier to sell the people on pacifism: they would never buy it from a professional politician whom, on the contrary, Americans would rather suspect of sacrificing the country's military needs to his greedy party's advantage. It would have been difficult for a civilian President to neglect America's strategic needs as dangerously as General Eisenhower did. But neither would it occur to an American to suspect a soldier of Eisenhower's fame and achievements: obviously, he *cannot* be a pacifist. But he is one. And no pacifist could be as effective in America as a general.

President Eisenhower, I think, will be remembered for one sentence primarily, "war is unthinkable." Eisenhower, the soldier, that is, has attained the immortality of an imperial conqueror; but Eisenhower, the President, has been not just an anemic mediocrity but a tragic failure in the one respect in which he seemed to qualify for political office—as leader of men.

There was hardly ever in times of trouble a man in power, in America or elsewhere, who had Eisenhower's alienation from eloquence, his embarrassing lack of articulation. A leader of men must be able, above all, to communicate. Eisenhower (whose sincerity in *private* conversation seems to have been always impressive) has in a lifetime of public service never uttered a single memorable phrase, not a single thought by which he can be identified. As a thinking (and speaking) man he is faceless. But this one sentence—"war is unthinkable"—will remain. It is a deeply moving sentence, with an air of beautiful helplessness about it. It is a sincere sentence, and it reaches for the heart. It is also logically without meaning, morally untenable, and politically suicidal.

If it seems strange that a famous soldier should be the author of this sentence, one ought to keep in mind that General Eisenhower's entire career in the Army was that of a military politician; and his characteristic function in World War II was that of a political general—the executive vice-president of a huge international establishment in charge of "human and public relations." His decisive job—and one must not minimize its importance—was to keep "the team" of a multinational army in a working state of co-operation. Neither strategic planning nor tactical command in the field was General Eisenhower's forte or fate. Luckier than most commanders in military history, he saw himself selected for the one job he could do better than anyone else—to manage a huge Allied army's "good will." It was also the only talent that qualified him for the presidency of the United States. And out of this talent grew the only memorable sentence he said as President. "War is unthinkable" is genuine Eisenhower (even if a ghost-writing journalist should have passed it on to the Chief Executive).

What makes this sentence on second thought so strange is first of all its grammatical incompleteness. Unthinkable—to whom? Thinking presupposes a thinker; and who is thinking in this case? Eisenhower? Then he should have said, "War is *to me unthinkable*"; and the statement of bewildered helplessness would have been even more moving—but also more visibly dangerous. For war, evidently, is not unthinkable to other people—Khrushchev, for instance. War, in fact, is not unthinkable to the high officers of the United States Department of Defense whose sworn duty and irreducible responsibility it remains *always to think of war;* and, let us hope, to think about it more realistically than anybody else in the world. For, if they do not, the United States is bound to lose the next war.

Now the amazing point is that President Eisenhower, when he said "war is unthinkable," did not for a second think of his former colleagues in the United States Army. With one sentence of three words he dismembered it. For how can an army stay thinkable if war is no longer? Obviously, to say "war is unthinkable" is to say that no war must ever be fought again. If "unthinkable" means anything at all, it means that the unthinkable thing's occurrence must not be tolerated. And to say that no war must ever be fought again is to say that armies must be disbanded—as dangerous archaic remainders from a past in which wars still were thinkable. In the new world, in which wars are unthinkable, the mere survival of archaic armies would establish an intolerable hazard to the only conceivable course, namely, pacifism.

The axiom of "war is unthinkable" has vital consequences for the conduct of United States foreign policy. Indeed, the decision of a government to consider wars unthinkable contains inherently its decision to *abandon* foreign policies; for there has never been, and there cannot be, a foreign policy that is not backed by a government's determination to go to war in an ultimate pursuit of this foreign policy. Without such a determination, a government may express its vague preferences for certain arrangements of international relations; but it cannot pursue a foreign policy. Indeed, all philosophers of eternal peace—beginning with Immanuel Kant —have considered the abolition of national sovereignties and the establishment of a world government as the basic requirements of eternal peace—precisely because national sovereignties (and corresponding foreign policies) presuppose a willingness to go to war. If wars are unthinkable, foreign policy is unthinkable—and, therefore, national sovereignty.

This, of course, President Eisenhower did not say and, most likely, did not mean to say. But since the day he pronounced his momentous statement there could not have been a single chancellery in the world that did not begin—to borrow John Foster Dulles's phrase—"an agonizing reappraisal": *can* the United States have a foreign policy? For what makes United States relations additionally difficult is that the outside world has the habit of drawing conclusions from statements made by responsible United States officials.

When Mr. Dean Acheson, in a speech he delivered as Secretary of State, did not include Korea among the specified areas of the world which his government would defend militarily, the Bolsheviks, quite rationally, took this for a signal to attack Korea: After all, Mr. Acheson must have anticipated exactly such a development when he omitted Korea! It is not too difficult to persuade an American that Mr. Acheson had most likely *nothing* in his mind—that he thoughtlessly blundered into a catastrophe; but it is absolutely impossible to persuade a European or an Asiatic that United States policies are so gaily irresponsible in conception and execution.

When President Eisenhower in a solemn declaration—movingly and desperately, as if he were taking his aching heart in his hands—announces that "war is unthinkable," the entire outside world must seriously ponder the possibility that he may mean it. It must assume that, if not he, his learned policy staff has been aware of the inherent consequences of such a discovery. It must assume that the United States, a great power, draws realistic conclusions from its own observations.

And so the entire world must have assumed that, the moment war had become unthinkable, the United States was abdicating as the sovereign bearer of a foreign policy. The world, I am afraid, has begun to catch up with the most momentous fact of recent years: that, under General Eisenhower, the policy of the United States Government has been based, earnestly and sincerely, on crude pacifism. And the world has begun to understand the appalling aspects of this fact: The survival of the free world is linked to the military preparedness of a government which is intellectually incapable, in the words of its own chief executive, to visualize a situation in which its armament would be used.

The truly pernicious results of America's resignation from foreign policy, under Eisenhower, are becoming visible in Germany. By its geography and its collective experience, Germany should be the decisive center around which a Europe, determined to resist communism, must form. Germany, and nothing else, is the barrier against a Soviet expansion into western Europe. Given Germany's strength, Europe can hold; if it softens, Europe falls.

This is, above all, Germany's geographic destiny: it happens to be the center of the Continent. But it is also Germany's political destiny: it happens to be the only western nation that has been mutilated by the Soviet Union. Still dismembered, thirteen years after the war's end, Germany has a vital claim against the Soviet Union—that the illegally occupied German territory of the Soviet zone be restored to the German Republic.

Here is Europe's fatal wound. If Germany—and with Germany Europe—were ever to resign itself to the Soviet usurpation of East Germany, the struggle with communism would be over; for the lasting and acknowledged sovietization of East Germany would in the end pull *all* of Germany into the Soviet camp. Any serious collapse of West German prosperity must multiply the German craving for national unity; and if in that quite unavoidable situation the West has already acknowledged the finality of Soviet control over European heart land, then the irresistible urge for German unity must tend toward the east. This, one should think, is the factor uppermost in every responsible German mind. But it is not.

Germany's open wound—hardly felt by the prosperous Germans who, on the contrary, do not want to be reminded of anything that smells of trouble—the continued violation of German sovereignty, could be turned, by statesmen of genuine political talent, into Germany's and the West's greatest factor of healing: A firm western policy, coordinated with a firm German posture, could make East Germany the place of the first communist defeat in decades.

For a determined western policy, willing to put all western military might behind the legitimate German demand for the overdue restoration of German national integrity, would most likely obtain a Soviet withdrawal from East Germany. No one can say how long this would take and what kind of pressures must be applied; but no one who understands the nature of communism can seriously doubt that the Soviets would in the end withdraw rather than fight a war over East Germany. As usual in history, the area of the gravest challenge is at the same time also the area of the decisive promise. Treated correctly, Europe's open wound may induce total cure. Treated incorrectly, or not at all, it will result in a deadly gangrene.

Amidst the well-being that cottons all German life, a sensitive observer feels the chills from the east. The question of German "reunification" remains the one German problem for which Dr. Adenauer has shown no profound understanding or, at any rate, no special political talent. In his heart of hearts he knows that the United States, certainly Eisenhower's United States, will not back a determined German drive for the restoration of usurped German territory; and as Adenauer has based his whole policy on a loyal cooperation with American intents, he remains anxiously silent about his country's and Europe's gravest problem.

He can even afford, from time to time, to announce publicly that West Germany, to please American wishes, is willing to refrain from announcing its claim. For instance, when President Eisenhower, in the winter of 1957-58, seemed enchanted with the prospects of an early "summit meeting" with Khrushchev, Adenauer, prompted by Dulles, obliged with a polite assurance that he was not going to spoil those prospects by insisting that "the German question"—as the United States was officially committed to demand—be put on the agenda of a "summit conference." There is nothing, one sometimes thinks, Adenauer could not afford in the present climate of German political life; but it is most unlikely that Adenauer's successor can continue that game—and it cannot be continued, even by Adenauer, once German prosperity subsides.

While I was in Germany there was only one moment of political distress for Adenauer—the passionate *Bundestag* debate about previous chances (alleged chances, to be sure) for German "reunification" allegedly wasted by Adenauer's policies. The facts, it soon turned out, were entirely on his side; but for days a pale Dr. Adenauer was taking it on his chin, silently, almost numb. And one

could sense that underneath the air of satisfaction the German
public was suddenly restless and confused and agitated by a re-
surgent emotion. In the end, the *Bundestag* opposition lost its case,
mainly because it had so blatantly overstated it. But no one who
has witnessed this scalding debate will ever doubt again that the
continued Soviet occupation of East Germany remains the great
trauma that may erupt into Germany's and Europe's next violent
upheaval.

Perhaps a man of greater political genius than Adenauer could
have compelled the United States to second a firm German policy
of restoration. But Bismarcks are not born every century; and
Dr. Adenauer, at any rate, is what he is—a solid German *Bürger,*
an enthusiastic European, a loyal ally of the United States. He is
all this—and no more. It may be considered Germany's good luck
that its first real leader in this unstable century was a patriarch who,
in pursuing his policy of extreme precaution, had tremendous
courage. And then, again, the near future may discover that
Adenauer's courage was wanting: had he more readily responded
to the challenge of a time that required daring, he might have
forced the right decisions on the United States and thus might have
saved Europe.

And it is true that only Germany, of all American allies,
would have been strong enough a power to press the United States
into a policy rather than always follow its lead. But it is also true
that Adenauer, with his incorrigible revulsion against a policy of
daring, has inoculated the German people with a sense of political
humility and has thus restored a new European trust in Germany.
Above all, it is incontrovertibly true that, whatever Adenauer's
mistakes may have been in regard to "reunification," they were all
obedient responses to American conduct: At the bottom of all
German hesitations and blunders are American strategy decisions—
if one can call "strategy" a continued embarrassment of hesitations
and fears.

By geography and fate Germany is the space in which the conflict between East and West will reach its climax. The modish

efforts to prove that India, or the Near East, or Africa, or some other exotic area, is the area of strategic world decision is as popular a parlor game as it is absurd. Outside the United States the Continent still remains the powerhouse of the world; and he who controls Europe still owns the world. The Communists have never doubted this nexus. They may *tactically* choose detours, through Africa or Asia, to reach their real goal—the control of Europe; their *strategy* has never changed. Since Lenin's conquest of power, in 1917, the Communists have always understood that the world revolution will have triumphed with the conquest of Germany, and not before. ("When the revolution has triumphed in Germany," said Lenin in 1920, "the center of world communism will move from Moscow to Berlin.") Europe cannot be held against the Soviets once Germany is lost; and without winning Germany, world communism is not secure.

This is the crucial parallelogram of forces in the struggle between world communism and the West. Whether or not the Germans want to withdraw from history, whether or not the United States tries for a few more years to neglect the basic fact of world strategy, will not really matter. What matters is that Communists, hard-headed realists, will of necessity pursue the conquest of Germany. They must—or else all preliminary triumphs will finally mean nothing.

And not for a day have the Soviets forgotten their central strategic assignment. They may be occasionally impressed by such technological American armament advances as the hydrogen bomb; but they are *truly* afraid of German military might, even when that might, for a while, looms as a mere potential. A Germany believably poised for an active policy in eastern Europe remains the most effective and perhaps the only effective check on Soviet expansion; but a Germany in a state of disarmed "precaution" and "neutralist" illusions is most dependably the final short cut to the communist conquest of Europe.

It seems the fatal mistake of United States policies not to have understood, ever, the central function of Germany in the defense of the West; and the truly unpardonable crime of Adolf Hitler is that he made it almost inescapable for the civilized West to underrate Germany's congenital role in the power structure of the West. It may well be an irreparable crime. The Soviets, at any rate, have profited from it ever since 1933; and even in the fifties, half a generation after Hitler's end, it may prove impossible to persuade the West that Germany has remained, and at last must be treated as, the West's mightiest citadel on the Continent.

As to America's German policy, it has been determined for the last ten years by nothing so much as a "public relations" aspect—the desire to do nothing and to allow nothing in Germany that might arouse "suspicions" in Europe. And by "Europe" the United States policy makers keep meaning the Europe of 1945—a continent united by American force and anti-German furor. Several members of the United States Foreign Service whom I have met in Europe throughout the last year are personally very much aware that thirteen crucial years have passed since that desperate moment of "liberation"; and that not only the Germany of 1959 is an altogether different nation from the ghastly human ruins Hitler left behind but also that the Europe of 1959 has little in common with the multilingual hordes of proud beggars who in 1945 cried for bread and revenge—American bread and revenge on the Germans. But those intelligent observers of the United States Foreign Service know better than to try to apply their superior knowledge to their official conduct; and I doubt very much whether the State Department in Washington has over the last years received a fraction of the considerable wisdom I could gather from a few members of the United States Foreign Service in Europe in securely private conversations.

At any rate, many a United States diplomat in Europe agrees that, whether or not our German policy ought to please European prejudices, these European prejudices have substantially changed since 1945. The Europe of 1959 is by no means the quivering mass of anti-German hatred and fears our policy makers still seem to imagine. I have found, in the Europe of 1958, much less wariness in regard to Germany than in Washington. I do not intend to say that, for example, the French of today love the Germans. They do not. But the French of today love nobody, not even the French. Yet there is all over Europe an air of reasonableness, of unemotional realism that may become Europe's greatest asset.

Europe, it seems to me, is entirely ready to let a new Germany assume its role—the role it has always played. And this, of course, is not because Europe suddenly adores the nation that was stopped running amuck just fourteen years ago. No one in Europe has forgotten the unforgettable (particularly not the Germans). But there is no sane person in Europe who, in 1959, was still afraid of another act of Teutonic aggression in his lifetime. There is, on the other hand, no sane person in Europe who does not consider communist expansion a deadly threat to European security. And there is, finally, no sane person in Europe who doubts that Germany, in 1959, has become by far the strongest, the decisive continental power in any attempt at a European defense.

The fundamental change in Europe's attitude toward Germany is nowhere more impressive than in the military and political structure of NATO. Even before Germany had effectively rearmed, it was already considered, accepted, and appreciated as NATO's military essense: 16 of the 30 divisions NATO hopes to count in 1961 will be Germany's contribution; and even today the only serious man power the NATO command has at its call are the five United States divisions stationed on the Continent and the growing bulk of the new German army. The remarkable fact is that—except for a few demonstrations in France and Holland that were unmistakably arranged by the local Communists—all of western Europe welcomed the German contribution to the military preparedness of the Continent with a calm comprehension that would have seemed inconceivable a few short years ago.

There are, naturally enough, not unimportant groups in western Europe whose vested interests demand that anti-German sentiments be perpetuated. For instance, one must not underrate the political weight of what likes to call itself *"la résistance"* in France. This curious political formation became in the Fourth French Re-

public what Freemasonry was in the Third—a tightly knit, ubiquitous, and rather ruthless organization of people who were banded
together by the exclusive aim to protect each other's jobs and
positions. *La résistance* was never quite the heroic and selfless
elite of France that it was hailed as in America. Opportunists,
careerists, and downright criminal elements joined true French
patriots in 1944 and 1945; and soon they outgesticulated the
genuine kind.

The Fourth Republic, that never ceased to suffer from such
illegitimacy, was to a large extent manned by the volatile
heirs to *la résistance;* and some of the worst scars in postwar
France's political face have been cut by the atrocious caricature
of justice these false *résistants* have forced upon the Republic.
Nothing ties men so closely together as guilt shared; and if it were
only for the fear that a truly reoriented France may punish the
operators of *la purification*—the terrible purge that from 1944 to
1948 destroyed thousands of innocent French lives and for which,
unfortunately, the great Charles de Gaulle is as responsible as anyone else—the adventurers of 1945, respectable today, have serious
vested interests in common. They will work hard to keep the anti-
German flames glowing in France, so that ignoble deeds stay hidden
in murky shadows. In short, no one who knows something of
French postwar politics will minimize the resolution of *la résistance*
to feed and exaggerate the country's anti-German apprehensions.

Yet there is today perhaps more readiness in France to coalesce
with a revitalized Germany than in any other country of the Continent—in spite of France's historically most justifiable grudges
against a Prussianized Germany; in spite of hideous German conduct in France during the last war; in spite of all clever demagoguery
of selfish French politicians. And the reason for such French
reasonableness is simply a growing French disgust with Europe's
habits of self-destruction. I do not mean to say that the French
people, in an altogether improbable act of mass rationalization,
have decided on an intimate French friendship with Germany; but
the French have accepted Germany's reborn strength as a fact of

European significance and they feel no longer threatened by German military strength.

This is true for all of western Europe. Of course, that calm climate may change. Adenauer's death, the possible rise of another "dynamic" German leader, the tremors of a serious European economic crisis, some new and fundamental mistakes of United States European policies, an unpredictably ferocious Soviet move—any number of factors may undo the present moderation of Europe's temper. But short of such violent turns, all of western Europe is for the time being prepared to accept Germany for what it is— the strongest segment of the Continent, Europe's indispensable guarantor against the East.

Were the United States to give Germany the central position in its system of alliances which Germany merits—on grounds of geography and history as well as because, in strength and capacities, it qualifies as America's senior partner in Europe—the United States would move, not against, but with the rest of Europe. An open American alliance with Germany would, in fact, disperse the remaining European suspicions of Germany: a Germany endorsed and advised by the United States could not possibly, ever again, erupt in nationalistic megalomania; and German policies executed in open agreement with the United States would encounter a European confidence which now suffers from memories of the German past and from Europe's distrust of American ignorance of things European.

Moreover, an open American alliance with Germany—which, of course, would invite the participation of any other western nation that is willing to accept the terms and share the objectives of such an alliance—would without a doubt constitute the most effective check on Soviet expansionism the West has ever created. A Germany that acts with unmitigated American endorsement can at last dare approach its "reunification" problem seriously; and faced with such a radical change of the continental parallelogram of forces, the Soviet Union, for the first time in decades, would be on the defensive.

The immense force of such an American-German alliance is beyond doubt. Its promise as a decisive turning point in the cold war is self-evident. In its way are not European but American prejudices. This is why it seems to me an imperative American duty to take a careful look at the new Germany and to investigate its worthiness as a senior partner of United States policies in Europe.

CHAPTER NINE

The Task

＾＾＾＾＾＾＾＾＾＾＾＾＾＾＾＾＾＾＾＾＾＾＾＾＾＾＾＾＾＾＾＾＾＾

From October 1954 to the end of 1957 Germany spent about DM 10 billion ($2.4 billion) on its military establishment. But these were just the token expenditures of planning rather than doing. With the beginning of 1958 the costs multiplied. For the fiscal year 1957-58, German defense was budgeted with another DM 10 billion. From 1958 to 1961—when the German forces are supposed to reach their peak in size and effectiveness—a minimum of another DM 45 billion will have to be spent—DM 15 billion per year. And after 1961, considering the ever-increasing cost of modern armament, West Germany's military budget will remain at least at the same magnitude—i.e., around 7.5 per cent of the national gross income. (The United States defense budget in 1957 was about 8 per cent of the United States national gross income.)

These defense expenditures in Germany amount to about DM 300 per capita and year ($76.00) compared to $220 per capita and year in the United States. But the purchasing powers of currencies do not correspond to the exchange-rate indices; and a mark equals 50 rather than 24 cents. In terms of German living standards, therefore, the average German spends about $150 a year on his military establishment. This is still less than the American's defense expenditures, but more than is being spent on the armed forces in most other western nations.

The available information on the programmed German military "hardware" is rather meager—not because Germany's defense minister, Franz Josef Strauss, is particularly secretive but because his planning staff simply does not know enough about the future. The finally chosen type of German armament will obviously depend on the military posture West Germany, NATO, and the United States will assume between 1958 and 1961. But a few relevant facts seem to be established even now.

West Germany expects to purchase before 1961 about 33,000 motorized army vehicles, including jeeps, and about 10,000 tanks. About DM 1.6 billion, or slightly less than $400 million, have been appropriated for the acquisition of United States tanks, type M 48. The naval construction program foresees 12 destroyers, 39 speed boats, 12 submarines, 34 small protective coastal craft, 120 special craft (including freight vessels), 13 service boats, 12 landing boats, 2 mine sweepers, and about 400 midget boats for various special uses. About DM 10 billion are allocated for the construction of barracks, air bases, training grounds, hospitals, and office buildings. And there are no intelligent estimates of the number and type of aircraft (let alone missiles) the German Army may purchase during the next few years. The German air force, to be effective at all, will have to remain fully coordinated with the United States air force establishment in Europe; and so long as no one knows—in this impenetrable confusion concerning intercontinental missiles, of nuclear weapons, and "international disarmament"—what kind of assignments the United States air force will have in the next few years, the German air force seems compelled to a makeshift existence.

The total costs of building an effective German army from scratch will not exceed the sum of $18 billion (DM 73 billion) by 1961, spent over the preceding five years. For this kind of money the Germans hope to have developed by 1961 an army of about 20 battle-ready divisions, an adequate naval auxiliary, and an air force of considerable firepower. Even in 1958, one year after the first military cadres were formed, the German military contribution to NATO exceeded the weight of any other NATO contingent, except the United States establishment in Europe.

No doubt the $18 billion invested from 1957 to 1961 in Germany's military might—paid entirely by the Germans themselves—will represent the greatest military bargain in NATO history. For one must not forget that the United States spent in the cold war from 1946 to 1958 close to $80 billion in foreign aid; and whatever the military effects of such stupendous expenditures may have been—most of the United States foreign aid has been justified as military rather than economic aid—their effect cannot possibly begin to equal that of $18 billion paid by Germany for its own rearmament.

And yet, Germany's military policy suffers from the very same predicament that may make all of NATO an ultimate failure: German rearmament, like NATO, is a venture without realistic purpose. The treaty that called NATO into being, and still supplies its only instrument of direction, does not even suggest the co-ordination of Europe's military forces against communism as NATO's *raison d'être*. The only formative idea, the only justification in the NATO concept—and in the German rearmament rationale—is a nebulous notion of "defense." And for this reason, it seems to me, NATO as well as Germany's rearmament remain essentially impotent.

I do not mean here to go into a semantic discussion of the obvious—that a defense that refuses to identify the only likely aggressor is doomed. That much is known to even the most "prudent" German and NATO commanders; and at least for the last two years, under United States General Norstad and German General Dr. Speidel, NATO quite openly adjusted itself to the only likelihood of conflagration. Neither NATO nor Germany diffuses its vastly limited powers even further by preparing for those abstract "eventualities" old-fashioned general staffs kept training for. NATO as well as Germany proceeds from the axiomatic certainty that there is only one conceivable European conflagration—a Soviet attack. In recent years there has not been a single European maneuver based on the supposition that one western nation may have to fight another; even the fictitious objective of neutral Switzerland's maneuvers of 1957 was to investigate the problems Swiss forces would have to face, in cooperation with French and German detachments, should an "eastern" aggressor push into Central Europe.

But to know the foe is one thing; to comprehend his intentions, and to prepare for them, is quite another. Neither NATO nor Germany can conceive of another aggressor than the Soviets. Yet neither NATO nor Germany has based its policies on the only realistic interpretation of communist strategy: that, as long as Europe and the United States are armed, the Soviets will never attack militarily; and that, therefore, a European defense enterprise which was created to function only in case of a *military attack,* must remain utterly futile.

The very heart of all communist policies—and this, as I said before, the West has completely failed to comprehend—is their determination to *avoid* armed conflict. The western "experts" may continue to ignore the obvious; the western peoples will not. The growing popular reluctance throughout the West to carry the great burden of armament is not entirely the frivolous thoughtlessness of democratic masses; it contains a great deal of instinctive comprehension: Why, indeed, should the West pile up those mountains of weapons if the only conceivable aggressor is believably determined to avoid war?

And this is precisely one of the strategic Soviet objectives: Western public opinion, or so the Soviets hope, will gradually cave in and disembody, if not abolish, the western defense establishment—in which case, of course, the Communists would no longer avoid conflagration but, indeed, launch a military attack that will encounter no defenses and therefore incur no risk.

To make any sense at all, a military establishment set up to counter communist expansionism must be built on the concept of *offensive.* There is undeniably some truth in the argument that western peoples have a congenital revulsion against a policy of offensive and, in fact, fight magnificently only when attacked. But

there is even more truth in the consensus of all careful observers—
namely, that the western nations are growing dangerously tired of a
military preparedness that, on the face of it, makes no sense. The
West's policy makers will have to choose between two "unpopular"
courses: They will either have to continue, against a vehemently
growing popular resentment, the construction of an obviously futile
military establishment, meant to serve in a case that will never
occur; or they will have to persuade an obstinately pacifistic public
opinion that, to end the intolerable communist threat, the West
must assume the offensive.

Does this mean that I propose "preventive war"? Of all the
catch phrases that confuse this age, none is more poisonously
loaded, and none meaner. By "preventive war," I take it, is meant
a conduct that does not prevent but deliberately starts a war: a
government unloads its arsenal of annihilating weapons on the un-
suspecting antagonist, so that he cannot launch an attack of his
own. If this is meant by "preventive war," I am clearly not advo-
cating it—but I also should like to show up the phrase for all its
shallowness and confusion.

In the first place, there is nothing morally repugnant—beyond
the moral repugnancy of war itself—in an attempt to disable an
irreconcilable foe before he strikes first. On the contrary, our joint
chiefs of staff would be remiss in their duty if, once they have
forceful reasons to expect a serious military attack on this country,
they would not most seriously ponder our capacities of rendering
that anticipated attack powerless by striking first. If the war itself
is morally defensible, and our victory in this war not only another
token of national glory but the condition of national survival, then
the strategy that secures victory is the soundest; and if that strategy
requires to shoot first, we would have to shoot first.

The only relevant question in this context is whether or not the
enemy attack can indeed be reliably anticipated. What enters here
is a problem of judgment—not of morality. The *moral* problem of
"preventive war" is pre-empted in a nation's decision not to surrender, not to adhere to the sectarian principles of non-violence,
but to fight. If it is considered morally correct to use all available

force in overpowering an enemy after he launches his attack, then, surely, the use of that force at an advantageous moment of your own choice can neither add to, nor subtract from, your moral responsibility for making war at all. The essence of your predicament is just this: How can you be reasonably certain that your foe means to attack at a moment of *his* choice?

And it is precisely within the confines of this practical question that I cannot be possibly considered a proponent of "preventive war." Were I persuaded that the Soviets intend to shower us with intercontinental missiles on December 7, 1959, I would most fervently advocate that we disable them, by what is called "preventive war," *before* that date. But I am not so persuaded. On the contrary, I am trying to prove in this book that the Soviets are deathly *afraid* of an all-out conflagration, are profoundly disturbed by the mere prospect of a serious armed conflict. Consequently, I propose to build our strategy on a posture and a conduct that keep the Soviets constantly confronted with the likelihood of such a conflict, unless they renounce their habitual provocations and withdraw from usurped western territory.

Short of doing violence to language, this cannot possibly be called a strategy of "preventive war." Most specifically, I do not suggest our launching a surprise attack on the Soviets. Rather, I suggest the *only* course that may ultimately save our world from an atomic catastrophe: I suggest an increasingly impressive posture of military might, put behind an increasingly forceful and entirely frank political offensive that demands a Soviet retreat from the obvious areas of intolerable irritation.

I have been trying to prove in this book that the Soviets must avoid the growing perils of a conflagration rather than take a chance on losing "history's mandate" altogether in a conflict of unpredictable outcome—that the forty-one years of the history of Bolshevism in power make this choice not only probable but inherently inescapable. But of course this may be a wrong assumption; and it is conceivable that the Soviets would *not* retreat. In this case we shall have to fight. But we then would be fighting, not because *we* have chosen war; we would be fighting because the Soviets would have changed their basic approach to their own destiny: They now would fight a major war rather than retard their schemes for world conquest. And in that case we shall *have* to go to war, whatever our preceding policy may have been, unless we decide to surrender.

An advocate of "preventive war" is interested in one question only: what is the most advantageous moment for us to launch the missiles? But this is not, in truth, America's problem. Our task, I think, is to make the Soviets retreat. And there is no alternative to this strategic commitment, unless we are willing to yield. If the Soviets do not retreat in response to our determined policy—if, that is, they have changed their fundamental strategy of forty-one years—then the conflagration has become unavoidable. And in this case, having in time attained an impressively offensive and superior posture, we would enter the unavoidable conflict in optimum condition.

It remains the tragic folly of all western policies vis-à-vis communism that they are confined to military planning, and *defensive* military planning to boot. All over western Europe—and nowhere more dangerously than in "realistic" Britain—there is that popular revolt against any further military investment in the cold war. In France, all military strength is employed to secure North Africa, and the installation of the Fifth Republic under Charles de Gaulle will soon be tantamount to a formal French warning that NATO can no longer reckon with a substantial French contribution. The British government, under Macmillan, has officially committed itself to a "slim-down" which, by 1961, will have reduced Britain's total military man power to 165,000 men, hardly enough to protect the British Isles, certainly not enough to provide a military guarantee for any British commitment abroad. And should the Labor party ever succeed the Conservatives, one must expect an even more catastrophic contraction of Britain's military power. Italy's military strength remains (to characterize it as charitably as possible) a small fraction of Switzerland's. Europe's small northern nations—Holland, Denmark, Norway, Belgium, Luxembourg—are in a constant mood to reconsider even their minute man-power loans to NATO. And Germany's rearmament efforts must be viewed with this general decomposition of the West's military posture in mind.

Rearmament remains indubitably Adenauer's least popular policy. There prevails in Germany a condescending indifference in regard to all military matters that is well-nigh incredible to anyone who remembers another Germany. Of course, that the German Social Democracy—more than one third of the nation, after all—has not liquidated its traditional "anti-militarism" is neither astonishing nor significant; it seems incapable of ever reforming itself and, in all fairness, its unwillingness to revise the party's traditional suspicion of German militarism is quite understandable so soon after the last war. The truly astonishing fact is the air of bitter embarrassment inside Adenauer's majority party whenever military problems must be considered. The attitude the non-socialist German assumes toward the new German army is polite contempt. This, I suspect, has very little to do with "anti-militarism"; though he, too, may have become a pragmatist, the typical Adenauer voter has been educated with deep-rooted respect for military might. What makes him doubtful about his new army is precisely its smell of impotence.

I made it a point to ask as often as I could about the German rearmament rationale; and with hardly an exception I always heard the same answer: Germany rearms merely to comply with American wishes. The Germans, it seems, see no primary national interest involved in their rearmament. On the contrary, this is the one area in which they still consider themselves a people without self-determination. When Germans talk about their new army, they shrug their shoulders: "What can one do, don't you see, if the Americans insist on our playing soldiers?" The tacit implication, and quite often the articulate argument, is simply that Germany, if it did not want to lose United States military protection, had to comply with United States wishes and put up a token army. But this army makes in itself very little sense to the Germans. Should a full-fledged Soviet attack on West Germany ever materialize, the United States would retaliate with all its might—or Germany would be lost.

Consequently, a separate German army is, at best, an auxiliary American force. So far, a majority of Germans are sufficiently persuaded that Germany needs United States protection to tolerate the idea of German rearmament in compliance with United States wishes.

But even a militarily gifted nation will have prohibitive difficulties in developing an effective military policy with such a rationale. And matters have been further complicated in Germany by the "disarmament" maneuvering Dr. Adenauer has lately considered necessary. Since "disarmament" became the professed main objective of the Eisenhower administration, the German Government felt itself obliged, or was pressured by United States foreign policy, to emphasize at every occasion that it is also guided by the same "ideal." But to the extent that the Germans take such protestations seriously, they comprehend Dr. Adenauer's armament policy even less: why, indeed, should the nation be committed to the unpleasantness of a new German "militarism," and to the very considerable expenses and discomforts of armament, if Adenauer himself announces every few weeks that he is "quite confident" about the prospects of international disarmament "under effective mutual controls"? To which Adenauer replies: "Yes, but such a disarmament can be achieved only if we are strong."

And it is a persuasive reply, as far as it goes. The psychological trouble remains, however, that no German can *really* believe that his new army, as it is being conceived and trained, will be a factor of decisive strength—certainly not as a countervailing force against Soviet military might. And so the German returns to his initial doubt: Why arm at all, if disarmament is the objective of our policy and if, short of attaining that objective, the German military force could not possibly affect the outcome of a United States-Soviet duel?

German professional soldiers, to be sure, have done their own thinking on the subject; and their rationale is neither Adenauer's nor that of German public opinion. They do not believe that "disarmament" is a realistic possibility; and they assume that this generation will have to live in a constant state of preparedness for the eventuality of Soviet attacks. Nor do the competent strategic minds of Germany believe that a German army will be merely an appendix to United States might. On the contrary, these Germans presume that a situation will soon develop in which the United States will be neither committed nor willing to guarantee German security against *all* possible Soviet provocations.

In particular, these German soldiers assume what seems to be the likeliest communist strategy of aggression—increasing military provocations executed, not by the Soviets, but by the armed forces of sovietized East Germany, the "German People's Republic." Consequently, West Germany's military establishment, in the opinion of these German military thinkers, must fulfill two functions: it must contribute appropriate forces to NATO and adequate bases to the United States; and it must, additionally, provide adequate military means to enable the German Government to secure German territory against all possible adventures of the East German Communists. German soldiers, in other words, begin to provide if only in theory, for *both* German commitments—the loyal participation in joint western defense policies *and* an independent German obligation to protect German sovereignty and German integrity.

But the officially defined magnitude of the future German army could not possibly suffice for these two commitments. By 1961 Germany is ordered to supply 16 divisions to the NATO command —just about the total strength of the German military establishment then in being. And certain western politicians have made no bones about their deliberate intention to put *all* of Germany's future military strength at NATO's exclusive disposal, to make sure that no German government could ever embark upon an effective foreign policy of its own.

These are not simply some last echoes from the era when the Allies were flirting with the "Morgenthau Plan" and other absurd schemes aimed at the extinction of Germany as a European power; rather, the current plans of monopolizing all German military force for NATO is part of the Macmillan-Eisenhower strategy "to reduce tension with the Soviet Union": A Germany with no force at its sovereign government's disposal could not possibly interfere with an Anglo-American appeasement of the Soviet Union which, quite likely, would include a formal recognition of the "German People's Republic."

Thus the *real* problems of German rearmament—those problems no "responsible" German politician dares discuss in public—contain all the tensions and stresses of world policies. As currently conceived, the German rearmament, impressive though it is, will remain indeed the futile appendix of a futile United States policy. For, completely absorbed by NATO, the 16 or 20 divisions Germany may have in 1961 will participate in NATO's inescapable frustration. Earmarked for nothing but a "Soviet attack" that will never occur, NATO's total military establishment is bound to atrophy; and West Germany's military might will atrophy with NATO. If, on the other hand, German armament is to make sense —objectively as well as in the German minds—it would have to go far beyond the German NATO commitment. In fact, it would have to be the result of a profound change of United States policies in regard to Germany as well as to NATO.

The professional work done by NATO commanders in recent years is impressive. And yet, having no positive purpose, NATO cannot be anything but an international town meeting ruled by unanimous consent. Like the United Nations Security Council, it is controlled and regulated by a single member's veto power; only in the Security Council the veto power is at least limited to the world's big powers, while NATO depends on the consensus of Europe's smallest nations. Denmark, in fact, can, if it wants to, determine NATO's conduct—which is exactly what happened at the Paris NATO meeting of December 1957: the President of the United States was graciously permitted to recite a few pious generalities, but the defiantly announced unwillingness of the Danish Government to allow rocket bases on its territory determined the fate of the conference. Its result was the unforgettably pathetic NATO begging for *"rapprochement"* with the Soviet Union.

And it does not matter a bit that unanimity is not formally required in NATO's statute: it is *politically* indispensable. A genuine alliance, defined in positive objectives, proceeds by the will of the

Allies who are agreed, in advance, on the direction of their joint policies. A loose conglomeration such as NATO, bound by nothing but a fervent desire of every member to be left alone, depends on the consent of its smallest and weakest partner. It is, in fact, precisely his weakness that assures him of an effective veto: a loose conglomeration, formed only by a desire to protect every participant's integrity, could never afford the forbidding effect of a majority rule that overrides the will of any of its members; and the weaker an opposing member, the more embarrassing would be its overruled complaint. For the multilateral partnership, meant to insure the national integrity of all its partners—*and to do nothing else*—would in such a case have *disavowed* the national integrity of a member who had no power to protect it himself. Thus, in the very act of a majority decision against the firmly stated preference of a small member, NATO would have destroyed its only franchise. And this is exactly what NATO cannot afford.

This is also why NATO will ultimately prove futile. All recorded history shows that, the more formidable and urgent the objectives of an alliance, the firmer and the more irrevocably committed must an alliance be. But to defeat a threat of truly cataclysmic proportions, the creators of NATO gathered a parliamentary assembly with built-in veto privileges of every single member, and especially the smallest.

I do not mean to advocate that the United States now reconsider the NATO pact. In spite of its basic structural fault—that it is no real alliance—NATO retains unequivocal advantages. It constitutes a promising venture of European cooperation with the United States. It has reduced to the point of disappearance the absurd kind of military competition among western governments that has characterized such a fateful part of European history between the two world wars. And it has even supplied a modicum of valuable military cooperation with the United States in the case of a western conflagration with the Soviets.

But NATO cannot perform the one function for which it is fraudulently credited in western public opinion: it cannot serve as the decisive tool of a determined western policy against the expansionist Soviet Empire. This NATO's central failure is not accidental, not avoidable, but the result of its very structure. Consequently, the United States should remain inside NATO for several advantageous reasons. But it should at last begin to forge the only effective tool of a determined policy—purposeful alliances, outside NATO, with powers that qualify as partners of such a policy. Such powers are Spain and Turkey on the two opposite ends of Europe; perhaps Great Britain, if it were still capable of stopping its downhill race toward self-emasculation; and most certainly Germany, the decisive continental power.

These alliances are entirely compatible with America's NATO obligations and even with the United Nations Charter that explicitly allows for all regional alignments which its members may deem necessary for their national security. And there is no reason why any western nation that would not be an immediate partner of such alliances should object—especially if the pacts, in defining their frank purposes, were to invite all powers that *share* the stated determination, and assume all the burdens of it, to join in due course. But even if, say, France or Denmark *were* offended, a United States alliance with Germany would clearly outweigh all their apprehensions.

It is always *pleasant* for United States policies to encounter friendly sentiments in France and Denmark; but to secure Germany's full potentials is *decisive* for the survival of the West. Applause in France and Denmark adds but little to the highly limited contributions these two lovable nations will make to the defense of the United States; while Germany's contribution is indispensable. A Germany mobilized with all its resources for a policy of western strength, in a close alliance with a determined United States, is a sufficient force to check any further Soviet expansion in Europe. *Without* such a Germany, no determined western policy in Europe is conceivable. Confronted with this central fact of international power relations, a sane United States could not possibly prefer "public relations" aspects to life necessities. France and Denmark are enjoyable company for the United States; Germany is its only senior partner in Europe.

It is by no means a safe partner. Left to its own devices, Germany is bound to sink into some kind of stupor; and soon. Its national vigor has been drained off by an ignoble defeat; its moral fiber has dangerously slackened in several years of an intoxicating prosperity; its youth is growing into a weirdly undirected if not cynical generation; its intelligentsia seems ready to substitute "neutralism" for Atlantic loyalty the moment Adenauer dies. West Germany, the Old World's strongest nation, is also its most endangered one. Unless it is aroused, pulled together, mobilized by a supreme American effort, Germany will catastrophically collide with a shrewd Soviet policy that knows of no higher task than Germany's "neutralization." And perhaps it is even now too late: perhaps German national indifference is so irreparable that even a determined turnabout of United States policies may not be enough to halt Germany's decay in helpless confusion. It is most certainly not too early to mobilize Europe's last reserve. And no other course is left than to underpin the German structure by an alliance with the United States that would give Germany a national purpose—the liberation of 17 million Germans who live under rapacious Soviet oppression.

Probably no nation can survive without a sense of destiny. The fall of Rome—one Rome after another—set in when the Romans had lost their sense of having a mission, when they could see no other meaning in their existence than personal comfort in prosperity. And most certainly the Germans cannot survive such shrinkage—not only because ingrained national traits must someday counteract Germany's present attack of pragmatism, but also because communism, Germany's next-door neighbor, will not allow the Germans to cultivate their garden in satiated indifference.

When the German intoxication with prosperity ends—as it someday must—the hangover will be desperate and there will be no other inspiration left than a suddenly upsurging desire for national unity. There can be no doubt that "reunification" will someday, and soon, become Germany's next rendezvous with destiny. The only question is whether the East or the West will be able to persuade the Germans of its capacities to solve that problem.

I propose that the West take the initiative. If the West does not, the East will.

The western solution of the problem is an American alliance with Germany that would make West Germany's pressure irresistible and, thus, roll back communism. The eastern solution of the problem is a "confederation" of the "two Germanys" that would make East Germany's pressure irresistible and, thus, topple western Europe. Our choice is not whether or not we want Germany to become the area of European decision. This is its inescapable function and fate. Our choice is only between a Germany that secures the final triumph of world communism and a Germany that leads the European offensive against Soviet expansionism. This choice is still ours; but not for long.

Had the Bonn government urged the admission of West Germany to the United Nations, certainly the United States and probably an overwhelming majority of all other U.N. members would have supported Adenauer. Why, indeed, now that even Japan, not to speak of Hungary, belongs to the least exclusive club on earth, why does Bonn still abstain? Even more: why does nobody in West Germany protest against the silly situation in which every little nomad government in the Near East, every former adherent of the Axis, the allegedly "fascist" Spain, tiny "neutral" Austria—in short: everyone who so much as expressed a wish—was admitted to the United Nations but West Germany, the Continent's strongest power, remains outside?

There was no German protest for the simple reason that official West Germany does not *wish* to join the United Nations. And it does not wish to because, in the opinion of official Germany, West Germany's admission to the United Nations would have to be followed by the admission of sovietized East Germany. Bonn never suggested membership in the U.N. because Bonn is profoundly convinced that Anglo-Saxon "realism" and Anglo-Saxon pacifism would be unable to resist Soviet pressures that would then demand the recognition of the "German People's Republic."

And it is by no means only membership in the U.N. that Bonn

has renounced out of such fears. Much more important than Adenauer's abstinence from contacts with Mr. Hammarskjöld is Bonn's anxious silence on the most absurd fact of recent history—that the United States has still no peace treaty with Germany, half a generation after the end of hostilities, and in spite of Germany's current weight in American affairs. West Germany is not only sworn and pledged, solemnly wedded to the United States by formal NATO treaties; it is also the closest friend and most reliable business partner the United States has in the Old World. And yet, no peace treaty; and no German holds that against us.

Why? Because, in Bonn's opinion, any formal negotiations concerning a peace treaty would activate an American and British and French readiness to acknowledge the existence of "the other Germany"—the section of Germany that is occupied by Soviet troops and a native Communist party.

Now there is, indeed, the Potsdam Agreement of 1945 that stipulates that "the Allied Nations" will negotiate and sign a peace treaty with defeated Germany only *unisono:* At a time when the United States Government was giving Stalin everything else he wanted, it gave him also the privilege to keep Germany out of normal relations with the West as long as he wanted to—which, of course, meant that Mr. Truman (who has learned a great deal since) conceded the Soviets a veto over United States policies. But this was in 1945. Three years later, in 1948, the United States, together with Britain and France, fully understood that the fastest possible integration of Germany into the western defense system was the single most important precondition of survival. Consequently, the western powers, having terminated the military occupation of Germany, not only recognized a fully sovereign government in Bonn but soon petitioned it to speed up its rearmament.

There it was: a sovereign government, actually the strongest sovereign government on the Continent, fully recognized and even courted by the United States—but still a government with which no peace treaty has been signed. And this absurdity makes sense to Washington as well as Bonn. Why? Because of the Potsdam Agreement—an agreement not only violated by the Soviet Union innumerable times but also an agreement which the United States, Britain, and France have completely discarded in all other respects.

Aften ten years of cold war, not a shred of the Potsdam Agreement remains legally valid. Is there anyone who would dare say that the United States cannot sign a peace treaty with its close friend, Germany, just because no understanding with the Soviets could be reached on its details? Since 1948 we have done everything else the Potsdam Agreement has ruled out; and we have done it for the forceful reason that the Soviets had violated every single one of its major stipulations, and crucially, long before we did. Besides, we did it because not to do it would have meant to lose Europe. Why, then, should the signing of an instrument that would synchronize and strengthen our policies in Germany be inadvisable?

That the Germans themselves are apprehensive is no excuse. On the contrary, the German fears are a serious *additional* reason to approach immediately the agenda of a formal peace treaty with Germany. For these German fears are rooted in the axiomatic assumption of most Germans that the United States will never openly defy the Soviet usurpation of East Germany. In many conversations with Germans I have not encountered a single one who was persuaded that the United States might be willing to tell the Soviets, unmistakably and with a show of force, that a continued Soviet occupation of East Germany is a violation not only of German sovereignty but also of international law—an inimical act against the United States. But this is precisely what we *should* tell them. And an immediate peace treaty with Germany would be a political feat of prime importance precisely because it would clarify the United States position in the crucial area of the world.

In particular, the peace treaty would first of all clarify that the *Bundesrepublik* is the legitimate, the *only* successor to the German Reich with which we were at war from 1941 to 1945. For the last decade the Bonn government has been treated by the United States —and by everybody else, including Israel and even the Soviets— as the only responsible successor to the government of the Reich: We have been holding it responsible for all the restitution and retribution the victims of the Reich could rightly claim. There was not the shadow of a doubt in anybody's mind that the Adenauer government, in historical continuity, is the legitimate heir to the government of belligerent Germany; and its *only* heir. That means, among other things, that its sovereignty is acknowledged over all territory which, by rights and even by our solemn declarations *during* the war, is inseparable from Germany.

In short, an American peace treaty with Germany will have to establish the fact that German sovereignty covers all territory that was internationally recognized as German by all powers of the world, including the Soviet Union, the day before Adolf Hitler took power. Conceivably, an American peace treaty with Germany may stipulate that Germany's *precise* border with Poland should be finally drawn after direct negotiations between the two nations. But with the sole exception of the German-Polish border (which was an unreasonable and irritating freak of willfulness long before Hitler) the peace treaty ought to clarify beyond any misinterpretation that Germany is the sovereign master of its *entire* territory. It must articulate the basic claim of Germany, the United States, and the entire West against the Soviet Union: that Soviet troops must cease the illegal occupation of the eastern parts of sovereign Germany.

It is exactly this clarification that would make an immediate American peace treaty with Germany a historic act of incomparable importance. There can be no unequivocal German and no intelligent United States policy in Europe, so long as there is the slightest doubt in Germany's or anybody else's mind that the United States *challenges* the Soviet occupation of eastern Germany. And no mere "policy statement" of the United States Government could dispel such doubts; far too many "policy statements" of the United States Government have been dismissed, forgotten, diluted, denied. Nothing short of a formal peace treaty will do—an act, that is, prepared in the limelight of open international negotiations and endorsed by the United States Senate.

What is needed here is the signature, not of the United States Government, but of America. For that peace treaty—and this is its significance—will have to initiate a new American policy in regard to the Soviet Empire. It would be signed in open renunciation of all the appeasement advocates who cling to the fallacious axiom that America's relations with the Soviet Union are still regulated by the Potsdam Agreement of 1945. It would at last restore not only German but American sovereignty. It would mark a complete change of the American posture in the cold war—from the defensive to the offensive.

In other words (to state the position in terms familiar to the permanent discussion of United States foreign affairs), I suggest a policy that is diametrically opposed to the conduct advocated by Walter Lippmann and George F. Kennan. Their concern and professed goal is an American recognition of the *status quo* in Europe and the whole world—an acknowledgment of the frontiers the Soviets have drawn for themselves by force, an acceptance of the "spheres of influence" as announced by world communism. I contend that any United States guarantee of the *status quo* is tantamount to America's resignation, first, as a world power and then, in fast consequence, as a free nation.

At the bottom of all Kennan-Lippmann plans is the mendacious syllogism that the Soviets, if only they had nothing to fear for themselves, would leave us alone. But the Communists mean to possess the world; and they mean it in dead earnest. In the face of their determination, crowned by unparalleled successes, to assume a change of communist heart is folly. Any American recognition of a *status quo* which leaves all the trumps, conquests, and usurpations in communist hands, is an unmistakable invitation to further communist advances.

There cannot be, and there never was, such a thing as the *status quo*. In history, which does not read Mr. Lippmann's column, and thus proceeds with its own prejudices, there is always one side that attacks and advances, while the other retreats and yields. Either our side will expand or the Soviets will. If *we* do not challenge communist supremacy over East Germany, the *Communists* will of necessity challenge democratic supremacy over West Germany. The eternal flow of history could never be arrested by agreement, even when both sides *honestly* agreed on arresting it; but when one side frankly means "to bury" the other, openly desires to own the *whole* world, to *remake* the whole world in the image of its belligerent utopianism, then the proposal to "agree" on a *status quo* is not merely intellectual inadequacy. It is sheer irresponsibility.

The Lippmann-Kennan school of thought contends, with rather moving despair, that, if the United States and the Soviet Union do not arrive at some such kind of agreement, the ultimate conflagration must result. They do not contend, in other words, that their proposal is *correct* or, at least, that it has chances of realization. They merely shudder. They keep telling the world that they shudder when they think what will happen if the historical trend is allowed to continue. They have never said that their proposals really can *stop* that trend; they merely assert that it "must" be stopped. Kennan and Lippmann, immensely learned gentlemen, have never suggested a policy. They have merely disguised their horror over the force of onrushing history with altogether incoherent *ad hoc* "proposals."

But it remains the one unequivocal working law of history that, if one side does not move, the other will—that neither time nor space can be arrested. The inherent consequence for all those who agree with Eisenhower that "war is unthinkable" remains that the Soviets will continue to advance and we will continue to withdraw.

I propose that our side at last begin to move—to move in and through Germany. This movement would start with a peace treaty that acknowledges the Bonn government as the sovereign master of all Germany as it existed on the day of Hitler's ascent to power; and, having so defined and recognized the inviolable sovereignty of Germany, the United States would immediately sign a bilateral pact of alliance with that Germany—an alliance which makes Germany America's senior partner on the Continent and openly pronounces as its goal the restoration of German sovereignty over all German territory. This treaty of alliance would be kept open for any other western power that agrees with its provision and is ready to embark, with the United States and Germany, on a European policy of determination. Endorsed by the United States Senate, such a treaty would create a new and cutting instrument of United States policy vis-à-vis the Soviet Union.

It would reverse the trend in Europe. The question of German "reunification" would no longer be the carrot-and-stick device in Soviet hands it is today. The issue that until now prevented the formation of a self-confident German policy, and consequently of a self-confident western policy in Europe, will now be restored to its true proportions and correct perspectives: Germany and the United States have a legitimate and profoundly serious claim against the Soviet Union—not a compromise to achieve, but an irreducible claim to settle.

No longer will it be a matter of the Soviets' impenetrable intentions whether, and when, and how urgently, the German people may dream of "reunification." Now the tables will be turned: now *the Soviets* will have to play the unnerving game of guessing how much pressure, at any given moment, the American-German alliance, adequately armed, will put behind their irreducible demand for the withdrawal of Soviet troops from German territory.

Allied by close agreement, Germany and the United States will massage the nerves and feed the apprehensions of the Soviets with a sometimes inscrutable, sometimes coldly forceful, always imaginative policy of incessant pressures and incessantly increasing urgency: get out of the territory of sovereign Germany, a senior ally of the United States! Now, for the first time, the *Soviet Union* would have to calculate and consider the risks of conflagration, to interpret feverishly the possible meaning of every move, every word, every gesture on the other side.

Knowing their timetable and their specific plans, the United States and Germany would calmly proceed with a war of nerves that, indeed, includes the risks of real war. But they would be committed neither to evicting the Soviet troops *forcibly* from German territory nor even to a precise *date* by which the eviction would have to be accomplished; yet they would clarify beyond a doubt that the liberation of East Germany is the *raison d'être* and the aim of their alliance; and that, if need be, they will achieve that aim, *at a time of their choosing,* by force.

The Soviets, for a change, will wonder and fret. Germany and the United States will coordinate pressures; invent methods of penetration; organize effective movements in the occupied zone; blanket the usurped parts of Germany with western literature, western broadcasts, and western modes of living. East Germany, in short, will be treated as the legitimate German territory it is— under foreign occupation, to be sure, and therefore it will be treated with due considerations of abnormal and dangerous conditions; but as a territory that must not for a moment doubt that someday soon the legitimate forces of the sovereign government will return, will punish all Quislings, and will exercise all sovereign powers. Clearly, and for all times, the United States and Germany will preclude any "confederation" with the Quisling government the Soviet troops have forced upon East Germany.

The crux of the matter remains that Germany, in spite of all solemn Allied declarations that their war aims exclude any country's aggrandizement at Germany's costs, lost in 1945 almost exactly one half of its territory and has not recovered it yet: the Soviets annexed outright 15,000 square miles, the Poles took more than 40,000 square miles, and the Quisling regime of communist East Germany controls more than 41,000 square miles—a total loss of more than 96,000 square miles, as compared to West Germany's total remaining area of 97,500 square miles.

Conceived in terms of political warfare, an American peace treaty with Germany would not necessarily stipulate whether or not some of the territory incorporated into the Soviet Union and Communist Poland could be reasonably traded in direct negotiations. The Communists will have to worry about this, for the time being. They may discover that it pays to become tractable and accommodating. And then, again, they may get so frightened by the undisclosed prospects of an increasing German pressure, seconded by the United States, that they may evacuate the stolen land outright rather than face the risks of a fatal collision. What may happen, once a determined American-German alliance has radically changed the power structure of Europe, is unforeseeable—which is precisely the immense promise of such a policy.

For the first time in forty-one years, simply by realizing that Europe's gravest wound could also become the area of its healing, the West would ride herd on communism. Conceived in terms of firmness and a spirit of offensive, the American peace treaty with Germany, followed by a firmly executed pact of alliance between the two nations, would have opened the second cold war—the one the West would have all chances of winning.

One must have lived for a while with the Germans to realize the complete change of climate such a reversal of policies must mean to them. This has been, for thirteen years, a dispirited and faithless nation; but at the same time a nation of almost unbelievable material potentials. For thirteen years the Germans could form no other purpose than to grow fat individually. But no other nation is less talented for private escapades than the Germans; and though they are trying hard to conduct themselves like time-honored pragmatists and sybarites, their troubled conscience shows through the thin varnish of their synthetic public opinion.

And then, after a decade of self-imposed blindness and undignified prevarications, a determined German government would at last rally the whole nation for a dedicated drive, coordinated with the world's strongest free country; a drive that means to restore freedom to the violated half of Germany and, thus, restore dignity and purpose to West Germany's conscience-stricken people. This, it seems to me, is the one way to organic German convalescence. And when Germany rises in a dedicated venture of advance in freedom, Europe rises.

I do not mean to say that such a reversal of policy would encounter no opposition in Germany. On the contrary, I am fully aware that formidable forces inside Germany would try to counteract the suggested total revision of Germany's course. There are, first of all, immense vested interests watching over Germany's strangely unbecoming inferiority complexes. (For, if it takes gracefulness to be attractively arrogant, it takes twice as much gracefulness to be humble without offending.) Germany's intellectual establishment could not possibly survive the change of climate: the gigantic interlocked structure of *Kultur* officers (editors, professors, celebrities, pastors, and prophets) would collapse; and before it collapses it would fight.

Important segments of the political opposition would also fight. The German Social Democracy is fundamentally a pacifistic formation; and a policy that frankly admits that it would rather take a chance on conflict than make surrender inescapable will, of necessity, arouse violent opposition on the German left. But by no means would it be the *entire* German left. The German Social Democracy has grown too large to remain monolithically pacifistic: if the nation rises in a true rally of dedication, massive segments of the German Social Democracy would unfailingly join—much the more as the Soviet-occupied German territory is a traditional fountain of Social Democratic strength.

In fact, the suggested reversal of German policies may be the only way of leading the opposition back into constructive cooperation. Though the Adenauer decade has brought not only prosperity but also social pacification to Germany, it has also alienated Germany's Social Democracy from what the Germans call *Staatsidee*— a sense of jointly belonging to a common concept of national destiny. And it was not just Adenauer's often insufferable righteousness that made the German Social Democrats withdraw ever more stubbornly, with an air of hurt self-esteem; it was also the somewhat repulsive atmosphere of bourgeois smugness that permeated German prosperity and made many a decent German cringe with disgust. But if German policy were at last dedicated to something more and greater than prosperity, a sense of liberation would grip Social Democrats as well as Adenauer voters.

And the Germans would never again use the defeatist term "reunification." To reunify would presuppose a preceding separation. But East Germany was never separated from West Germany—it was merely occupied, terrorized, kept captive. The problem was never—no matter what the metropolitan and "neutralist" German press habitually says—how to bring about "a merger"; the only problem was always how to restore legitimate German sovereignty over stolen German territory.

There never *were* two Germanys—there was only the one Germany, recognized as the legitimate government of *all* Germans by *all* civilized nations since 1948; the Germany that worked hard for the last ten years to resume its place among the civilized nations; the Germany that succeeded beyond anybody's dreams, and was now getting ready to recover its national integrity. There can be as little talk of "German reunification" as one can speak of reunifying a man with his stolen cash. The law has to see to it that the thief surrenders his booty. For thirteen years Germany kept quiet. Now, supported by the United States, it announces its unimpeachable claim. And it is going to get its own.

Were this the spirit in which a revitalized Germany, tightly allied with a revitalized United States, would conduct its affairs in the decisive two or three years ahead, the tide of defeat for the whole West may turn. A firm alliance between the United States and Germany would put steel into the flabby structure of NATO. The technical needs of United States preparedness in Europe center geographically on the German core of the Continent, not on the fringes to which the United States currently clings; and once these needs can be satisfied without the diplomatic horseplay that concedes the smallest European principalities a veritable veto power over United States policy, NATO, freed from these fantastic prerogatives of provincialism, may streamline its command.

Above all, a coordinated United States-German military policy and administration in Central Europe would spare NATO the most vexing problem of the fifties—where to place United States troops. American contingents, currently stationed all over western Europe, would then be employed in the only fashion that makes military sense and produces effective political pressure—namely, in Germany proper and right alongside the Iron Curtain. Germany would at last be what geography and history meant her to be—the massive bolt that locks Europe against any further Soviet advance, a bolt that can also be thrown wide open to release superior pressure into the Soviet Empire any time the United States and Germany decide to take the initiative.

Once and for all, the United States-German alliance would end Europe's "neutralist" machinations that freeze the anti-Soviet rally today, and will make it impossible tomorrow. For the West would at last have set a fact—a massive fact. "Neutralism," a moral malady, unfailingly responds to determined power. It forms like a fungus on the edges of futility, and it atrophies in the orbit of directed vitality.

When it erupted in megalomania, and obscenely dishonored its name, Germany opened the West to the Communist invaders. If America comprehends the chance, a new Germany that has restored its spirit and recovered its national integrity may yet save the West.

DATE DUE

DEC 11 '70			
JAN 11 '71			
FEB 27 '95			
DEC 13			
			PRINTED IN U.S.A.

GAYLORD